Not Even Past

{ Not Even Past }

The Stories We Keep Telling about the Civil War

CODY MARRS

JOHNS HOPKINS UNIVERSITY PRESS   BALTIMORE

© 2020 Johns Hopkins University Press
All rights reserved. Published 2020
Printed in the United States of America on acid-free paper
9 8 7 6 5 4 3 2 1

Johns Hopkins University Press
2715 North Charles Street
Baltimore, Maryland 21218-4363
www.press.jhu.edu

Library of Congress Cataloging-in-Publication Data

Names: Marrs, Cody, author.
Title: Not even past : the stories we keep telling about the Civil War /
    Cody Marrs.
Description: Baltimore : Johns Hopkins University Press, 2020. | Includes
    bibliographical references and index.
Identifiers: LCCN 2019020341 | ISBN 9781421436654 (hardcover)
    | ISBN 1421436655 (hardcover) | ISBN 9781421436661 (ebook) | ISBN
    1421436663 (ebook)
Subjects: LCSH: United States—History—Civil War, 1861–1865—Litera-
    ture and the war. | Race relations in literature. | United States—Race
    relations. | United States—History—Civil War, 1861–1865—Influence.
Classification: LCC PS217.C58 M35 2020 | DDC 813/.4093581—dc23
LC record available at https://lccn.loc.gov/2019020341

A catalog record for this book is available from the British Library.

*Special discounts are available for bulk purchases of this book. For more informa-
tion, please contact Special Sales at specialsales@press.jhu.edu.*

Johns Hopkins University Press uses environmentally friendly book materials, including recycled text paper that is composed of at least 30 percent
post-consumer waste, whenever possible.

Contents

Illustrations

Preface

We tend to think of the Civil War as something that happened in the past—in some other age, some other world. Textbooks, documentaries, and national parks all convey the idea that the Civil War was a series of battles that happened on specific dates a long time ago: a momentous fight that deserves to be remembered, and remembered in the right way.

The lesson of the twenty-first century is that the Civil War did not just happen in the past. It is not a milestone that must be recalled, or a bygone event with distinct "legacies." It is an enduring struggle, an unresolved conflict that rages through American culture. The Civil War continues to be contested every time slavery is discussed, state authority is invoked, and public spaces are renamed. It persists every time a monument is raised or destroyed, every time a Confederate flag is displayed or taken down. The fight has certainly shifted, but it is far from over.

The premise of this book is that this ongoing struggle is best apprehended through the stories that have been told about it. The multitude of films, poems, photographs, novels, folktales, and works of art about the Civil War are not just tokens of remembrance or pieces of an archive. They are active engagements with this enduring contest—living attempts to render it through words and images.

This book is about these narratives and the war out of which they've emerged, a war that, as William Faulkner put it, is not over; indeed, "it's not even past."*

*William Faulkner, *Requiem for a Nun* (New York: Vintage, 1994), 73.

Not Even Past

Introduction

ANDRÉ CAILLOUX MUST HAVE BEEN MORE THAN A little shocked when he looked down and realized what had just happened. He'd used that hand for so many things. Long before he became a captain in the Native Guard, the North's first black regiment, he used it to roll cigars and, every once in a while, to box. He used it to caress his children, including his baby who died as an infant. Years ago, he even used it to apply for manumission, after which Cailloux, born a slave in a Louisiana parish, got married, started a business, and became a central figure in the African American community of New Orleans.[1]

In the spring of 1863, all of that was far behind him. The self-declared "blackest man in New Orleans" had just been hit by a cannonball and his hand dangled, bleeding and mangled, by his side. Whatever dread or shock he might have experienced, he did not convey it to those around him. Instead, he steeled himself one final time and shouted, first in English and then in French, *"Still forward, and to the guns!"*[2]

The Confederate defenses proved too strong. The assault was repulsed, and Cailloux was killed by an exploding shell. When his fellow soldiers tried to recover his body, sharpshooters cut them off. So Cailloux's corpse, rather than finding its way home, was left uncovered and unburied for forty days. But he was far from unremembered. Once the North finally captured the fort, they ferried Cailloux's remains back to his loved ones, and New Orleans did what it does best, turning tragedy into festival. Mourners decked out in black regalia gathered en masse.

William Morris Smith, *Company E, 4th U.S. Colored Infantry, at Fort Lincoln* (1864).
Courtesy of the Library of Congress, Prints and Photographs Division.

After they adorned the coffin with flowers and candles, they led a mile-long procession through the streets, ensuring that no one would ever forget this man who died fighting for freedom.[3]

That effort to preserve Cailloux's memory—to provide in death if not in life the honor which he and other black soldiers were due—continued long after the funeral concluded. Rodolphe Desdunes, an African American writer whose brother served under Cailloux, dubbed him an "American Spartacus." That ancient Roman slave, Desdunes stated, "displayed no braver heroism than did this officer who ran forward to his death with a smile on his lips." The historian, soldier, and minister George Washington Williams also lionized Cailloux. Although Cailloux's "arm was shattered" and "his voice faint from exhaustion," Williams marveled, "he refused to leave the field." When he finally fell, he did so "in the advance with his face to the foe"; "it was a soldier's death."[4]

Poets, too, have sustained Cailloux's memory. In poetry Cailloux becomes a symbol of the Civil War itself, an embodiment of its meaning and significance. Paul Laurence Dunbar, the great African American lyricist, called men like Cailloux the war's unsung heroes for the manner in which they simultaneously represented emancipation and carried it out. Dunbar wrote,

> They fought their way on the
>   hillside, they fought their
>   way in the glen,
> And God looked down on their
>   sinews brown, and said, "I
>   have made them men."

Joseph Wilson, a writer who served in the war's most famous black regiment, the 54th Massachusetts, saw the dishonor bestowed upon Cailloux's remains as symbolic of the dishonor routinely bestowed upon blackness itself:

> He lay just where he fell,
> Soddening in a fervid summer's sun,
> Guarded by an enemy's hissing shell,
>
> . . . .
>
> A flag of truce couldn't save,
> No, nor humanity could not give
> This sable warrior a hallowed grave,
> Nor army of the Gulf retrieve.

Though no army could recover Cailloux's body at Port Hudson, we can do so now, the poem suggests. That is the grand task the poem sets for itself: to provide, through language, a hallowed grave. More recently, the actions of Cailloux and his compatriots have been recalled by Natasha Trethewey, whose poetry attempts to account for the "things which must be accounted for": "the unburied dead . . . exiles in their homeland," every "lost limb—and what remains, phantom / ache."[5]

From the nineteenth century to the twenty-first, writers have extolled Cailloux's actions and drawn attention to the pivotal role that black soldiers played in the Civil War. Yet, despite their efforts, these soldiers remain largely forgotten. Nearly everyone knows that the war revolved around slavery, but the actual wartime actions of African Americans have tended to be marginalized or erased. As Trethewey writes,

> The Daughters of the Confederacy
> has placed a plaque here, at the fort's entrance—
> each Confederate soldier's name raised hard
> in bronze; no names carved for the Native Guards—
> 2nd Regiment, Union men, black phalanx.
> What is monument to their legacy?[6]

The only monument, the only real record we have, are scattered acts of remembrance. And that record is much thinner, and far less visible, than the monuments that have been erected for Robert E. Lee, the Battle of Gettysburg, and the other cornerstones of white American memory.

That disregard began almost as soon as Cailloux fell. Some newspapers claimed that the black soldiers were forced to fight against their will, while others omitted mention of them altogether. *Harper's Monthly* devoted most of its coverage to the tactics and topography involved in the battle, while the *Atlantic Monthly* focused on the tragic deaths of several Harvard men, "young heroes who dropped the oar and took up the sword."[7] One of the most influential Civil War novels, John William de Forest's *Miss Ravenel's Conversion from Secession to Loyalty* (1867), depicted Port Hudson as a skirmish fought exclusively by white soldiers. Here is what the protagonist, Edward Colburne, does on the day that Cailloux led his fateful assault:

> At five o'clock . . . Colburne was awakened by an order to fall in. . . . [So he] proceeded to form his company, and, that done, ate his breakfast of raw pork and hard biscuit. He would have been glad to have Henry boil him a cup of coffee; but that idle freedman was "having a good time," probably sleeping, in some unknown refuge. For two hours the ranks sat on the ground, musket in hand; then Colburne saw the foremost line. . . . It was a long row of stern faces, bronzed with sunburn, . . . grave with the serious emotions of the hour, . . . and set as firm as flints toward the enemy. The old innocence of the

peaceable New England farmer and mechanic had disappeared from these war-seared visages, and had been succeeded by an expression of hardened combativeness. . . . [They were] as good men as the sun ever shone upon.[8]

This passage carries out a literary whitewashing. There is only one person of color, and he is a minstrel character, an "idle freeman" who sleeps through the battle. Colburne's men, in contrast, embody the ideal of American manhood, hardened and reborn through the war's violence. We are led to believe that the Siege of Port Hudson, like the Civil War itself, had nothing to do with black freedom and everything to do with the fate of white identity.

The novel is hardly unusual in that respect. Over time Port Hudson came to be remembered not as the first battle in which black soldiers played a significant role but as a turning point in military tactics. By the summer of 1863, many bloody battles had already taken place—most notably at Antietam, Gettysburg, and Chancellorsville, where tens of thousands were killed or injured—but Port Hudson represented a different kind of fighting. Cailloux died on the first morning of an attack that lasted forty-seven more days. It was a long, grueling assault determined not by acts of heroism but by small, strategic advances and the deprivation of resources. This was siege warfare—an early version of World War I. To defend the port (and retain control of the Mississippi River), the Confederates dug trenches, laced the ground with land mines, and created a series of angled fortifications that enabled them to repel the Union onslaught for weeks. When the siege finally concluded, it was because the North carried out a multipronged, multiphase attack from land and sea, slowly moving their cannons and batteries closer to the fort, chipping away at the Confederates' defenses and severing their supply lines.[9]

Many writers, artists, and historians have explored the battle's tactical and technological significance. The novelist-turned-poet Herman Melville viewed the Siege of Port Hudson as a sign and portent of war's modernization. Prior eras, like medieval Europe or Homer's Greece, may have celebrated heroism and valor, but such ideals, Melville suggests, no longer belong in the world remade by the Civil War. Now the only thing that matters—the only force that truly shapes history—is "plain mechanic power." This "was battle," writes Melville, yet "beyond the strife" there was

> No passion; all went on by crank,
> Pivot, and screw,
> And calculations of caloric.[10]

At Port Hudson, those calculations were conducted by Paul Francis de Gournay, a Cuban native who helped design the Confederate defenses. As he later recalled, the Confederates sought to take full advantage of the landscape through a "contracted line of defense." They placed the batteries on the high bluffs, using the rocks as a natural shield. When the fighting began, the darkness and the smoke "formed a curtain between us and the enemy. While we peered into this dark abyss, striving to catch the dim outline of the black hulls, the crest of our parapets . . . lighted up by the burning matches . . . were marked out in bold relief, their great elevation being their only protection."[11]

That scene is visually captured in Julian Davidson's oil painting *The Battle of Port Hudson* (1886), which shows the Confederate cannons firing on the Union ships and lighting up the Mississippi. There is beauty here, but little else. Orange lines reveal plumes of cannon fire and trace the fatal trajectory of falling shells. Davidson's painting depicts an orchestra of smoke and light. But there is no Cailloux, and no Native Guard. Nor is there anything to denote what caused this great tempest of metal and flame. What truly matters about Port Hudson—what must be recalled above all else, it would seem—is the strategic destruction that engulfed it.

So how should André Cailloux be remembered? As an individual, or a symbol? Was he a federal soldier, a freedom fighter, or just one more "calculation of caloric"? And what type of conflict claimed his life? Was Cailloux killed in a fight over resources and positions? Or was this part of a much broader struggle, a larger fight over race, liberty, or power?

These questions reveal the paradox of looking at the Civil War through

Julian Davidson, *The Battle of Port Hudson* (1886). Facsimile print by L. Prang & Co. Courtesy of the Library of Congress, Prints and Photographs Division.

literature. On the one hand, the war has been exhaustively depicted and discussed. There are Civil War films and Civil War poems, Civil War novels and Civil War paintings . . . and plays, and sculptures, and dioramas. Countless movies, letters, and memoirs recount the assault on Fort Sumter, William T. Sherman's March to the Sea, Abraham Lincoln's assassination, the political whirlwind surrounding the passage of the Thirteenth Amendment, and, of course, the Siege of Port Hudson. To limit the example just to printed texts, there have now been roughly 80,000 books published about the Civil War—the equivalent of a book per day printed for more than two hundred years.[12]

These works, however, do not yield a discrete, stable vision of the conflict. They interpret it in multiple ways, focusing on different people and attributing the violence to different causes. From the perspective of literary history, there is no single Civil War. Instead, several basic plots—primal stories that we tell each other again and again—continually compete for cultural primacy. The war is often remembered as an emancipatory struggle, as an attempt to destroy slavery in America now and forever. But it is also remembered as a fight for Southern independence, as a fratricide that divides the national family, and as a cruel war defined by its brutality.

This book retraces these narratives, from the 1860s to the twenty-first century. It reconstructs these stories' evolution, examining where they originated, how they developed, and why they acquired such lasting power. As we will discover, Robert Penn Warren had an excellent reason for describing the Civil War as "our only 'felt' history": this conflict, which has been incessantly revisited, never quite became history at all.[13] Even today it continues to unfold, persisting not merely as a cultural touchstone—the somewhat clichéd notion that the Civil War is always with us—but as an unresolved, and perhaps unresolvable, struggle through which we inevitably define ourselves. That lack of an ending fuels these plots. They all explore and try to illuminate some enduring connection between the past and the present, but they view that connection in radically different ways.

In the popular imagination, of course, the war came to a sudden and definitive conclusion on April 9, 1865, when Robert E. Lee surrendered to Ulysses S. Grant at Appomattox Court House. That moment has been broadly mythologized in American culture. It has been imprinted on stamps, preserved in paintings, and retold in children's books. It has been celebrated in films like Steven Spielberg's *Lincoln* and in histories like Jay Winik's *April 1865: The Month That Saved America*. It is even reenacted each spring by actors at Appomattox, which has become a national park and, for Civil War enthusiasts, a kind of mecca. These retellings of Lee and Grant's fateful exchange almost always depict it as a scene of fraternal grace and mutual honor that set the stage for postwar reconciliation. Indeed, Lee's surrender has come to be remembered as the moment when the Civil War finally, mercifully reached its end and the nation was renewed.

History has taught us to be wary of such commemorations. Not only did the fighting between the North and the South continue for months on end, but even the principle for which the North ostensibly fought—the abolition of slavery—was only partially secured. This is perhaps the greatest tragedy of André Cailloux and other African Americans who struggled to carry freedom forward: after 1865, slavery was altered rather than expunged. The rise of violent white terrorist organizations like the Ku Klux Klan, the modern prison complex, and the wage system ensured that slavery subsisted in spirit if not in name. It took another one hundred years to pass the Voting Rights Act, which finally procured the political liberties that were supposed to be guaranteed by the War Amendments, and that only begins to touch on the other consequences of Reconstruction's failure. The refusal to redistribute land and property to former slaves—to enact General Sherman's promise of "40 acres and a mule"—has effects to this day, impacting racial disparities in schooling, housing, and family wealth.

For all intents and purposes, the Civil War continues. If there was ever any doubt about the war's persistence, it evaporated in August of 2017, when right-wing forces descended on Charlottesville, Virginia, to protest the City Council's recent decision to remove the town's statue of Robert E. Lee and rename the park dedicated to the former Confederate general. In the newly rechristened "Emancipation Park," neo-Confederates armed with guns and battle flags marched in fervid demonstration, chanting "White lives matter!" and assaulting counterprotesters with sticks, fists, and makeshift weapons. One of the neo-Confederates bragged afterward, "Today [I] cracked 3 skulls open with virtually no damage to myself."[14] Another fascist drove his car directly into a group of counterprotesters, injuring nineteen people and killing one.

Charlottesville was an aftershock of the American Civil War. This is why the fascists sang "Dixie" as they marched through the park: the Civil War continues to be our political fault line, the shifting ground upon which everything is built. The idea that the Civil War *was* somehow resolved—that it concluded in 1865, giving form to a new nation and a new modernity—is one of the most powerful fictions that has been told about it. We keep telling stories about the Civil War, in part, so we can imagine it to be something other than what it really is: an unsettled conflict that will continue to be refought as long as American civilization exists.

We also keep telling these stories because we thirst for closure. Plots make it possible for experience to not bleed off into nothingness or flow beyond our meager grasp. They provide everything from the most private reflections to the most epic upheavals with a sense of coherence, fashioning contours for events that would otherwise remain amorphous and unremembered. This is true with a vengeance when it comes to the Civil War. From the story of emancipation to the myth of the Lost Cause, from *The Red Badge of Courage* to *The Amalgamation Polka*, these plots give the struggle shape and meaning, making it resonate on various frequencies into the twenty-first century and beyond.

By examining these narratives in juxtaposition, we can better understand how they assemble a cultural mythology for the Civil War, the symbols and themes of which have become such potent touchstones for American identity. In the United States, regional, national, and political sensibilities have long taken shape through the war and the epic significance that is attached to it—so much so that whenever we tell a story about the Civil War, we are almost always telling a story about ourselves. As the historian David Blight notes, the "United States, to an important degree, *is* the stories it tells itself about the Civil War and its enduring aftermath."[15]

If the stories we tell about the Civil War reveal who we are—not only who we have been, but who we wish to become—then literature is indispensable. Literature is a practice of storytelling that reframes the culture out of which it grows, providing a fictive order for people's most ardent longings, antipathies, and aspirations. When Scarlett O'Hara plucks a carrot from the earth and declares that she "will never be hungry again!"; or when W. E. B. Du Bois speculates about John Brown's awed reverence for the Bolshevik Revolution; or when Natasha Trethewey describes the "distant field," off the frame of Winslow Homer's *The Veteran in a New Field*, where "another veteran toils, / his hands the color of dark soil," they are taking cultural memory and turning the volume up.[16] From the nineteenth century onward, literature recasts the whirlwind of questions, passions, and ideals that have been unleashed by the conflict. Looking at the Civil War through its literary history gives us access to the stories, both factual and nonfactual, that have shaped people's understanding of the conflict and molded its memory.

That range of experience is recorded in the war's multivocal and multicultural literature. The following pages consider several highly canonical authors, such as Walt Whitman and William Faulkner, but I also focus on other, less famous writers like William Wells Brown, an African American novelist who penned a stunning chronicle of the "colored regiments." There are artists such as Edmonia Lewis, a Rome-based sculptor of Native American and Afro-Haitian descent; religious leaders such as Abram Ryan, a Catholic priest who became the foremost poet of the Lost Cause; and filmmakers such as D. W. Griffith. There are also statues, plays, paintings, histories, and odes from every corner of the North and South—indeed, from the whole international arena that comprised the war—which span more than 150 years. What fascinates me is how this astoundingly diverse chorus converges around a discrete group of plots—not ironclad taxonomies but fluid stories that have been remade and reimagined by many people almost ad infinitum.

Let us turn, then, not to the Civil War—for there is no single, over-arching conflict to be gleaned from literature—but to the multiple wars that emerge in literary history, beginning with the mythic story about brothers fighting brothers.

{1} A Family Squabble

THE CIVIL WAR TORE FAMILIES APART. IN COUNTLESS films, books, and TV shows, brothers divide their allegiances, fighting for the North and the South. Or fathers, out of love of country or region, renounce their sons. Or cousins, in a moment of terrifying recognition, suddenly see each other across the battlefield. The Civil War's status as a familial conflict has become so widespread that it now passes for basic common sense. If there is one thing that *everyone* knows about the Civil War, it is that—as Johnny Cash once put it—it was a "bloody brother war."[1]

Here's the rub: such family divisions were actually fairly uncommon. In the border states some families, such as the Breckinridges and Crittendens in Kentucky, did split their allegiances.[2] However, many Americans in the mid-nineteenth century hewed quite closely to their family's politics, even if they privately disagreed with one another. Allegiances, large and small, were far more local and family based than they became later on. So when the time arrived to choose a side in the struggle, there was often little choice involved. People who either witnessed or participated in the Civil War tended to feel as though they had been swept up in fate's mighty wave, an inexorable force that some called "God" and others "duty" or "necessity."[3] Stories of fractured families contravene the Civil War's actual history, providing us with narratives that bear little resemblance to the divisions that, in reality, fueled the conflict. So why have these stories endured? What grants them their lasting power and allure?

First and foremost, they bolster an important social fantasy: that the American nation is a family. That fantasy converts something that is purely accidental—the time, place, and circumstances of one's birth—into something that is profoundly significant. It allows one to see oneself, and countless others (including many who remain unknown and anonymous), as tied together in an intimate and inviolable bond. Such imagined kinship made it possible for Americans during and after the Civil War to see a hidden order, even a kind of destiny in the struggle's chaos. This narrative enabled the Civil War to be felt and remembered not as a total war that scorched the earth; not as a massive, industrial-scale bloodletting carried out with new repeating weapons and exploding shells; not as a struggle that emancipated a people, remade the government, and created lasting ideological divides; but, instead, as a kind of sibling rivalry.

The seductiveness of that story is also tied to its racial politics. Part of the reason the Family Squabble has been endlessly retold in every possible medium, migrating from life to text, from text to image, and back again, is because it places white Americans at the core of the conflict. As we will see, this is a crucial feature of most Civil War memory (with the notable exception of the Great Emancipation): it decenters and devalues black freedom.

Walt Whitman and the American Family

Few writers had a bigger hand in mythologizing the Family Squabble than Walt Whitman. By the end of the 1800s, the Brooklyn-born poet had become one of the country's foremost literary celebrities. Copies of *Leaves of Grass*, as well as images of the "Good Gray Poet" (with his flowing beard and expressive face), circulated throughout the Atlantic world. Artists made paintings of his likeness, and newspapers printed parodies of his distinctive voice.[4] When Whitman turned 70, Mark Twain wrote him a laudatory letter, pleading with him to "tarry yet a while" and continue writing about the earth's "marvels."[5] And one of the major themes to which Whitman repeatedly returned, using his cultural influence to shape public memory, was the Civil War. According to Whitman, it was not the American Revolution but the Civil War that made the

Mathew Brady, *Walt Whitman, half-length portrait, seated in chair, facing left* (1862). *Carte de visite.* Courtesy of the Library of Congress, Charles Feinberg Collection.

United States into a nation, henceforth bound together—like a massive family—by a shared history of love and sacrifice.

Whitman only acquired that perspective after massive emotional and intellectual upheaval. Initially, the Civil War almost destroyed him. Prior to the conflict, Whitman considered the United States to be a place of unprecedented social unity. In the 1850s he positioned himself as an American bard whose expansive vision and free-flowing voice mirrored the nation's communal, democratic ethos. As he attested (or "yawped") in 1855, "The United States themselves are essentially the greatest poem. In the history of the earth hitherto, the largest and most stirring appear tame and orderly to their ampler largeness and stir. Here at last is . . . not merely a nation but a teeming nation of nations."[6] In Whitman's view, what made the United States "the greatest poem" was the harmonious balance of power inscribed in the Constitution, a balance replicated in his grammar: the States, *plural*, are poetic because they generate unity out of difference.

The early editions of *Leaves of Grass*, Whitman's sprawling book of poems, celebrated the connections and attachments that flourish in this nation of nations. Sometimes, those connections could become quite intimate. He liked to directly address the reader as a comrade or lover: "Come closer to me, / Push close my lovers and take the best I possess, / Yield closer and closer and give me the best you possess." He envisioned the nation as a grand arena of love and affection:

> I dream'd in a dream, I saw a city invincible to the
>   attacks of the whole of the rest of the earth;
> I dreamed that was the new City of Friends,
> Nothing was greater there than the quality of robust
>   love—it led the rest,
> It was seen every hour in the actions of the men of
>   that city,
> And in all their looks and words.[7]

This invincible city is, in a way, the United States. Here, Whitman suggests, "robust love" has become universal, manifesting not only in the people's behavior but also in their very "looks and words."

The Civil War shook Whitman to the core. What if everything he had said about America—its innate sense of freedom, its almost spiritual cohesion—was utterly untrue? As the City of Friends collapsed on itself, he wondered, "Must I change my triumphant songs?" and "learn to chant the cold dirges of the baffled? / And sullen hymns of defeat?"[8] That fear was compounded when he heard that his younger brother, George, an infantryman in the Union Army, had been shot at the Battle of Fredericksburg (1862). When Whitman and his family received notice of George's injury, they initially had no clue how extensive it might be, so Walt traveled to Washington and scoured the city's hospitals. What he witnessed there filled him with pity and terror. The hospitals were cesspools of infection and disease—poorly sanitized, understaffed, and

overcrowded. The surgeons, still ignorant of germ theory, did not dis-
infect the saws with which they routinely amputated limbs (which were
buried in large piles, like mass graves for gangrenous hands and feet). For
beds, volunteers sometimes laid blankets on top of leaves.[9]

After days of searching, Whitman finally found his brother. A bullet
had split his cheek, but otherwise he was okay.[10] Upon recovering, George
went back to the front, but Whitman was haunted by the hospitals. So
he returned, working as a nurse and trying to ferry the sick back to
health—or in the more hopeless cases, comforting them in their darkest moments. "Every family," he remarked, "has directly or indirectly
some representative among this vast army of the wounded and sick."[11]
Whitman—ever fascinated by transformation—remade himself into this
army's fatherly caregiver. From 1862 through 1865 he washed, clothed,
fed, and soothed the wounded soldiers, sometimes bringing them books
or candy, or helping them write letters home. In the process Whitman
grew especially close to the men, some of whom came to see Whitman
not simply as a friend but as part of their family. Several of those soldiers,
upon returning home, even named their sons after him.[12]

That fierce attachment was entirely mutual. In his relationships with
the soldiers, he rediscovered the social bond that he feared had vanished
from the country and left him with nothing but the "sullen hymns of defeat." Rather than renouncing his faith in national harmony, he redirected
it, devoting himself and his poetry to the countless young soldiers upon
whom the war depended. For Whitman those soldiers, both Northern
and Southern, both living and dead, became the new representatives of
American nationality and brotherhood.

That vision of the war evolved, slowly and organically, out of Whitman's wartime experiences. As he tended to the soldiers, he came to
see many of them—as he once put it—as "*my* boys." A glimpse of that
intimacy can be seen in a letter that he wrote to the parents of Erastus
Haskell, a young soldier from New York who died in 1863:

> Dear friends, I thought it would be soothing to you to have a few lines about
> the last days of your son Erastus. . . . From the time he came to Armory

Whitman's letter to Mr. and Mrs. S. B. Haskell (1863). Courtesy of the
New-York Historical Society.

Square Hospital till he died, there was hardly a day but I was with him. . . .
[S]ometimes when I would come in, he woke up, & I would lean down &
kiss him, he would reach out his hand & pat my hair & beard a little, very
friendly, as I sat on the bed & leaned over him. Much of the time his breathing was hard, his throat worked—they tried to keep him up by giving him
stimulants, milk-punch, wine &c—these perhaps affected him, for often his
mind wandered somewhat—I would say, Erastus, don't you remember me,
dear son?—can't you call me by name? . . . I write you this letter, because I
would do something at least in his memory—his fate was a hard one, to die
so—He is one of the thousands of our unknown American young men in
the ranks about whom there is no record or fame, no fuss made about their

dying so unknown, but I find in them the real precious & royal ones of this land, giving themselves up, aye even their young & precious lives, in their country's cause—Poor dear son, though you were not my son, I felt to love you as a son. . . . [F]arewell, dear boy—it was my opportunity to be with you in your last rapid days of death . . . [ensuring that you did not] die among strangers without having one at hand who loved you dearly.[13]

As Whitman pens this testimonial, he slowly morphs into a sort of father for the lost boy. That transformation of a stranger into "one who loved you dearly" blooms and broadens as the letter reflects on the "thousands of our unknown American young men" who have died in similar circumstances. Whitman, it would seem, is a fatherly presence to each and all—someone able to mend, or at least console, the wounded nation.

Whitman provided a more lyrical depiction of the Family Squabble in *Drum-Taps* (1865), his book of poems about the conflict. The struggle that materializes in *Drum-Taps* is defined not by battles but by the experiences often disregarded as part of History with a capital *H*: unutterable doubts and dreams; sensations of awe; and the fervent, almost familial intimacies fostered by war. In one of the poems, Whitman restages the impromptu burial of a young soldier:

Vigil strange I kept on the field one night;
When you my son and my comrade dropt at my side that day,
One look I but gave which your dear eyes return'd with a look I
    shall never forget,
One touch of your hand to mine O boy, reach'd up as you lay on
    the ground,
   . . . . .
Till at latest lingering of the night, indeed just as the dawn
    appear'd,
My comrade I wrapt in his blanket, envelop'd well his form,
Folded the blanket well, tucking it carefully over head and care-
    fully under feet;
And there and then and bathed by the rising sun, my son in his
    grave, in his rude-dug grave I deposited,

> Ending my vigil strange with that, vigil of night and battle-field
>   dim,
> Vigil for boy of responding kisses, (never again on earth
>   responding,)
> Vigil for comrade swiftly slain, vigil I never forget, how as day
>   brighten'd,
> I rose from the chill ground and folded my soldier well in his
>   blanket,
> And buried him where he fell.[14]

What makes Whitman's vigil so moving is that it is directed, with all the commitment of a devoted father, toward someone whom he does not know at all: a young boy who has been mortally wounded. The poet's kindly acts—silently watching over him, then tucking him in as if he had simply fallen asleep, peacefully, at home—are complemented by his references to the soldier as his dear "comrade," or more intimately still, as "my boy" or "son." Whitman, it would seem, is this boy's surrogate father. Yet the poem also pushes that connection beyond the space of the page, encouraging the reader to view this boy, whomever he is, as the *nation's* lost son, now buried in the "chill ground." Here, and throughout his writings, Whitman depicts the Civil War as a family squabble that both solicits and requires remembrance.

Houses Divided

Although Whitman wrote from experience, he was also tapping into a cultural zeitgeist. In the Civil War era, many Americans felt an intense if often unvoiced desire, an urge bubbling up just under the surface of consciousness, to see the United States as a family not in spite but because of how fractured the country had become. If nothing really tied the states together other than a few pieces of paper (which, according to Secessionists, could be revoked at any time), it was hard to envision how or why any Union could persist. However, if citizens were bound to one another like members of a family, then discord—even the violent sort unleashed by war—could give way to reunion. The Family Squabble provided a way to make the nation cohere in the mind when it could not cohere in reality.

This narrative acquired some of its early flavor from Abraham Lincoln. In 1858, Lincoln famously described the nation as a "house" that cannot be "divided against itself." Later, Lincoln declared secession to be illegal because the states were bound together by "bonds of affection" that made "every living heart . . . all over this broad land" belong to "one national family." His famous conclusion to the Second Inaugural Address, "With malice toward none, and charity for all, . . . let us strive . . . [to] bind up the nation's wounds," is a kind of benediction given by a grieving father.[15]

Yet if Lincoln (who was frequently referred to as Father Abraham) presented himself as the nation's sad patriarch overseeing a struggle between his factious children, he was far from the only one who viewed the Civil War in such terms. Fratricide was a frequent topic of wartime rumors, which cropped up in everything from newspapers to private conversations. There were whispers about a Union captain at the Battle of Belmont (1861) who, shortly after imprisoning a number of Confederate soldiers, was shocked to discover that his own brother was one of them.[16] Rumors also flew about two brothers who fought each other at the Battle of Shiloh (1862). The Confederate sibling, the story goes, was shot and badly wounded, but he was whisked away to a nearby hospital, where his Union brother held him in his loving arms until he passed. Still other stories, reported at second or third hand, surreptitiously entered the American imagination. As Richard Devins reported in his *Pictorial Book of Anecdotes and Incidents of the War of the Rebellion* (1866), an "eye and ear witness relates an occurrence at the battle of Shiloh, which shows . . . the peculiar frightfulness of the 'family war' growing out of the Southern rebellion." Apparently, after two regiments from Kentucky "fought each other with terrible resolution," a Union infantryman "wounded and captured a man who proved to be his brother, and, after handing him back, began firing at a man near a tree, when the captured brother called to him and said: 'Don't shoot *there* any more—that's *father!*' "[17]

As such rumors accumulated, they began to be taken as events that

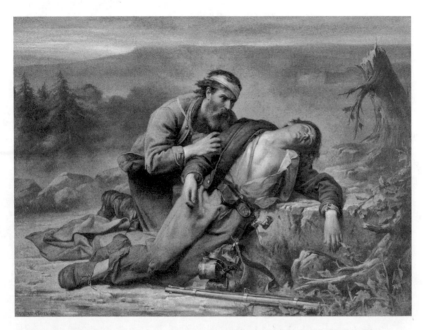

Constant Mayer, *Recognition: North and South* (1865). Oil on canvas. Courtesy of the Museum of Fine Arts, Houston.

were not simply factual but utterly emblematic. Fratricides real and imagined were woven into American culture, appearing in speeches, poems, stories, and songs. The war's status as a family tragedy—or, as one newspaper put it, an "afflicting spectacle of brother shedding brother's blood"—acquired a robust multimedia life, moving between text, image, and utterance.[18] These stories about fratricide were visually complemented by woodcut prints, charcoal sketches, and paintings, such as Constant Mayer's *Recognition* (1865). In Mayer's scene, a Confederate soldier is stunned and saddened to realize that this slain Union fighter, whom he may have just shot, is his own brother. As is suggested by the painting's scale (it is nearly eight feet long) and subtitle ("North and South"), this image is supposed to symbolize the entire Civil War. The recognition evoked in Mayer's scene is the realization that the struggle is a collective, familial loss—and a deeply unnatural one at that. That unnaturalness is underscored by Mayer's symbolism: the broken tree, whose severed trunk lay next to the Union soldier's lifeless body, mirrors the soldier's bloodless death.[19]

That family tragedy, grimly staged in *Recognition*, was retold by the war's poets. In 1862, shortly after the Battle of South Mountain—in which Union and Confederate forces fought across treacherous terrain, killing each other in rocky gaps and narrow passes—*Harper's Weekly* printed the following lines about two brothers felled by "each other's blow," only to reconnect in their final moments:

> Each thought of the mystic token—
>   The talismanic sign;
> Each recognized a Brother!
>   Two firm right hands entwine!
> The fire of the noble order
>   Touched not their hearts in vain.
> All hate fades out, uniting
>   Two hearts with the triple chain![20]

Brotherhood, these lines suggest, is a permanent and mystical relation, an underlying order that supersedes even the most violent acts.

This literature prompts one to wonder where, exactly, loyalty should reside. Are you first and foremost a member of a nation, a family, or a region? For most people, that question is deeply troubling. It asks one to do the impossible—to choose between relationships, to elevate one type of fidelity above another. By expanding the nation to encompass kinship itself, the Family Squabble offers a solution to this problem: if the nation is a family, then one does not have to choose at all. Commitments to one's country, family, or state can instead be viewed as overlapping and harmonious.

For people who lived through the war, this family narrative carried real emotional resonance. It offered a way to see purpose in all of the suffering. That desire to put the pieces back together—to find some wholeness amid the rubble—became so acute, and so widespread, that men as different from one another as William Seward and John Brown Gordon, opposing architects of the Union and Confederate war machines, could both remember the war in familial terms. When Seward, who served as Lincoln's secretary of war, spoke at the dedication ceremony for the National Cemetery in Gettysburg in 1868, he described the Civil War as an immense "graveyard . . . filled with brothers," a "fratricidal war" that the nation required to finally realize its "great destiny."[21] Gordon, who served under Robert E. Lee (and later became a member of the Ku Klux Klan), similarly recollected the conflict, stating that everything that happened in those "four years of fratricidal war"—every letter sent, brother lost, and son mourned—ultimately strengthened the national family.[22]

After 1865 it became increasingly clear that if the Family Squabble was once a misty by-product of rumor and rhetoric, this was no longer the case. It was quickly morphing into something else, something bigger and more coherent—a mythology through which America's past and present could be reconciled and understood.

The Family Squabble after the Civil War

The story of that mythology's abiding appeal is also the story of what happened to the country after the Civil War. When the South surrendered, Herman Melville described the United States as a would-be conqueror with "Law on her brow and empire in her eyes":

Power unanointed may come—
Dominion (unsought by the free)
    And the Iron Dome,
Stronger for stress and strain,
Fling her huge shadow athwart the main;
But the Founders' dream shall flee.[23]

He could not have been more prescient. The United States expanded into the West, often through violent means, going to war against native peoples and annexing their land. This expropriation had already been going on for quite some time, most famously with the forced removal of the Cherokee in the 1830s, but the unification of the North and South intensified it beyond measure. By the end of the nineteenth century, the United States had added thirty new states, as well as territories in the

Pacific, the Caribbean, and South America, more than quadrupling the nation's size and extending its borders beyond the edge of the continent.[24] That massive change to the nation's contours does not even begin to touch on the social, cultural, and technological changes wrought during these years. The spread of the railroad, the creation of factories, the advent of electric lighting, and the emergence of major cities altered the United States in unprecedented ways, as did the influx of immigrants from Germany and Italy, from Russia and Eastern Europe, and, before the 1882 Exclusion Act, from China. These changes collectively transformed what had been (and was constitutionally designed to be) a mostly agrarian, white supremacist republic into a modern, multicultural empire.

This transformation stoked fear and anxiety in many white Americans. They responded by restricting immigration, segregating public spaces, forming nativist political parties, and, on occasion, resorting to physical violence. They also attempted to reorder the changing world—to make it more recognizable and inhabitable—in more subtle ways. Civil War memory became a medium for negotiating new experiences. As the country changed in unprecedented ways, the Family Squabble enabled white Americans to look back to the past and see themselves reflected in it. It allowed them to place themselves at the center of the nation's story and imagine that this most momentous struggle—the war that led to black freedom and set modern America into motion—was, in fact, about white men.

The brotherhood theme became especially popular in didactic mediums like children's stories and young adult novels. Lee & Shepard's "Blue and the Gray Army Series" featured several interlinking novels by Oliver Optic. The first installment, *Brother against Brother* (1894), follows two Northern brothers who move south shortly before the war, only to be torn apart by the conflict when their sons join opposing sides. In the follow-up novels *In the Saddle* (1895), *A Lieutenant at Eighteen* (1895), *On the Staff* (1896), *At the Front* (1897), and *An Undivided Union* (1899), those sons become cavalrymen; fight in the war's major battles; and, after a great deal of toil and terror, reconcile, leading the Secessionists to become Unionists and the two families to reunite. The Civil War thereby becomes, for the family and the nation alike, a kind of initiation ritual through which political and personal maturity are acquired. As Optic puts it, the war "transformed the older boys of the day into men" and enabled them to realize "the blessings of AN UNDIVIDED UNION."[25]

Fraternal discord and American history similarly dovetail in John Musick's *Brother against Brother; or, The Tompkins Mystery* (1887). Published as part of Ogilvie & Company's "Fireside Series," Musick's novel has a familiar setup: two Northern brothers, George and Henry Tompkins, move to the South, marry Southern women, and become slaveholders. The story focuses on three sets of internal divisions: George, who is cool and rational, is at odds with his brother Henry, who is "naturally overbearing and cruel"; George's sons, Abner and Oleah, disagree over the Civil War and join opposing armies; and that decision fractures George's marriage. All of these internal conflicts crystallize around the war, but that struggle also brings about their tidy resolution. Once the war concludes, the sons reconcile and make the family whole again. Toward the end of the novel, Musick—sounding like the stilted voice-over in a bad film—writes, "There are the brothers, Abner and Oleah, with all their old brotherly affection renewed. . . . They sit at the common table—the soldier of the North and the soldier of the South—as though they were, as they are, of one family. Dear reader, . . . let us rejoice that the time has come, when this great Nation, North and South, is united once more in the firmest bonds of friendship—one brotherhood."[26]

The United States was far less united than Musick stated. In the late nineteenth and early twentieth centuries, unbrotherly acts abounded, shadowing these hopeful stories about national fraternity. The novels by Optic and Musick were published during the lynching crisis, in which more than four thousand African Americans were murdered in grim, public spectacles of death and power.[27] Some of those murders were photographed by white participants, who placed images of the lynchings on greeting cards that circulated throughout the country, in the North as well as the South. Such brutal acts were supplemented by more official forms of white supremacy, from immigration quotas to the Supreme Court's ruling in *Plessy v. Ferguson*, which made the idea of "one brotherhood" little more than a fiction based on a highly selective understanding of who can, or should, count as kin.

The Family Squabble is a Northern version of the Lost Cause. Like its Southern counterpart, it reframes the conflict as a war fought by and for white people. It is hardly a coincidence that this literature rarely features African Americans: that's a feature, not a bug. That is why the brothers in Mayer's painting—like the brothers in wartime rumors and the brothers who populate scores of Civil War novels, poems, and plays—are all white. It is also why, in Whitman's *Drum-Taps*, an entire book of poems about the Civil War, there is not a single black presence. To correct the error, Whitman later added a poem titled "Ethiopia Saluting the Colors" (1871), but it does little to remedy the situation. In it, Whitman wonders quizzically why this woman—who he says is "hardly human"—would salute the flag at all:

> Who are you, dusky woman, so ancient, hardly human,
> With your woolly-white and turban'd head, and bare bony feet?
> Why, rising by the roadside here, do you the colors greet?[28]

It's not her country, Whitman seems to suggest, and the war was not really about her, so why does she pay her respects? All of Whitman's sympathy—all of the care he lovingly bestowed on the white soldiers—is suddenly absent, cut short by race.

The racial content of the Family Squabble changes little over time; what does change are the uses to which this mythology is put. The narrative played a particularly important role in the celebrations of the Civil War's Centennial. From 1961 through 1965, the United States was awash in Civil War exhibits, reenactments, and commemorations, many of which recycled the brotherhood theme. On the eve of the celebrations, Ulysses S. Grant III, grandson of the famous general and chair of the Centennial planning commission, opined, "The war did not divide us. Rather, it united us, in spite of a long period of bitterness, and made us the greatest and most powerful nation the world had ever seen." The notion that the war was about unity rather than disunity—a struggle between quarreling white brothers—was reiterated in the Library of

Congress's Centennial catalogue. The title page displays a Union flag and a Confederate flag peacefully intertwined, and the historical overview squarely places the blame for the war on unbrotherly extremism: "[Political] minorities, North and South, [were] led by men of sincere but extreme points of view. . . . Moderation and compromise failed; emotionalism replaced reason; and the growing nation was plunged into its greatest internal crisis."[29]

A slew of books were published to mark the war's one-hundred-year anniversary. *The Civil War Centennial Handbook* (1961), designed as a general guide for the average American, commenced with an epigraph about family ("Here brothers fought for their principles / . . . And a united people will forever cherish / the precious legacy of their noble manhood") and described the war as a tragic fratricide: "beliefs . . . had become so firm that they transcended family ties and bonds of friendship—brother was cast against brother." It included an entire chapter devoted to such fratricidal acts. Here is a snippet:

> PRESIDENT LINCOLN, the Commander-In-Chief of the Union Army, had four brothers-in-law in the Confederate Army, and three of his sisters-in-law were married to Confederate officers. . . .
>
> The Battle of Lynchburg, Virginia, in June 1864 brought together two future Presidents of the United States—General RUTHERFORD B. HAYES and Major WILLIAM MCKINLEY, U.S.A.—and a former Vice-President—General JOHN C. BRECKINRIDGE, C.S.A. [Confederate States of America]. Five other Union generals later rose to the Presidency: ANDREW JOHNSON, U.S. GRANT, JAMES A. GARFIELD, CHESTER A. ARTHUR, and BENJAMIN HARRISON.
>
> The four Secretaries of War during the eleven years prior to the Civil War were all from the South. All four later held office in the Confederate government. . . .
>
> In 1859 WILLIAM TECUMSEH SHERMAN was appointed the first president of what is today the Louisiana State University. Although his chief claim to fame was the destructive "March to the Sea," a portrait of the Union general occupies a prominent place in the Memorial Tower of this Southern university.[30]

These paragraphs—or more accurately, nuggets of loosely connected information—enlist an elastic definition of brotherhood. The implicit claim is that all white Americans are, in a way, brothers; the Civil War was simply a strange, tragic moment in which they did not recognize each other as such. The Centennial thereby becomes, in this *Handbook* and in the anniversary's other texts, an opportunity to revisit and reclaim this white national fraternity—a Cold War–era fiction of consensus and consanguinity.

Although one wouldn't know it by reading the *Handbook* and other Centennial writings, all of these texts were produced during the civil rights movement. While the Centennial's planners were celebrating the war's legacies, protestors were testing those legacies and putting them into practice. For many of the participants in the civil rights movement, memory needed to be accompanied by action. Martin Luther King Jr. (whom we'll revisit in chap. 4) underscored this link between struggle and remembrance in his 1962 speech to New York's Centennial Commission. The problems that gave rise to the war, King argued, were never resolved. The "rebellion against equality continued into the second half of the nineteenth century and into the twentieth century, diminishing the authority of the Federal government and . . . contaminat[ing] every institution of our society."[31] The integrationist sit-ins, boycotts, legal suits, and registration drives sought to curb that long rebellion and carry the freedom movement of the 1860s into the 1960s.

The story of the Family Squabble and the story of emancipation were not merely opposed. These contrasting interpretations derived from different lived experiences, and they had real-world consequences. If the Civil War was indeed a conflict between white brothers as the Centennial's celebrants imagined, then the issue of racial discrimination had nothing to do with the war, whose proper memory was fixed in time. During the Civil War itself, the Family Squabble provided a way to see unity—to discern a nation somehow, someway—in the midst of disunity, and it performed a similar function now, a century later. Whenever it gets retold, this story supports a potent fiction: that the United States is a completed Union, perennially bound and sealed.

Even some of the more skeptical works occasioned by the Centennial, such as Robert Penn Warren's *The Legacy of the Civil War* (1961), recycled this theme. Warren's book is in many respects an anticentennial meditation, an exercise in demythologizing the war. Toward the outset, he writes that slavery constituted the war's heart and soul: "However we may assess the importance of slavery in the tissue of 'causes' . . . slavery looms up mountainously and cannot be talked away." It was slavery, not debates about tariffs or federal law, that provoked "all the mutual vilification, rancor, self-righteousness, pride, spite, guilt, and general exacerbation of feeling that was the natural atmosphere of the event, the climate in which the War grew." Warren also takes to task the war's two most insidious legacies: for the South, a "Great Alibi" that "explains, condones, and transmutes everything" (so that racial segregation and discrimination can be seen as traditions); and for the North, a "Treasury of Virtue," a "psychological heritage" that enables Northerners to feel redeemed by the war and cleansed of history's sins.

But *The Legacy of the Civil War* is also built on a familiar narrative. As Warren writes,

> Before the Civil War we had no history in the deepest and most inward sense. There was, of course, the noble vision of the Founding Fathers articulated in the Declaration and the Constitution—the dream of freedom incarnated in a more perfect union. But the Revolution did not create a nation except on paper; and too often in the following years the vision of the Founding Fathers, which men had suffered and died to validate, became merely a daydream of easy and automatic victories, a vulgar delusion of manifest destiny, a conviction of being a people divinely chosen to live on milk and honey at small expense. The vision [of the Founders] . . . had not [yet] become a national reality. It became a reality, and we became a nation, only with the Civil War.

The Civil War, in other words, finally made America real. It converted ideals that had been merely fictive, even dreamlike, into something concrete. There is no language of brotherhood here, but the underlying story is the same: the war made the United States into the national family it was always supposed to become. It was the birth moment of the union—the "true community," in Warren's words, "the spiritually significant communion"—to which we now belong.[32] Warren enlisted a mythology of the war to critique the mythologies that the war produced.

That probably says less about Warren than it does about the Family Squabble's enduring hold on the American mind. This story—and this is perhaps the truest measure of its cultural clout—has not merely reframed the Civil War as a domestic conflict, through and through. It has reframed Americanness itself as a legacy of that conflict. For Warren, and for many others, American identity only became a reality when fratricide gave way to reunion, yielding a community reborn. No matter how far the conflict dissolves into the past, it continues to be remembered as the founding moment for modern America. Perhaps that is the secret of the story's boundless success: it provides nationality with an origin story, depicting Americanness as a relation that can never be undone. Indeed, if the Civil War was carried out within a single family, and that family was reunited, then the nation is as inexorable as kinship itself—a house not simply undivided but utterly indivisible.

Father Abraham

From the nineteenth century onward, many of these stories converge around Abraham Lincoln. In numerous works, Lincoln is not simply a major player in the war's drama; he is the event's paradigmatic embodiment. His acts, both public and private, come to stand in for the nation's history, transmuting America's experiences—of pain and bafflement, of hope and disappointment—into the life of a single man. In these strands of cultural memory, Abraham Lincoln, for all intents and purposes, *is* the Civil War.

To be sure, there are many Lincolns. There is the monumental president whose stern face and giant body loom over the Lincoln Memorial. There is the freedom fighter commemorated alongside Che Guevara and Fidel Castro in Havana's Museum of the Revolution. There is the white savior of the Freedman's Memorial, standing benevolently with his outstretched hand above a meek ex-slave. There is the operatic hero

Alexander Gardner, *Abraham Lincoln and his son, Theodore (Tad)*.
Photograph (April 1865). Courtesy of the Library of Congress,
Prints and Photographs Division.

of Aaron Copland's *Lincoln Portrait* (1942), whose song for modernity
("The dogmas of the quiet past are inadequate to the stormy present. . . .
As our case is new, so we must think anew, and act anew") has been
recited by James Earl Jones, Neil Armstrong, and Margaret Thatcher.[33]
There is also the Lincoln who has appeared on television shows from
Star Trek to *The Simpsons*, as well as the animatronic president who for
more than forty years delivered a speech at Disneyland about "the love
of liberty" and "reverence for the law." These texts and performances
established several well-known types, such as Lincoln the Pioneer and
Lincoln the Emancipator. But one of the most powerful and abiding
characters is Lincoln the Patriarch.

Lincoln's status as a surrogate father for the grieving nation—preserved in that peculiar appellation, "Father Abraham"—first crystallized in the midst of the war when Lincoln's family, like so many others, was touched by the conflict. One of his sons, Robert, joined the Union Army, and another, Willie, died in 1862 at the age of 11, sending Mary Todd—and perhaps Lincoln himself—into a deep depression.[34] That suffering grounded Lincoln's interpretation of the war. The Gettysburg Address is as much about death, and how to process it, as it is about freedom. According to Lincoln, loss bestows a sacred legacy upon a place and a people—whether it's a vast nation or a single family. That is why, in Lincoln's words, "we can not dedicate—we can not consecrate . . . this ground": death itself bestows meaning.

Lincoln's dual role as head of the family and head of the state only acquired its fullest elucidation upon his death. Immediately after his assassination, Lincoln was mourned as a father and his murder denounced as a parricide. In New York, people put up black streamers, as well as banners declaring "Alas! Alas! Our father Abraham Lincoln is Dead." That sense of loss, *Harper's Monthly* declared, was "the feeling in all true hearts and homes," a sentiment articulated by prominent poets such as Henry Howard Brownell ("Aye, the wars are all over,— / But our good Father is gone"), as well as more obscure writers who lamented the death of this "father of the state."[35]

As the Lincoln mythology took shape, he became a figurehead for the Family Squabble writ large. Artists, writers, and filmmakers took up Lincoln as the symbol of sacrifice par excellence—a father around whom the nation's brothers can rally and abandon their differences. Much of that mythology can be traced (yet again) to Whitman. As Whitman later recalled, whenever he thought of the Civil War in all of its totality—whenever he remembered those four years in which entire "centuries of native passion" were somehow compressed—he inevitably thought of Lincoln: "Looking over all, in my remembrance, [is] the tall form of President Lincoln, with his face of deep-cut lines, with the large, kind, canny eyes, . . . and the tinge of weird melancholy saturating all." For Whitman it was not simply Lincoln's representative sadness that made him so significant—though he did seem to express the country's collective grief. It was the way he embodied a fatherly commitment to the Union:

> He leaves for America's History and Biography . . . [its] greatest, best, [and] most characteristic . . . Personality. . . . The tragic splendor of his death, purging, illuminating all, throws round his form, his head, an aureole that will remain and will grow brighter through time, while History lives, and love of Country lasts. By many has *this* Union been conserv'd and help'd; but if one name, one man, must be pick'd out, he, most of all, is the Conservator of it, to the future. He was assassinated—but the Union is not assassinated. . . . The soldier drops, sinks like a wave—but the ranks of the ocean eternally press on. Death does its work, obliterates a hundred, a thousand—President, general, captain, private—but the Nation is immortal.[36]

What Whitman describes would be impossible to truly memorialize. But Whitman believed that poetry, at its best, could express the inexpressible. So after Lincoln's death, Whitman returned to verse, devoting his *Sequel to Drum-Taps* (1865–66), in its entirety, to the martyred president. The *Sequel*'s crowning poem, "When Lilacs Last in Dooryard Bloom'd," uses a trinity of symbols—a star (Lincoln), a lilac (rebirth), and a warbling bird (Whitman, singing through his grief)—to capture the assassination, as well as the tempest of emotions it unleashed. We watch as the "sad orb" sinks into the darkness, never to rise again. Then Lincoln's great black coffin passes through the country, uniting people through their grief:

> With the pomp of the inloop'd flags, with the cities draped
>   in black,
>   . . . .
>
> With processions long and winding, and the flambeaus of
>   the night,
> With the countless torches lit—with the silent sea of faces,
>   and the unbarred heads,
>   . . . .

With dirges through the night, with the thousand voices
   rising strong and solemn;
With all the mournful voices of the dirges, pour'd around
   the coffin,

.   .   .   .

Here! coffin that slowly passes.
I give you my sprig of lilac.[37]

Everyone grieves in unison, including Whitman, who places a "sprig
of lilac" (i.e., the poem itself) on Lincoln's coffin. Nonetheless, as the
poem unfolds, it becomes increasingly clear that it is both about Lincoln
and not about Lincoln. Whitman depicts the president's death as representative of all the other deaths—the "million dead," as Whitman said
elsewhere, now buried in "clusters of camp graves" or in "the woods or
by the road-side, (hundreds, thousands, obliterated)—the corpses floated
down the rivers . . . [or lying] at the bottom of the sea":[38]

I saw battle-corpses, myriads of them,
And the white skeletons of young men—I saw them;
I saw the debris and debris of all dead soldiers;
But I saw they were not as was thought;
They themselves were fully at rest—they suffer'd not;
The living remain'd and suffer'd . . .[39]

"Lilacs" may have been sparked by Lincoln's assassination, but this poem
is an elegy for "all [the] dead soldiers," delivered to those who remain.
This is what makes the poem so effective, and so memorable: it converts
Lincoln's death into a vast symbolic loss.

    Whitman's Lincoln poems were met with acclaim. Whitman even went
on tour, performing lectures and recitations at various public venues—
and everyone wanted to hear his Lincoln material (so much so that it
became a bit of a sore spot for the poet). Whitman had clearly tapped into
something buried deep within the country's troubled soul. In the spring
of 1865, when the bloodletting of the past four years was finally starting
to wind down, people wished to feel—they needed to feel—that these

countless deaths were not only necessary from a political or historical standpoint but also spiritually meaningful. Many Americans discovered that spiritual significance in Lincoln's death, and in the mourning and sense of peace that followed. Then, as ever, tragedy became "Death's outlet song," allowing the most fraught of human emotions to be processed, turning suffering into sentiments that the soul is better equipped to carry.

The public's grief over Lincoln's murder eventually became less vehement, less intractable, but it did not disappear. Instead, it blended into the cultural landscape. Long after everyone with direct experience of the assassination passed away, Lincoln remained ingrained in American memory. Versions of Lincoln permeate the Civil War's narratives and anchor many of its texts, books, and performances. (Even Thomas Dixon and D. W. Griffith, the neo-Confederate mythmakers behind *The Clansman* and *The Birth of a Nation*, were avid Lincoln fans.) However, Lincoln became particularly vital to—and in the American mind, inseparable from—the Family Squabble.

For storytellers who saw the war as a conflict over national unity, Lincoln proved indispensable. In countless works, Lincoln became a symbolic father through whom the national family is either saved or remade. In the film *Of Human Hearts* (1938), Lincoln counsels a surgeon in the Union Army (played by a young Jimmy Stewart) for neglecting his obligations of his family. That fatherly Lincoln, whose chief concern lies in family cohesion, was a linchpin of some of the earliest silent films, such as *The Reprieve* (1908), *Abraham Lincoln's Clemency* (1910), and *The Sleeping Sentinel* (1914).[40] In other narratives, such as Irving Bacheller's novel *Father Abraham* (1925)—one of several novels written by various authors under that same title—Lincoln becomes a parental substitute and political idol. Bacheller follows Randall Home, a fatherless teenager on the cusp of adulthood, as he travels to Springfield and then declares his love for Lincoln. In response, the future president calls Randall "my son" and invites him to "come some morning at eight o'clock" for a game of catch. "Two days later," Bacheller writes, "at eight o'clock in the morning, Randall found Mr. Lincoln with his small boy, Tad, playing

barn ball back of his house. He was throwing the ball against the side of
the barn and catching it as it came down. Tad, an energetic little lad of
seven, raced for the ball with merry shouts when his father missed it."[41]
Randall briefly takes Tad's place, becoming a sort of adopted son for
Lincoln (and foreshadowing his subsequent election as patriarch in chief).

These stories created a character who exists almost exclusively in the
imagination: Father Abraham, America's great murdered patriarch. That
view of Lincoln is now so widespread and well established that it seems
altogether natural. However, nothing is less natural than cultural memory. It works by transforming violence, loss, and conflict—experiences
that, in their raw form, are exceedingly difficult if not impossible to
process—into symbolic narratives. It converts trauma into mythology.
And that is certainly the case with Lincoln, whose wartime actions contrast quite radically with Bacheller's surrogate father or Whitman's heav-
enly soul. He suspended habeas corpus and established new presidential
powers, creating a model for the "unitary executive" that has come to
dominate American politics in the twenty-first century. He sanctioned
scorched-earth tactics—the burning of fields and homes, the destruction
of roads and railways—that resulted in the deaths of many civilians and
slaves. He instituted a massive draft from which the rich were exempt,
and he refused multiple offers of peace. Even his support for emancipation was slow to develop: he initially backed emigration schemes that
would have sent African Americans to South America or the Caribbean,
only embracing emancipation once it became clear that it offered a strategic advantage. In 1862, Lincoln—still dreaming of emigration—told a
group of black delegates, "You and we are different races . . . [and] this
physical difference is a great disadvantage to us both, as I think your race
suffer[s] . . . by living among us, while ours suffer[s] from your presence.
In a word we suffer on each side." As Frederick Douglass opined, "He
was preeminently the white man's President, entirely devoted to the
welfare of white men."[42]

The real Abraham Lincoln, in short, had to be remade into Father
Abraham. His words had to be reassembled and his actions reframed in
order to be reborn as a grand national patriarch, and literary history pro-

vides a rich and wide-ranging record of that cultural rebirth. It is largely through literature that Lincoln becomes a living, breathing symbol of the family tragedy.

To transform the historical Lincoln into Father Abraham, stories tend to collapse any distinction between his public and private lives. Irving Stone's *Love Is Eternal* (1954), for instance, views Lincoln's political acts and military decisions through the lens of his romantic life. As the novel recounts the courtship and subsequent marriage of Abraham and Mary Todd Lincoln, the Civil War becomes a domestic event—a conflict that is not so much fought as it is discussed. Even Lincoln's death, that final act of Confederate violence, is depicted as a family loss that leads Mary Todd to recall, with both pleasure and melancholy, the "companionable, confiding hours" they had spent together, and the moments when, in his pain, she "comforted him."[43] That family-nation analogy is flipped in Gore Vidal's *Lincoln: A Novel* (1984). In Vidal's fictive world, politics swallow up domesticity: the novel affords views of Lincoln as a father and a husband, but they are subordinated to the novel's lengthy dialogues about the Civil War. But Vidal, too, crafts a vision of Father Abraham by folding Lincoln's private and public acts into one another, thereby transforming the Civil War and its myriad dilemmas into a narrative of closure and resolution.

The only moment when the domestic life of Vidal's Lincoln supersedes his political life is when his son, Willie, dies. Once Lincoln sees the boy's corpse, small and shrouded, he "pull[s] back the sheet" and discovers that "the boy's eyes had been closed; the hair combed. Delicately, with a forefinger, Lincoln touched his son's brow . . . [and tears began] to flow down leathery cheeks that looked as if they had never before known such moisture." Lincoln says, almost to himself, "It is hard to have him die," and then turns to his son, whispering "in a voice that was oddly conversational," "We loved you so."[44] Lincoln's grief for his son becomes a generalized grief for the war's dead, a lamentation for the nation's many lost sons. Lincoln thus becomes Father Abraham not simply by leading the nation into war but by sacrificing his own son to it (much like his biblical namesake). That grief-rooted sense of

Lincoln's symbolism continues to shape recent literary treatments (such as George Saunders's 2017 novel, *Lincoln in the Bardo*) and influence our contemporary view of the war. In the twenty-first century, Lincoln may no longer be remembered as a calm pardoner or baseball-throwing dad, but he continues to be hyperidentified with the Civil War and the family tragedy that it occasioned.

The Lincoln we now imagine is still very much Father Abraham. *Mr. Lincoln's Wars* (2003), Adam Braver's collection of thirteen Lincoln-related vignettes, centers on this saddened patriarch: "His face looked sunken, cheekbones drawn out in a sharp cut, with thin jowls of flesh formed under his eyes that locked off to the distance. . . . His boy, Willie, had died three years ago at the age of twelve, and Lincoln had been right by his bedside." The Lincolns, Braver writes, are just one more set of grieving parents, just "one more family behind a set of doors where a plague not seen since the likes of Pharoah has stolen a son from every home. On both sides of the border, North and South, the bodies are piled high and the tears of [their] parents wash the black from the night into their hearts."[45] Lincoln's status as the Civil War's griever in chief is secured in each of the stories—which feature divided brothers, a young wife in mourning, and several other people from the war's peripheries—but comes into particularly sharp focus in "The Undertaker's Assistant," a story about the man who dressed Lincoln's dead body and his son's before him.

"It was in the summer of 1862," the undertaker recalls, "not too long after his son Willie had died," that he met the president and expressed his condolences for his "fine-looking boy." Lincoln, stunned, asks him who he is and then, upon finding out, pleads, "Tell me everything." "Since Willie died," Lincoln says, "All I've done is walk the floors all night," pacing back and forth, "counting off the steps until light breaks through the window and I have an excuse to be awake." "See," he explains, "the thing is, . . . I don't eat these days, Mr. Jackson, and I sure as hell don't sleep. And the boy's mother is reduced to a saddened state. . . . I'm in charge of a divided nation where boys on both sides seem to have been born to just pass through too quickly. Maybe that's why the Lord put them here, I don't know. But He included my twelve-year-old boy, and I don't understand. . . . There's some part of me that believes Willie's dying was somehow a part of all the soldiers dying."

Braver's Lincoln is at once familiar and unfamiliar. This president is a far cry from the superlatively eloquent and levelheaded orator of the Gettysburg Address. Instead of discerning some hidden Providential reason for "all the soldiers dying," he fixates on his own ignorance ("I don't know"; "I don't understand"). Instead of directing and justifying the war, he is swayed and broken by its violence ("I don't eat . . . and I sure as hell don't sleep"). Yet as Lincoln's grief for his son takes hold, compelling him to accost anyone who has ever had any contact with Willie, it also expands, enveloping the nation in its mournful embrace. As he puts it, "There's some part of me that believes Willie's dying was somehow a part [of the war]"—a loss that, in its generality and representativeness, turns Lincoln into a suffering father for the entire war-torn country.[46]

Lincoln's capacity to embody the Family Squabble is similarly explored in Steven Spielberg's 2012 film *Lincoln*. Although the movie purports to be (and was roundly celebrated as) a story about emancipation, its true subject is something decidedly less enthralling: compromise.[47] Written by Tony Kushner amid the spirited debates about the Affordable Care Act, *Lincoln* presents the Civil War as a historical lesson about the dangers of excessive passion. Pulled between two vehemently opposed camps, the radical abolitionists and the proslavery Democrats, Lincoln negotiates a third way that outlaws slavery while initiating a reunion with the South. The film's politics are lodged just as much in its domestic scenes—especially the exchanges between Lincoln and his wife, who has been carried away by grief—as they are in its political dialogues. At one point, Mary Todd falls to her husband's feet, begging him to forbid their son, Robert, from joining the Union Army. She then accuses Lincoln of being heartless and uncaring after Willie died, whereas she revealed "what heartbreak, real heartbreak, looks like."

Lincoln (played by Daniel Day-Lewis) replies, "I couldn't tolerate you grieving so for Willie because I couldn't permit it in myself, though I wanted to, Mary. I wanted to crawl under the earth, into the vault with his coffin. I still do. Every day I do. . . . [But] I must make my decisions, Bob must make his, [and] you yours." That response, which toes the line, in a rather heartbreaking way, between sorrow and stoicism, captures the film's broader view of compromise: it is not a mere tactic but a veritable end in itself, a principle that squares the head with the heart. *Lincoln's* various exchanges in the residential wings of the White House, in the Senate chambers, and near the battlefield parallel one other, forging a collective impression of the war as a struggle between passion and reason. And it is a struggle, of course, in which the principal actors are almost all white. The film thus updates the Family Squabble that has been cycling through American culture for generation after generation, recasting the Civil War as a conflict carried out within a single white family, headed in this case by Lincoln the father, who becomes, long after his martyrdom, all the more majestic and symbolic in his grief.

The sheer persistence of that story is more than a little strange when you look at it from a certain remove. A nation, to state the blindingly obvious, is very much *not* a family. None of the things that define a nation—whose members are strewn about and linked only through legal fictions—resemble the intimate bonds and everyday rhythms that collectively create a family. One could attribute this metaphor's abiding popularity to many different causes—the tendency of political rhetoric, for example, to take on a life of its own, or the way that American culture almost invariably makes wars into moral parables. But more than anything else, the remarkable endurance of the family tragedy derives from the sense of community that it provides by turning violent change into a story of belonging and persistence.

That story became all the more important in the wake of the war. After the North's victory, the newly consolidated nation underwent a massive transformation, expanding its territory and modernizing its economy. Yet there was always a contradiction at its core: the country created by the American Revolution and the Constitution had destroyed itself. The Family Squabble lets us quietly pass over that contradiction or imagine our way around it. If the nation is fundamentally a family, then the Civil War was simply a domestic quarrel, a temporary falling out that ultimately brought everyone back together. Is that an impossible (and slightly embarrassing) fiction—a story belied by history and logic alike? Of course. But in the end that might be the secret to its appeal. It says something that people know on some level isn't true but profoundly want to believe. It functions as a kind of national wish fulfillment, converting common assumptions about race, community, and the American past into fictions that feel like history. In that respect, the Family Squabble is no mere conceit: it is a living mythology that continues to take form even now, after all this time.

{2} A Dark and Cruel War

IF THE CIVIL WAR WAS SUPPOSED TO BE A DEFINING moment in American history, no one ever told Mark Twain. When the violence erupted in 1861, the famed humorist was still Samuel Clemens—an unpublished, 20-something riverboat pilot from the hamlet of Hannibal, Missouri—and he responded with decidedly little interest or enthusiasm. As he later recalled in "The Private History of a Campaign That Failed" (1885), a fictionalized account of his wartime experiences, there are a "great many people who did something in the war," but he was not one of them. He "entered the war, got just a taste of it, and then stepped out again permanently." Twain joined a group of Confederate volunteers who called themselves the Marion Rangers, which turned out to be nothing more than a ragtag crew of fifteen guys, none of whom had a lick of military experience. They viewed the war as a kind of holiday and spent most of their time on a farm far away from the carnage. While residing there, Twain learned to ride a horse, but only barely. He also tried, and failed, to train a mule— which repeatedly dumped him on the ground and brayed. Eventually he grew so bored that he simply packed up his things and went home.[1]

In Twain's one encounter with the enemy, the enemy did not even bother to show up. After receiving word that an attack was imminent, the Marion Rangers, in all of their out-of-place absurdity, debated "which way to retreat." Everyone, Twain writes, was so flustered that they couldn't fathom what to do, or how to react. "Except Lyman. He explained in a few calm words that, inasmuch as the enemy was approaching from

Abdullah Frères, *Samuel Langhorne Clemens*.
Photograph (1867). Courtesy of the Library of Congress,
Prints and Photographs Division.

over Hyde's prairie our course was simple. All we had to do was not to retreat *toward* him." That retreat did not turn out very well. They fled into the dark woods until one of them lost his footing, "and then the next person behind stumbled over him and fell, and so did the rest, one after another." These human dominoes promptly lost their guns, their powder keg, and any remaining pride. Then they heard a sound, which they feared could be the enemy, but it turned out to be "several dogs . . . bounding over the fence with great riot and noise." Humiliated and terrified, each of the Marion Rangers then "blackguarded the war . . . and everybody connected with it, and gave himself the master dose of all for being so foolish as to go into it."[2]

To commemorate this mock-epic battle, Twain draws a map. In its very simplicity it satirizes the grand, intricate maps of Civil War battles that were

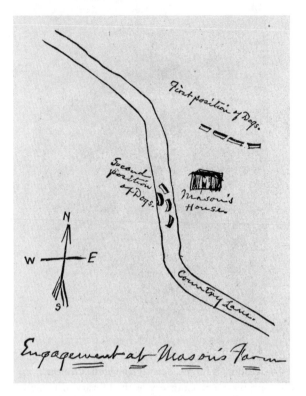

Engagement at Mason's Farm. From Mark Twain's "The Private History of a Campaign That Failed" (1885).

popular in the late nineteenth century—maps that often tracked the armies' byzantine routes and positions, visually indexing the war's tactical complexity. If this map is a joke, it is not directed merely at Twain's younger self. It is also directed at the Civil War. For Twain, the war is defined by its absurdity, and that point is underscored by this image of absence and inaction.

Twain's story is funny, but it also has a dark edge. That's how Twain's writing works: we laugh, and then we discover that the joke is ultimately on us. Twain was a satirist who took as his subject "the whole damned human race." That is undoubtedly the case in "The Private History of a Campaign That Failed." Twain's story is actually punctuated by a murder—an accidental one, but a murder nonetheless. In the middle of the night, the Marion Rangers hear a rumor that the enemy is fast approaching. In characteristic fashion, they decide to just stay in bed—but they soon grow worried and anxious. Then, as if moved by some "unvoiced impulse," they look outside. They can barely see anything—the moonlight is just bright enough to trace the hazy outline of objects—but they hear the "muffled sound" of "hoof beats." That's when it happens. A blurry figure suddenly appears. No one can see it—"it could have been made of smoke, its mass had such little sharpness"—but that does not stop them from reacting, mostly out of sheer fright: "I got a hold of a gun in the dark, and pushed it through a crack between the logs, hardly knowing what I was doing, I was so dazed with fright. Somebody said 'Fire!' I pulled the trigger, I seemed to see a hundred flashes and a hundred reports, then I saw the man fall down out of the saddle."

Shocked by what has just occurred, the Rangers wander out of the cabin. When they find their victim, they discover him lying on his back with his arms askew, his mouth agape, and his chest heaving up and down as he desperately tries to breathe. His blanched white shirt "was splashed with blood," writes Twain, and the "thought shot through me that I was a murderer, that I had killed a man, a man who had never done me any harm. That was the coldest sensation that ever went through my marrow." Out of horror and sympathy, he kneels down by the man, "helplessly stroking his forehead," feeling as though he "would have given anything," even his own life, "to make him again what he had been five minutes before." The other Rangers apparently felt the same way:

> They hung over him, full of pitying interest, and tried all they could to help him, and said all sorts of regretful things. They had forgotten all about the enemy, they thought only of this one forlorn unit of the foe. Once my imagination persuaded me that the dying man gave me a reproachful look out of the shadow of his eyes, and it seemed to me that I would rather that he had stabbed me than he had done that. He muttered and mumbled like a dreamer in his sleep about his wife and his child, and, I thought with a new despair, "This thing that I have done does not end with him; it falls upon them too, and they never did me any harm, any more than he."

Twain's narrator shoots the stranger out of fear and ignorance; his sole wish is for self-preservation. Nonetheless, Twain is clearly unnerved by this act. As it turns out, this unlucky soldier might not have even *been* a soldier. "The man," he notes, "was not in uniform and was not armed. He was a stranger in the country, that was all we ever found out about him." The horrifying truth of the situation haunts Twain—"the thought of him," he says, "got to preying on me every night"—and leads him to reflect more broadly on the strange cruelty of sanctioned violence: "It seemed an epitome of war, that all war must just be the killing of strangers against whom you feel no personal animosity, strangers who in other circumstances you would help if you found them in trouble, and who would help you if you needed it."[3] Twain's sobering suggestion, derived from his Civil War experiences, is that war is never a principled fight for ideals. At its core, it is always the merciless act of killing strangers.

In this regard, Twain's story exemplifies another narrative of the conflict, which emphasizes the war's shocking brutality. This story has been told many times from many perspectives. Its architects include a motley crew of Civil War veterans, novelists, and other memory makers. Some observers, like Twain, abhor the violence, while others embrace it, viewing killing as inevitable and the Civil War as a case study in modern warfare. But these accounts all share the same, bone-deep sense that the Civil War was unusually brutal and its meaning resides in that brutality. As the Union general William T. Sherman declared during his March to the Sea—a scorched-earth campaign designed to inflict terror on the South—this war is "dark and cruel" and "you cannot refine it."[4]

There are several reasons why the story of the Dark and Cruel War took root. Like most of the Civil War's narratives, it centers American memory around white perspectives. If the struggle's meaning is embedded in the white soldiers who participated in battle and experienced its horrors firsthand, then slavery and emancipation become secondary considerations at best. The Dark and Cruel War mirrors the Family Squabble and Lost Cause in that regard: these narratives all reroute American memory by elevating white suffering over black freedom. It also offers, or *seems* to offer, a way to remember the war without explicitly wading into politics: here, the story goes, one finds people instead of causes. Yet, as we will see, this narrative is intimately connected to the history of race, violence, and empire in the United States.

Scenes of Suffering

The most well-known version of the Dark and Cruel War is Ken Burns's. In his nine-part documentary *The Civil War* (1990), Burns recounts almost every aspect of the Civil War, from its music and literature to its medical practices and military tactics.[5] The series' appeal derives from its personalized feel: Burns familiarizes us with the daily lives of former slaves, Ulysses S. Grant's drinking habits, Nathan Bedford Forrest's strategic mind (several of his well-known adages are repeated and explained by Shelby Foote, in his charming Tennessee drawl), and Morgan Freeman's booming voice almost seems to bring Frederick Douglass back to life.

Burns's documentary, however, is also a story, and that story revolves around the experience of suffering. For Burns, this is what links the Civil War's participants: the war was a great crucible of affliction out of which America was formed. The title theme is "Ashokan Farewell," a melancholic waltz, and the first episode begins with a quote about "the incommunicable experience" shared by the war's participants. That quote is actually drawn from two speeches by Oliver Wendell Holmes Jr., who, long before he became a Supreme Court justice, served in the Union Army and was shot in the chest at the Battle of Ball's Bluff (1861). As Holmes recalled decades later, "We have shared the incommunicable experience of war"; "the generation that carried on the war . . . has been set apart by its experience. Through our great good fortune, in our youth our hearts were touched with fire. It was given to us to learn at the outset that life is a profound and passionate thing . . . and it is for us to bear the report to those who come after us."[6] That emphasis on unspeakable suffering also anchors Burns's documentary, which regards pain and destruction as the Civil War's defining legacy.

That viewpoint grew out of the war, which swallowed up countless lives in waves of grief. The fighting that engulfed the United States from

1861 to 1865 resulted in the deaths of approximately 750,000 soldiers and
50,000 civilians. And those numbers only hint at the untold suffering
unleashed by the war: the injuries and amputations, the deaths by disease, torturing and starvation, the suicides and near suicides, the utter
destruction of the land, and the mass animal deaths that fueled the war
machine (horses killed, pigs consumed, etc.).[7] The war was so devastating and so lethal that it transformed American mourning practices
and funeral rituals. To take just one example, the Civil War gave us embalming. At first, embalming provided a way to preserve the bodies of
soldiers who had been killed so they wouldn't rot before arriving back
home; only later, after the war, did it become a routine way to treat and
prepare the deceased.[8] It was not without reason that Lincoln called the
war a "mighty scourge."[9]

Whitman, always sensitive to the zeitgeist, summed up the sense of
loss and woe many Americans felt:

> THE DEAD in this war—there they lie, strewing the fields and woods and
> valleys and battle-fields of the south . . . Antietam bridge—the grisly ravines
> of Manassas—the bloody promenade of the Wilderness . . . the number-
> less battles, camps, hospitals everywhere—the crop reap'd by the mighty
> reapers, typhoid, dysentery, inflammations—and blackest and loathesomest
> of all, the dead and living burial-pits, the prison-pens of Andersonville . . .
> (not Dante's pictured hell and all its woes, its degradations, filthy torments,
> excell'd those prisons)—the dead, the dead, the dead—*our* dead—or South
> or North, ours all, . . . the corpses floated down the rivers, and caught and
> lodged, (dozens, scores, floated down the upper Potomac, after the cavalry
> engagements, the pursuit of Lee, following Gettysburg)—some lie at the
> bottom of the sea—the general million . . . the infinite dead . . . not only
> Northern dead leavening Southern soil—thousands, aye tens of thousands,
> of Southerners, crumble to-day in Northern earth.[10]

Whitman struggles to pack all of the unthinkable horror into language.
The passage brims with death, which warps Whitman's sentences into
a heap of fragments. What Whitman describes bears little resemblance
to the Family Squabble that he gracefully memorializes elsewhere in

his writings; this is a vast, unreasoning affliction unleashed upon an entire nation.

Whitman was also distressed by the manner in which "our dead" had been killed. One of his most unnerving dispatches from the war concerns a massacre in Virginia's wilderness. A Northern medical convoy, transporting sixty wounded soldiers, was suddenly ambushed by Confederate guerillas. As soon as the Northerners surrendered, the Confederates ransacked the train and murdered the injured soldiers in cold blood. Some of them "were dragg'd out on the ground on their backs," Whitman writes, and the guerillas took turns "stabbing them in different parts of their bodies. . . . Some had been effectually dispatch'd, and their bodies lying there lifeless and bloody. Others, not yet dead, but horribly mutilated, were moaning or groaning." Nor did the violence stop there. A force of Union cavalry arrived, placed the Confederates under arrest, and then decided to publicly execute them the next day:

> The seventeen [captured] men were . . . placed in a hollow square, half-encompass'd by two of our cavalry regiments, one of which regiments had three days before found the bloody corpses of three of their men hamstrung and hung up by the heels to limbs of trees. . . . Now, with revolvers, they form'd the grim cordon of their seventeen prisoners, . . . and the ironical remark made to them that they were now to be given "a chance for themselves." A few ran for it. But what use? From every side the deadly pills came. In a few minutes the seventeen corpses strew'd the hollow square. . . . Multiply the above by scores, aye hundreds . . . light it with every lurid passion, the wolf's, the lion's lapping thirst for blood, the passionate, boiling volcanoes of human revenge for comrades, brothers slain—with the light of burning farms, and heaps of smutting, smouldering black embers—and in the human heart everywhere black, worse embers—and you have an inkling of this War.[11]

Is it any wonder that Whitman was drawn to the Family Squabble? That story provides some solace, some semblance of hope and connection. *This* war, on the other hand, is just an animalistic slaughter.

The Dark and Cruel War appears in many of the photographs taken of the conflict. Daguerreotypists such as Mathew Brady, Alexander Gardner, and Edward T. Whitney recorded the carnage of war for the first time, doing something that was not technologically feasible even as recently as the Mexican-American War of 1846–48, and the images they captured tended to efface or challenge the war's ideological pretexts. Some of the photographs reveal bodies askew in blood-soaked fields or buried en masse. Others show solitary soldiers who died in trenches, their limbs already stiffening into their final, quartz-like state, or bodies strewn in strange, inhuman lines. One of Gardner's most affecting photographs shows the savagery at Antietam, which left more than 20,000 men killed, injured, or missing. The most intense fighting took place in a road (afterward dubbed the "Bloody Lane") where scores of soldiers were slaughtered and their bloodied bodies fell on top of one another, forming a hideous pile. This image is harrowing. People are turned into either blurred observers of death or inanimate ravine matter, nearly indistinguishable from the natural debris that surrounds them. This photograph conveys the raw, impersonal force of mass violence—the power of sanctioned murder that civilizations, with their gift for euphemism, call "war." The brutal reality cloaked by that term is laid bare in such images, which impart the hostility of warfare to the very violability of the human self.[12]

Other photographs impart a similar story, shedding light on events like the Battle of Gettysburg. Gettysburg has gone down in cultural memory as a defining moment for several reasons: it was the deadliest battle of the war, it was where Lincoln delivered his famous speech, and it was militarily significant, squashing any hopes for a Confederate victory. In the summer of 1863, Robert E. Lee decided to invade the North, with Pennsylvania as the point of entry. The Union Army parried Confederate attacks until July, when the two sides converged, just outside of Gettysburg. A riot of death ensued: over the course of three days, about 11,000 men were killed, another 29,000 wounded, and Lee's northward push was repulsed.[13] It was celebrated as a Union "victory," but such terms ring hollow in the photographs of the battle, which convey unfathomable suffering.

That suffering permeates Lincoln's Gettysburg Address. After hark-

Alexander Gardner, *Confederate Dead in a Ditch on the Right Wing* (1862). Courtesy of the Library of Congress, Prints and Photographs Division.

Timothy O'Sullivan, *A Harvest of Death, Gettysburg, Pennsylvania* (1863). Courtesy of the Library of Congress, Prints and Photographs Division.

Timothy O'Sullivan, *Dead Confederate Soldier in Devil's Den, Gettysburg* (1863).
Courtesy of the Library of Congress, Prints and Photographs Division.

ening back to the American Revolution ("Four score and seven years
ago . . .") and invoking the country's place in global history ("Now
we are engaged in a great civil war, testing whether . . . any nation
so conceived and so dedicated, can long endure"), Lincoln focuses on
the battle's human toll. The heart of the speech is Lincoln's lament for
the dead: "We have come to dedicate a portion of that field, as a final
resting place for those who here gave their lives that that nation might
live. It is altogether fitting and proper that we should do this. But, in a
larger sense, we can not dedicate—we can not consecrate—we can not
hallow—this ground. The brave men, living and dead, who struggled
here, have consecrated it, far above our poor power to add or detract."[14]
Part of what makes the Gettysburg Address so effective is its rhetorical
sleight of hand. On the one hand, Lincoln says that to properly honor
the dead, we must let their actions speak for themselves. We, the living,
must resist the idea that we can somehow "add or detract" from these

deaths. On the other hand, Lincoln does precisely that, interpreting the soldiers' deaths—even Confederates'—not as deaths but as willed sacrifices for democracy. That pivot provides the Gettysburg Address with its astounding emotional charge: Lincoln converts a grim orgy of blood, death, and pain into a kind of ritualistic offering. Lincoln's speech is an eloquent attempt to cleanse the Dark and Cruel War, to baptize it in the name of democracy.

Many people who lived through the struggle saw it as something far more mysterious and momentous than a "civil war." Abolitionist speeches, religious sermons, and political poems were littered with apocalyptic imagery that cast the war as a calamity of biblical proportions, a red-tinged augur of God's final reaping. For Christians schooled in the idea of Providence, the struggle appeared to be nothing less than a divine intervention, and Northerners and Southerners alike were struck by this possibility. Henry Timrod declared that the North's zealots, "blinded in their rage," were fighting against God himself, who clearly sided with the South. Julia Ward Howe, an abolitionist from New York and author of "Battle Hymn of the Republic" (1861), saw the struggle as a sublime bloodletting, a vengeful release of God's "fateful lightning" on the sinful southland.[15] Nonetheless, such assertions provoked an array of questions. If God was indeed intervening, how could the purpose of that intervention be apprehended by human minds? And more troublingly, what if God sided with one's enemy?

Those questions plagued Lincoln. By the end of the conflict, he embraced the notion that God's will, though ultimately unknowable, was manifesting itself in the war's violence. In his Second Inaugural Address of 1865, Lincoln declared slavery to be an offense against God and deemed the war a "mighty scourge" unleashed on "both the North and the South" as the "woe due to those by whom the offense came." Earlier in the conflict, Lincoln was not so certain about God's role. As he wrote in 1864,

In great contests each party claims to act in accordance with the will of God. Both *may* be, and one *must* be, wrong. God cannot be *for* and *against* the same thing at the same time. In the present civil war it is quite possible that

God's purpose is something different from the purpose of either party—and yet the human instrumentalities, working just as they do, are of the best adaptation to effect His purpose. I am almost ready to say that this is probably true—that God wills this contest, and wills that it shall not end yet. By his mere great power, on the minds of the now contestants, He could have either *saved* or *destroyed* the Union without a human contest. Yet the contest began. And, having begun He could give the final victory to either side any day. Yet the contest proceeds.[16]

One can see Lincoln's legal mind at work, trying to piece together the strange machinations of God's purpose. The possibility exists, Lincoln admits, that both the North *and* the South are contravening God's will—that perhaps His "purpose is something different from the purpose of either party." (The qualifiers that crop up midway through the reflection are quite telling: "I am *almost* ready to say that this is *probably* true.") Lincoln is trying to excise his doubt—to repress or expel it—by reading Providence through history. The very fact that the war exists, when God easily could have preserved or destroyed the nation without it, means that His will is at work, and Lincoln, like so many others, is attempting to make sense of that will and discern a pattern in its unfolding.

The Dark and Cruel War also disturbed, and fascinated, Emily Dickinson. Although she lived most of her life in her native Amherst, Dickinson was deeply interested in the world around her, and her poems—whether concerned with nature's melodies or the metaphysics of pain—record those passionate engagements. Dickinson believed that to tell the truth one must "tell it slant": knowledge, that is, can only be conveyed elliptically. Her commitment to slanted insight is evident in the poems that she wrote about the Civil War, which tend to work by way of metaphor: battle is a "horrid Bowl"; survivors are "Pawn[s] for Liberty"; autumn is a bloody field ("An Artery – opon the Hill – / A Vein – along the Road –"). In the spring of 1863, she wrote the following lines:

They dropped like Flakes –
They dropped like Stars –
Like Petals from a Rose –

When suddenly across the June
A Wind with fingers – goes –

They perished in the seamless Grass –
No eye could find the place –
But God can summon every face
On his Repealless – List.[17]

With its natural figures and hymnal melody, the poem initially imparts a sense of peace. However, that peacefulness is undercut by Dickinson's metaphors: these falling flakes and petals are men mowed down by bullets. God is a force not of love but of violence, a point hinted at in the second line. Stars dropping from the sky present an apocalyptic image. (It's also Miltonic. In *Paradise Lost*, the war between heaven and hell is signaled by angels "dropt from the Zenith, like . . . falling Star[s].")[18] As these men fall like flakes of snow or stars crashing to the earth, the very boundary between the human and the inhuman is blurred, perhaps irreparably.

The fact that this poem seems to be simultaneously about and not about the war says a great deal about Dickinson's view of the conflict. As she stated in a letter, "War feels to me an oblique place." *Oblique*, according to the *Oxford English Dictionary*, describes something that diverges "from a straight line or course"; it is a state of being askew. Dickinson's sense of the war's obliqueness—to her as well as to individual reasoning more generally—is evoked by another poem she wrote in 1863, after the pitiless battles at Chancellorsville and Gettysburg, where men died by the thousands:

If any sink, assure that this, now standing –
Failed like Themselves – and conscious that it rose –
Grew by the Fact, and not the Understanding
How Weakness passed – or Force – arose –

Tell that the Worst, is easy in a Moment –
Dread, but the Whizzing, before the Ball –
When the Ball enters, enters Silence –
Dying – annuls the power to kill –[19]

Who, or what, is sinking? And what does "it" (or "this" or "that") denominate? The second stanza offers a clue. Most infantrymen used balls of melted lead for bullets, and the poem's second half describes the effect of those bullets on the body and the mind. Dickinson transports us to a battlefield where, once again, men are sinking and their deaths are associated with the force of nature. The scene that Dickinson describes here is not a struggle for union or emancipation. The only knowledge that can even be attained is disturbingly negative: dying leads not to glory or freedom; it just "annuls the power to kill." For Dickinson the war is a massive erasure, an upheaval marked by undoing and annulment.

Other depictions of the Dark and Cruel War abounded. Joseph Lawson, a free black barrel maker from Fredericksburg, saw in the conflict an unnerving, animalistic violence. As he recalled in a later interview, he was alarmed one night to discover people running around trying to find shelter, or, if they couldn't find any, escaping into the woods. Shortly afterward, the town was bombarded by "Yankee cannon" and "the gunners could shoot the bombs and balls just where they wanted to": "I know two people was killed dead in bed that morning—an old man and an old woman." Lawson's neighbors fled to his house, which quickly filled with women and children. Then a single "solid shot—a twelve-pounder," struck his house, cutting "one of the big house timbers plumb in two." When the assault finally ceased, he went outside and saw the scores of dead lying on the ground. Many of his former neighbors were now scattered about, some still recognizable and looking as though "they [were] fast asleep," while others had been mangled beyond recognition. "When a man had been hit by a shell that exploded," Lawson recalls, "it bust him up in such little pieces you would n't 'a' known he was ever the shape of a man. A good many bodies was all laid in a row side of the stone wall with blankets over their faces. I saw some old gray fellers among the dead. They had no business to be in the war at their age. Out in front of the stone wall was the Yankees where they'd fallen one 'pon top of t' other." For Lawson, the war is a reasonless bloodletting defined by unspeakable violence, an event that made him never "want to see no mo' war."[20]

A similar distress is recorded in Mary Chesnut's *Diary*. Initially written in the 1860s and then expanded in the 1880s, Chesnut's diary has become one of the most prominent works of Confederate literature. She belonged to the upper crust of South Carolinian society—her father was a governor and senator, her husband was one of the signatories of the Confederate Constitution, and she counted the wife of Jefferson Davis among her intimate friends—and her diary certainly reflects that social position. She hails Confederate victories and mourns Confederate losses, which "stun [us]" and "fill [us] with . . . hate." Yet for all of Chesnut's partisan sympathies, her diary is mostly concerned with the war's psychological impact.[21] Likening herself to Cassandra, the ancient prophetess who foretold the Fall of Troy, Chesnut depicts the Civil War as the tragic destruction of an immense domestic world, an upheaval that spreads from the battlefield to the hearth, the salon, and the dining hall. "When we read of the battles in India, in Italy, in the Crimea," she remarks, "what did we care? Only an interesting topic like any other to look for in the paper. Now you hear of a battle with a thrill and a shudder. It has come home to us. Half the people that we know in the world are under the enemy's guns." Every telegram leaves one "pale with fright": "You handle it, or dread to touch it, as you would a rattlesnake—worse—worse. A snake would only strike you. How many, many, this scrap of paper may tell you, have gone to their death. When you meet people, sad and sorrowful is the greeting; they press your hand, tears stand in their eyes or roll down their cheeks, as they happen to have more or less self-control. . . . And this thing now seems never to stop."

This onslaught came home to her too. Chesnut was devastated when her "gallant and gay" nephew, Johnny, joined the army. Her diary also recounts her family's increasing destitution as the war progresses. One night, as she sits by the window trying to think pleasant thoughts, she discovers that she cannot hold onto them, even for a little while. "A man began to play on the flute, with piano accompaniment. First 'Ever of

Thee I Am Fondly Dreaming,' then 'Long, Long, Weary Day.'" Initially, the music felt like "a complement to the beautiful scene, and it was soothing to my wrought-up nerves. But von Weber's last waltz was too much. Suddenly I broke down. Heavens, what a bitter cry. Such floods of tears. The wonder is, there was any of me left."[22]

Even observers who were far removed from each other politically or geographically shared this view of the war's cruelty. Chesnut's take, for example, is echoed by none other than Nathaniel Hawthorne, that most Northern of Northern writers. More than a decade after writing *The Scarlet Letter* (1850), Hawthorne took to the pages of the *Atlantic Monthly* to say something about the conflict that had swallowed up the republic and slowed his literary output. There is no longer any "remoteness of life and thought," he lamented, "no hermetically sealed seclusion, except, possibly, that of the grave, into which the disturbing influences of this war do not penetrate." The only way to escape the war, the only way to truly disenthrall oneself of its influence, Hawthorne suggests, is to die. And even *that* is no guarantee. For Hawthorne, the war amounts to a massive threat to privacy; it is an upheaval of all the things—all the everyday acts and rhythms—that make up one's life and make that life worth living.[23]

The war's brutality is epitomized by a group of Confederate prisoners Hawthorne meets, none of whom seemed to have the faintest understanding of the conflict. There was not a "trace of hostile feeling in the countenance, words, or manner of any prisoner there," Hawthorne writes; "it is my belief that not a single [one] . . . had the remotest comprehension of what they had been fighting for, or how they had deserved to be shut up in that dreary hole." There is more than a little classist condescension in Hawthorne's commentary (he calls the Confederates "peasants" and "simple, bumpkin-like fellows"), but his essay also suggests that *everyone*, in both the North and the South, is similarly mired in ignorance. Not only does the war, by destroying privacy, remove any opportunity for reflecting on the war's real significance; there is also no record of a "human effort, on a grand scale," that has yet "resulted according to the purpose of its projectors"—indeed, the war epitomizes our inability to ever effect what we desire.

That includes securing freedom, either for ourselves or for others. So far, Hawthorne notes, the war has yielded little in the way of emancipation, and it seemed unlikely to do so in the future: "whoever may be benefited by the results of this war, it will not be the present generation of negroes . . . who must henceforth fight a hard battle with the world, on very unequal terms." Its only result—the only transformation that has definitively occurred, in Hawthorne's view—is destruction. "Around all the encampments, and everywhere along the road," Hawthorne remarked, "we saw the bare sites of what had evidently been tracts of hardwood forest, indicated by the unsightly stumps of well-grown trees not smoothly felled by regular axe-men, but hacked, haggled, and unevenly amputated, as by a sword, or other miserable tool, in an unskillful hand." The armies, it would seem, were laying waste to nature itself:

Fifty years will not repair this desolation. An army destroys everything before and around it, even to the very grass; for the sites of the encampments are converted into barren esplanades, like those of the squares in French cities, where not a blade of grass is allowed to grow. As to other symptoms of devastation and obstruction, such as deserted houses, unfenced fields, and a general aspect of nakedness and ruin, I know not how much may be due to a normal lack of neatness in the rural life of Virginia, which puts a squalid face even upon a prosperous state of things; but undoubtedly the war must have spoilt what was good, and made the bad a great deal worse. The carcasses of horses were scattered along the way-side.[24]

As Hawthorne describes it, Civil War America is a kind of apocalyptic wasteland, a place not of promise but of desolation.

Hawthorne was so disturbed by the Dark and Cruel War that he was never able to transmute it into fiction. But later writers did so frequently and voluminously, producing a wide array of stories about the conflict. As those stories developed, views of the Dark and Cruel War split apart, forming two major camps. One camp, the Philosophers, connected the violence to broader questions about human nature. The other camp, the Soldiers, moved in the opposite direction, viewing the struggle as a tactical contest.

Let us turn, first, to the Philosophers.

The Civil War's "Awful Machinery"

If the Civil War yielded little more than pain and misery, then it is a revelatory conflict, an upheaval that reveals elemental truths. That is how Mark Twain, Ambrose Bierce, Stephen Crane, and some fellow travelers viewed the war: a struggle that disclosed dark but important insights into humanity's insatiable appetite for violence.

The most widely read work in this vein is Stephen Crane's *The Red Badge of Courage* (1895). It revolves around Henry Fleming, a young soldier who wants to test his mettle and attain his manhood. "His busy mind," Crane writes, "had drawn for him large pictures extravagant in color, lurid with breathless deeds," and he believed "that the only way to prove himself was to go into the blaze." Fleming's naive fantasy has to do with the notion that maturity can somehow be acquired through battle, and Crane's novel is a record of that fantasy's unraveling. After he joins the army, Fleming finds that the dreams bear little resemblance to the reality: the men alternate uneasily between camp life and battle, neither of which presents much of an opportunity for self-growth. The further that Fleming descends into the depths of war—fighting, then fleeing, then rejoining the fray to sate battle's "blood-swollen god"—the more his identity disintegrates into the Dark and Cruel War. Swept up in an endless "blue demonstration," he becomes a cog in a massive machine, one of the "many feet" of a "moving monster."[25]

The war staged in Crane's novel has no discernible cause. There are no debates about slavery, freedom, or the Constitution. The only reason we even know that Fleming fights for the North is because of his blue uniform, and even that minor detail shores up the novel's broader interpretation of the war, suggesting that it is really just a bunch of men dressing up in different colors and senselessly trying to murder each other. The remoteness of what's at stake is conveyed by Crane's depictions of the army as monsters, animals, and other inhuman creatures. On the battlefield Fleming's regiment resembles "huge crawling reptiles," and every trace of human personality is expunged:

> Presently he began to feel the effects of the war atmosphere—a blistering sweat, a sensation that his eyeballs were about to crack like hot stones. A burning roar filled his ears. . . . The men bending and surging in their haste and rage were in every impossible attitude. The steel ramrods clanked and clanged with incessant din as the men pounded them furiously into the hot rifle barrels. The flaps of the cartridge boxes were all unfastened, and bobbed idiotically with each movement. The rifles, once loaded, were jerked to the shoulder and fired without apparent aim into the smoke or at one of the blurred and shifting forms which upon the field before the regiment had been growing larger and larger like puppets under a magician's hand. . . . The men dropped here and there like bundles . . . leaving bits of dark "debris" upon the ground. . . . The torn bodies expressed the awful machinery in which the men had been entangled.[26]

This is not a description of men in battle. It is a description of humanity being stripped away. Fleming is deafened by the "burning roar"; his eyes might "crack like hot stones." None of this obeys the dictates of reason: the cartridge boxes bob "idiotically," the rifles (acquiring an agency all their own in Crane's passive syntax) are "jerked to the shoulder and fired without apparent aim," and the bullets are hurled not toward soldiers but toward puppets, "blurred and shifting" in the smoke.

What lesson can be drawn from such a war? *The Red Badge of Courage* famously subverts the classical ideal of war-born glory, the ethos of *dulce et decorum est pro patria mori* (it is sweet and honorable to die for one's country) that Wilfred Owen similarly contested after World War I.[27] Crane's novel also lodges a more specific critique of the Civil War, implying that perhaps this event that has loomed so large in the American imagination is a kind of abyss. If the war even has a rationale (and within *The Red Badge of Courage*, that is very much in doubt), it is either unknowable or incommunicable. Crane conveys a similar skepticism in one of the poems he wrote on the edge of the twentieth century:

There was crimson clash of war.

Lands turned black and bare;

Women wept;

Babes ran, wondering.

There came one who understood not these things.

He said, "Why is this?"

Whereupon a million strove to answer him.

There was such intricate clamour of tongues,

That still the reason was not.[28]

It's unclear whether this "crimson clash" refers to the Civil War or some other struggle, but that's precisely the point: the Civil War, Crane suggests, was war plain and simple, and war is just malignant, unreasoning violence. The darkest and cruelest aspect of the Civil War, according to Crane, is that it had no point.

To the extent that Crane identifies a source for the Civil War, he attributes it to people's inner animality. Across his writings, Crane suggests that war—whether in the 1860s or after—unchains an inborn lust for carnage, a thirst for violence that is as savage as it is irrepressible. Henry Fleming experiences this lust as a "red rage" that transforms him into a "pestered animal": "He wished to rush forward and strangle with his fingers. He craved a power that would enable him to make a world-sweeping gesture and brush all back. His impotency appeared to him, and made his rage into that of a driven beast." There is no manhood attained here; everything resembling a human self falls away and gets supplanted by an almost reptilian appetite for destruction. The Civil War becomes a deeply impersonal and ferocious conflict—a "dark pit," in Crane's words, into which human "animals [are] tossed for a death struggle."[29] If Crane is right, then almost everything we have told ourselves about the Civil War—all the stories we have shared about its historical and political significance, in his day and our own—are really just elaborate lies, consoling half-truths that let us pretend to be something other than violent animals that constantly go to war against each other . . . and then do it again, and again, and again.

In this respect, Crane's perspective resembles Mark Twain's. Humanity's quenchless appetite for war, Twain once remarked, obliges us to rank *Homo sapiens* among the lowest order of animals. "The higher animals," he explained, occasionally "engage in individual fights but never in organized masses. Man is the only animal that deals in that atrocity of atrocities, War. He is the only one that gathers his brethren about him and goes forth in cold blood and with calm pulse to exterminate his kind." Twain developed this perspective in response to the rise of the American empire. When the Confederacy collapsed, violence did not cease; it just shifted westward. The US Army, often with the aid of Civil War veterans, warred against numerous tribes of Native Americans, killing thousands of Cheyenne, Apache, and Lakota and laying claim to their land. In 1800, the United States was a relatively small republic consisting of sixteen states poised along the Eastern Seaboard; by 1900, it was a massive empire composed of forty-five states that spanned the entire continent.

After subduing the West, the American military exerted its power abroad, invading Samoa, the Philippines, Cuba, Nicaragua, Haiti, and other countries across the Western Hemisphere. The historian Frederick Jackson Turner, born in the first year of the Civil War, saw this appetite for bloodshed as an integral and defining part of the American character. Americans, he said, tend to view bloodshed as something that is *redemptive*, even identity forming; the history of the United States is essentially a long story of "regeneration through violence." Considering the astoundingly violent past of the United States—which, since its inception, has been at war for 93 percent of the time—it is hard to disagree.[30] It is that bellicose spirit to which Twain vehemently objects. The Civil War, he suggests, was no different from any of the other wars through which the United States has defined itself.

Twain provided his most biting critique of American warfare in "The War Prayer." Penned in 1905, shortly after the United States had annexed new territories in the Pacific and the Caribbean, "The War Prayer" conjures up the feeling of war fever in a Sunday service—"in every breast burned the holy fire of patriotism," stoked by a preacher who asks God to bless their soldiers—only to savagely subvert it. A grizzled stranger walks in, takes over the pulpit, and translates the pastor's supplication:

> O Lord our God, help us to tear their soldiers to bloody shreds with our shells; help us to cover their smiling fields with the pale forms of their patriot dead; help us to drown the thunder of the guns with the shrieks of their wounded, writhing in pain; . . . help us to wring the hearts of their unoffending widows with unavailing grief; help us to turn them out roofless with little children to wander unfriended the wastes of their desolated land in rags and hunger and thirst, sports of the sun flames of summer and the icy winds of winter, broken in spirit, worn with travail, imploring Thee for the refuge of the grave and denied it.[31]

With its shrieking guns, wailing widows, and fields of patriot dead, the stranger's satiric prayer seems to be about the Civil War and about warfare more broadly. That connection between the particular and the general, between the Civil War and war as such, tells us something important about the conflict and about ourselves. For Twain and Crane, this is what makes the Civil War dark and cruel: it stands in for war itself, symbolizing our capacity to kill strangers. These writers make us wonder, What if war and murder are always, inevitably, the same thing—sanctioned and unsanctioned versions of the same unspeakable crime? And what if the foremost historical legacy of the United States is not freedom but something far crueler: our endless appetite for violence and our equally endless ability to justify it?

Twain explored this connection between wars past and present in *A Connecticut Yankee in King Arthur's Court*, his 1889 novel about a factory foreman who is spirited back to the year 528, in the midst of King Arthur's mythical reign. On the one hand, the novel unfolds at a conspicuous remove from the Civil War: the narrator, who becomes known simply as The Boss, takes down Merlin, travels the countryside with Arthur, and uses science and engineering to bring modern technology to premodern England. On the other hand, Twain constructs eerie parallels between The Boss's adventure (which concludes with a bloody civil war) and American history. The Boss is not simply an American; he is a self-proclaimed "Yankee of Yankees" (a "practical" man almost "barren of sentiment"), and he sees Britain as a benighted hellscape plagued by slavery. Most people, he states, "were slaves, pure and simple," and almost everyone, from King Arthur on down, believed that this institution was divinely ordained. So The Boss, an enlightened Yankee if ever there was one, decides to emancipate the slaves and spread freedom throughout the land. At one point he even issues a Lincolnesque "Proclamation" declaring the end of feudalism and the return of "all political power . . . to its original source, the people of the nation."[32]

The war in *A Connecticut Yankee* is a restaged version of the Civil War, and the only thing this conflict yields—its only indelible result—is pain and suffering. The Boss, wishing to rid the world of knights (a class that closely resembles the Old South's aristocratic slaveholders), kills them with bombs, revolvers, and, in the novel's climactic scene, an electric fence. That scene, the "Battle of the Sand-Belt," is utterly terrifying. The knights, fully armored and marching by the thousands, converge on The Boss, who has surrounded himself with charged wires. When the knights touch the fence, they become "a whirling tempest of rags and fragments." The Boss—as if mimicking Samuel Clemens in "The Private History of a Campaign That Failed"—then goes out to view his handiwork, only to discover that it is impossible to describe. "Of course," he remarks, "we could not *count* the dead, because they did not exist as individuals, but merely as homogeneous protoplasm, with alloys of iron and buttons."[33]

What does it mean if that inhuman reduction is the war's chief consequence? Twain's story has less to do with whether the war is right or wrong (although the violence captured here certainly imparts a sense of transgression and cruelty) than with an argument about belief. "Inherited ideas," The Boss declares, "are a curious thing. . . . I had mine, the king and his people had theirs. In both cases they flowed in ruts worn deep by time and habit, and the man who should have proposed to divert them by reason and argument would have had a long contract on his hands." In this respect, the war was an unavoidable struggle, an inevitable clash of inherited ideas that were as distinct as they were ineradicable.

Ambrose Bierce shared Twain's skepticism. During the war, Bierce served as an infantryman and topographical engineer in the Union Army. He participated in the battles at Philippi, Stone River, and Shiloh—where, he later recalled, the exploding shells left a "wretched debris" that "littered the spongy earth"—and then suffered a headshot (from which he eventually recovered) at Kennesaw Mountain.[34] After the war, he became a writer of considerable range, composing works of speculative and supernatural fiction, as well as numerous fables, essays, maxims, novellas, poems, and epigrams. Bierce's most compelling works, though, are his short stories about the Civil War, collected in *Tales of Soldiers and Civilians* (1891) and *Can Such Things Be?* (1893). These stories draw on Bierce's wartime experiences, and they construct a distinct account of the Dark and Cruel War, emphasizing the limits of individual perception and the absolute power of chance.

In "Chickamauga," Bierce reconstructs a ferocious battle he had witnessed decades earlier. The Battle of Chickamauga (1863) was the deadliest skirmish after the Battle of Gettysburg (1863), yielding more than 30,000 total casualties and scarring Bierce for the rest of his life. The battle is retold from the perspective of a six-year-old boy, the son of a poor Southern planter who gets so absorbed in play that he strays from home and falls asleep in the woods. When he wakes up, he is perplexed by what he sees: bears—many of them—traversing the earth with a "shambling, awkward gait." They are, of course, not bears but men, gravely injured and unable to walk, now crawling toward the river to drown themselves. "All their faces," Bierce writes, "were singularly white and many were streaked and gouted with red. Something in this . . . reminded him of the painted clown whom he had seen last summer in the circus, and he laughed as he watched them." Assuming that the soldiers are playing a game, he mounts one, hoping to go for a ride. "The man sank upon his breast, recovered, flung the small boy fiercely to the ground as an unbroken colt might have done, then turned upon him a face that lacked a lower jaw." Terrified, the child runs away, and the jawless man rejoins the procession: "And so the clumsy multitude dragged itself slowly and painfully along in hideous pantomime—moved forward down the slope like a swarm of great black beetles, with never a sound of going—in silence profound, absolute."[35]

In describing these men as an inhuman mass—bear-like creatures or swarms of beetles thirsting for death—Bierce evokes the war's terrible violence while depriving it of a rationale. Human bodies are reduced to animal matter, and there is no underlying cause. The war's remoteness to human understanding is underscored in the setup: we only learn what is happening from a young boy who turns out to be deaf. The story ends when he discovers his mother's corpse and, in his distress, releases "a series of inarticulate and indescribable cries—something between the chattering of an ape and the gobbling of a turkey—a startling, soulless, unholy sound." This is the sound of mourning, but for Bierce it is also the sound of the war—the acoustics of reasonless violence. In this regard, the child is Bierce's paradigmatic Civil War survivor. We are, he suggests, all versions of this boy, surrounded by devastation but unable to assign it any coherent meaning.

Of Bierce's stories, few are as acerbic—or as darkly humorous—as "Killed at Resaca." Bierce narrates the life and death of Herman Brayle, a valiant lieutenant (and apparent dimwit) who liked to display his courage by standing directly in the line of fire. "He would sit his horse like an equestrian statue," Bierce writes, "in a storm of bullets and grape, in the most exposed places . . . [even] when, without trouble and with distinct advantage to his reputation for common sense, he might have been in such security as is possible on a battlefield in the brief intervals of personal inaction." Even when he was on foot, his conduct was the same. "He would stand like a rock in the open when officers and men alike had taken to cover . . . facing in the direction of the sharpest fire." Brayle is a living embodiment of Henry Fleming's outmoded ideal—the Homeric soldier steeled by bravery—and the Civil War is where such ideals come to die. During the Battle of Atlanta (1864), the inevitable finally occurs: Brayle gallops out to the edge of a field, presenting an easy target to the enemy, so they shoot him. His death garners no glory, nor does it propel the regiment forward. He simply dies, and in doing so, he demonstrates the inviolable power of chance. As Bierce puts it,

"He who ignores the law of probabilities challenges an adversary that is seldom beaten."[36] For Bierce the Civil War is but a manifestation of the universe's underlying chaos, a violent disorder that the human mind is inherently incapable of grasping.

Strategizing Death

Another group of writers, the Soldiers, moved in the opposite direction. Instead of being horrified by the Dark and Cruel War, they embraced it. For the Soldiers, the Civil War's meaning resides not in its ethical or philosophical dimensions but in the lessons it imparts about modern warfare.

This more bellicose version of the Dark and Cruel War discovered its greatest advocates in former generals, captains, and other officers who composed autobiographies about their Civil War experiences. Periodicals like *Scribner's* and the *Southern Historical Society Magazine* routinely featured essays by or about former officers and their tactical decisions. In the 1880s, the *Century* ran a popular series, "Battles and Leaders of the Civil War," in which Northern and Southern commanders reflected on their wartime experiences. Autobiographies of some of the most prominent officers also began to appear as soon as the war concluded. Scores of these books were printed up through the early twentieth century, composed by the generals of the Army of the Potomac, the Army of the Valley, and the Army of Tennessee; the admirals of the Mississippi River Squadron and the James River Squadron; and leaders of numerous other fleets, regiments, and divisions.

In these officers' memoirs, the human personality tends to be stripped away. They contain few if any reflections on their inner life; indeed, nearly all of the things that constitute a private self are conspicuously absent. What one finds instead are detailed accounts of battles, the backstories of military commissions, verbal exchanges between commanders, and an abundance of maps and graphs. What one finds, in short, are men of the gun, men whose lives were shaped by warfare before and after the events of 1861–65, and who were far less interested in questions of history or identity than in matters of military planning and execution.

These books were on the mind of Robert Underwood Johnson, the editor of the *Century*, when he stated that "current literature abounds in minute studies of the separate campaigns and engagements of the great civil war, most of them purely military . . . [and] so extended as to bewilder the reader with [a] multiplicity of details." Johnson saw the work he shepherded into the world as a corrective to this tendency, but what he describes—the minute attention paid to battles, the proliferation of impersonal detail after impersonal detail—are underlying features of the genre, and they convey a view of the war as a martial testing ground. One of the *Century's* selections, David Thompson's narrative of the Battle of Antietam (1862), provides a vivid rendering of these minutiae. It commences by describing the landscape ("the student of that battle knows one corn-field only," but "there were woods, too, and knolls, and . . . other corn-fields") and then segues into an account of the fighting that ensued:

A Confederate battery discovered our position in our corn-field, as soon as it was light enough to see, and began to shell us. As the range became better we were moved back. . . . The general plan of battle appears to have been to break through the Confederate left, following up the advantage with a constantly increasing force, sweep him away from the fords, and so crowd his whole army down into the narrow peninsula formed by the Potomac and Antietam Creek. Even the non-military eye, however, can see that the tendency of such a plan would be to bring the two armies upon concentric arcs, the inner and shorter of which must be held by the enemy, affording him the opportunity for reenforcement by interior lines—an immense advantage only to be counteracted by the utmost activity on our part, who must attack vigorously where attacking at all, and where not, imminently threaten. Certainly there was no imminence in the threat of our center or left—none whatever of the left, only a vague consciousness of whose existence even seems to have been in the enemy's mind, for he flouted us all the morning with hardly more than a meager skirmish line, while his coming troops, as fast as they arrived upon the ground, were sent off to the Dunker Church.

To the degree that this battle has any importance, it resides in its strategic coherence. General McClellan's plan—to shatter Lee's left flank and then push him away so as to pin in the Confederate forces—was unsound since it risked bringing the "two armies upon concentric arcs." That is indeed what occurred: Lee shifted his lines, which enabled him to repel Burnside's forces.[37] For Thompson, the Battle of Antietam is significant because of *how* rather than *why* it was fought; its entire meaning resides in the fact that it was a tactical blunder.

Viewed through these writings, the Dark and Cruel War is a dehumanizing force that robs people of their ability to love, dream, or feel any kind of meaningful intimacy. In his narrative, Thompson becomes little more than a set of eyes, an observer of the war's defining movements and countermovements. Even the more fleshed-out versions of this genre, like Ulysses S. Grant's *Personal Memoirs* (1885–86), frame the war in similar ways. After blaming the conflict on political demagogues ("There is little doubt in my mind now that the prevailing sentiment of the South would have been opposed to secession in 1860 and 1861, if there had been a fair and calm expression of opinion"), Grant devotes much of the book to his generalship, providing extended accounts of numerous battles, sieges, and campaigns. To complement these descriptions, Grant includes no fewer than forty-three maps. Forty-three! It does Grant's *Personal Memoirs* only a slight disservice to say that it is less an autobiography than an annotated series of topographic charts.

Grant's most thorough annotation describes the Battle of Shiloh. In the spring of 1862, Grant was leading his army through Tennessee when the Confederates launched a surprise attack. He recounts the fierce fighting as the Union forces tried, and initially failed, to hold their positions. "A number of attempts were made by the enemy to turn our right flank, where Sherman was posted, but every effort was repulsed with heavy loss. But the front attack was kept up so vigorously that . . . the National troops were compelled, several times, to take positions to the rear." Eventually, Grant's men were reinforced by three more divisions, and because of their superior numbers and positions, they were able to repel the Confederate assault. As Grant summarizes it, "The situation at the close of Sunday was as follows: along the top of the bluff . . . Colonel J. D. Webster, of my staff, had arranged twenty or more pieces

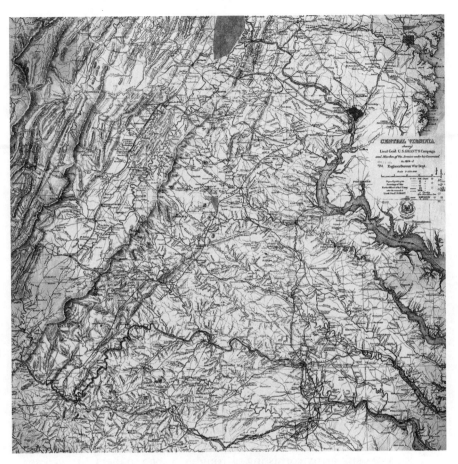

Map of Central Virginia. From Grant's *Memoirs* (1885–86).

of artillery. . . . Hurlbut with his division intact was on the right of this artillery, extending west and possibly a little north. . . . McClernand came next in the general line, looking more to the west. . . . Sherman came next, his right extending to Snake Creek." Against this arrangement, no Confederate victory was possible. The South's forces "made a last desperate effort to turn our flank, but was repulsed. . . . Before any of Buell's troops had reached the west bank of the Tennessee, firing had almost entirely ceased; anything like an attempt on the part of the enemy to advance had absolutely ceased."[38]

Other officers shared Grant's strategic view. Edward Porter Alexander, a Confederate artillery officer, remembered the Battle of Mechanicsville (1862) as a contest of positions. The Confederate forces, he writes, attempted to "deceive the enemy by making him think that our game was to reinforce Jackson strongly up in the Valley, and have him make a vigorous attack on Washington itself." They withdrew multiple divisions, only to have them stand ready near the railroad stations. Everything "was so planned that by railroad and by marching, they would all be back, and all of Jackson's original men with them, concentrated at Ashland. . . . There the battle order took them in hand at 3 am on June 26th, and started them to march around the enemy's flank at Beaver Dam and to cross the creek above it and to take the enemy in rear, while A. P. and D. H. Hill crossing by Meadow Bridge and Mechanicsville roads threatened its front."[39] Once again, the fighting's meaning consists in its plans and stratagems. This is a war not merely defined by its martial particulars; it is fundamentally *about* the manner in which it was fought.

William T. Sherman, too, saw the war as a war of strategy. Through his writing as well as his tactics, Sherman played a vital role in shaping the story of the Dark and Cruel War. By the fall of 1864, Sherman and Grant were convinced that as long as the South desired to fight and had the ability to do so, the war would continue. So they shifted tactics, directing their violence toward the South's infrastructure and morale. With a massive army consisting of roughly 60,000 soldiers—as well as thousands of ex-slaves who had fled their plantations and sought refuge in the Union's lines—Sherman marched through Georgia and South Carolina, laying waste to the heart of the Confederacy. In this March to the Sea, Sherman instructed his men to upend railways, forage liberally, take guns and ammunition and horses, and demolish houses and mills and cotton gins, in order to sever the Southerners' supply lines and break their will to fight.

Sherman's army became a kind of traveling city, a moving civilization that transformed the landscape. As E. L. Doctorow writes in *The March* (2005), Sherman's forces were so numerous "that they overflowed the street and spread themselves through the yards like a river widening its

George N. Barnard, *Charleston, South Carolina. Ruins of Cathedral of St. John and St. Finbar and Secession Hall* (1865). Courtesy of the Library of Congress, Prints and Photographs Division.

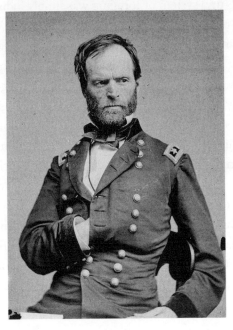

Maj. Gen. William T. Sherman (between 1860 and 1865). Courtesy of the Library of Congress, Prints and Photographs Division.

banks. White canvas wagons pulled by teams of mules appeared, the mule skinners with their sleeves rolled, and behind them caissons, the gun barrels catching the late-afternoon sun with sudden, sharp shards of light that suggested their propulsive murderousness." To this day, in many parts of the South, Sherman continues to be widely reviled and regarded as a heartless butcher.

Sherman's writings are just as illuminating as his military decisions. In his memoirs, which he completed more than a decade after his March to the Sea, Sherman describes the war as a vast, malformed chaos and the army as a brute instrument of order. For Sherman the army is not a democratic outgrowth of the people but something much colder: an "animated machine," an "instrument" that depends on what all machines require—energy, efficiency, and interlocking parts. This utilitarian perspective infuses Sherman's book (which he describes as a collection of "materials"), from his battle commentaries to his tactical recommendations. "No army can be efficient," he opines, "unless it be a unit for action, . . . and the more simple the principle, the greater the likelihood of a determined action"; "The great question of the campaign was one of supplies"; "[my] system of foraging was simply indispensable to our success. By it our men were well supplied with all the essentials of life and health, while the wagons retained enough in case of unexpected delay, and our animals were well fed."[40] In this machine, every soldier, from the lowliest private to the highest general, is but a gear or cog—part of a massive system of guns, trains, and supplies that uses chaos as fuel.

Sherman's sparse prose mirrors his utilitarian outlook. He seems to have carried his theory of war into the realm of language, composing his book by simplifying the syntax and approaching each paragraph as a kind of regimental unit. One must not mistake Sherman's utilitarianism for a full-fledged philosophy, though. The seeds of modern warfare are certainly laid here, gesturing toward the asymmetric and guerrilla-style conflicts of the post-WWII era, but for Sherman all of this developed as a kind of automatic response to the war's particular set of circumstances. His foraging expeditions, urban bombardments, and scorched-earth methods emerged out of a need for uncompromising efficiency. "Very few of the battles," he writes, "were fought as described in . . . text-books, viz., in great masses, in perfect order, maneuvering by corps, divisions, and brigades." His soldiers (or cogs) were "generally in a wooded country, and, though our lines were deployed according to tactics, the men generally fought in strong skirmish-lines, taking advantage of the shape of ground, and of every cover." The war's unpredictability was also magnified by the Confederates' superior geographical knowledge ("they were always ready, had cover, and always knew the ground to their immediate front; whereas we . . . had to grope our way over unknown ground") and by the infrequency of classic, textbook-style battles: "Rarely did the opposing lines in compact order come into actual contact . . . [and] when the lines did become commingled, the men fought individually in every possible style, more frequently with the musquet clubbed than with the bayonet, and in some instances the men clinched like wrestlers, and went to the ground together."[41]

Sherman sums up this fighting with a resonant insight: "War is cruelty, and you cannot refine it." This statement comes from his correspondence with John Bell Hood, which contains some of his sharpest reflections on the Dark and Cruel War. When Sherman's animated machine finally reached Atlanta in 1864, he wrote to Hood, the Confederate commander in charge of the city, asking him to remove the civilians. Hood heeded the request and then took Sherman to task, haranguing him for his promise to attack Atlanta even if the civilians were not relocated. "And now, sir," declared Hood, "permit me to say that the unprecedented measure you propose transcends, in studied and ingenious cruelty, all acts ever before brought to my attention in the dark history of war. In the name of God and humanity, I protest, believing that you will find that you are expelling from their homes and firesides the wives and children of a brave people."

Sherman responded in kind, answering Hood's rebuke with his own. "You style the measures proposed 'unprecedented,'" Sherman replied, "and appeal to the dark history of war for a parallel, as an act of 'studied and ingenious cruelty.'" But the evacuation is "not unprecedented; for General Johnston himself very wisely and properly removed the families all the way from Dalton down, and I see no reason why Atlanta should be excepted. Nor is it necessary," he added, "to appeal to the dark history of war, when recent and modern examples are so handy. You yourself burned dwelling-houses along your parapet, and I have seen to-day fifty houses that you have rendered uninhabitable because they stood in the way of your forts and men." As for protesting in the name of God, Sherman says,

> In the name of common-sense, I ask you not to appeal to a just God in such a sacrilegious manner. You who, in the midst of peace and prosperity, have plunged a nation into war—dark and cruel war—who dared and badgered us to battle, insulted our flag, seized our arsenals and forts that were left in the honorable custody of peaceful ordnance-sergeants, seized and made "prisoners of war" the very garrisons sent to protect your people. . . . You cannot qualify war in harsher terms than I will. War is cruelty, and you cannot refine it; and those who brought war into our country deserve all the curses and maledictions a people can pour out. . . . You might as well appeal against the thunder-storm as against these terrible hardships.[42]

Sherman touches on several themes, asserting that the war has clouded the distinction between soldiers and civilians; that a just God would have no role in such a struggle; and that, like a great storm, it cannot be stopped—only weathered. All of this seems to absolve Sherman himself of any ethical responsibility (hence his sly rechanneling of agency: "You yourself burned dwelling houses," "You . . . have plunged a nation into war," etc.). But Sherman's description of the war also yields a fairly coherent account of the conflict. He presents it as a great, unreasoning force—a maelstrom of cruelty that cannot be altered or resisted.

Sherman's perspective on the war harmonizes with James Longstreet's. A former Confederate general, Longstreet likewise views the war as a struggle over tactics, but for this commander the conflict's lesson has to do with the value of trench warfare. In his 1895 memoir *From Manassas to Appomattox*, he even critiques Robert E. Lee for his decisions at the Battle of Chancellorsville (1863), often considered to be Lee's crowning strategic achievement. "Considered as an independent affair," Longstreet admits, "it was certainly grand," but Lee entertained an outmoded view of fighting and did not commit to entrenched battle.

If he had, Lee would have been able to fortify his positions and, even after Hooker's assault, hold "his army solid behind his lines, where his men would have done more work on the unfinished lines in a day than in months of idle camp life." As a stand-alone fight, Longstreet continues, the battle was undoubtedly "brilliant, and if the war was for glory could be called successful, but, besides putting the cause upon the hazard of a die, it was crippling in resources and of future progress, while the wait of a few days would have given time for concentration. . . . This was one of the occasions where success was not a just criterion."[43] In his assessment of Lee's generalship, Longstreet advances a rather remarkable claim: that the point of the battle, its true value, lay in securing superior positions and wearing down the Northern forces. The war revolved not around glory, freedom, or even victory, but around logistics.

Longstreet's commitment to trench warfare tells us something about his broader view of the war. For Longstreet, as for Sherman, the war is ultimately a struggle over limited positions and resources. It is not a fight for unity, whether regional or national—nor is it personal. Here is how Longstreet describes his momentous decision to join the Confederacy (which turns out to be decidedly unmomentous): "On the 29th of June, 1861, I reported at the War Department at Richmond, and asked to be assigned for service in the pay department, in which I had recently served. . . . On the 1st of July I received notice of my appointment as brigadier-general, with orders to report at Manassas Junction, to General Beauregard."[44] There is no decision to even be made. Longstreet simply moves from military machine to military machine. There are no drawn-out philosophical reflections or political ruminations because, for Longstreet and these other commanders, they do not belong in the war. The latter is a cruel struggle that can only be understood through martial maneuvers and techniques—in short, through the logistics of killing strangers.

The Tactical War: Revivals and Afterlives

The Soldiers' perspective persists in later literature and culture. Stories about Civil War strategy have thrived in recent decades. Films such as

Gods and Generals (2003)—which focuses on the commands of Stonewall Jackson, Joshua Chamberlain, and Robert E. Lee—apply the great man theory of history to the war's memory, presenting the conflict as a series of consequential decisions made by brilliant, if flawed, men. Television programs such as *Civil War Combat* (History Channel, 1999–2003) reconstruct the famous battles at Petersburg, Shiloh, Antietam, and Cold Harbor in all of their martial complexity, explaining the various envelopments, flank attacks, and force concentrations that defined the war and determined its outcome. Histories such as Shelby Foote's *The Civil War: A Narrative* (1958–74) and John Keegan's *The Civil War: A Military History* (2009) give more nuanced accounts of those tactics and their development, and numerous novels, from James Reasoner's *Chancellorsville* (2000) to Newt Gingrich's *Gettysburg* (2003), similarly construe the war as a conflict whose meaning resides, almost entirely, in its martial schemes.

The enduring appeal of this genre is due in no small part to the rise of the military-industrial complex. As the government and the economy in the United States became increasingly intertwined, it reshaped the more private aspects of American life, normalizing and domesticating everything military. There is a thread of connection between the militarization of the police, airports, and sporting events and the uptick in this strain of Civil War memory, which frames the conflict as a clash of technologies and stratagems. There is also the vital issue of politics. Approaching the conflict as a sequence of battles whose import lies in their tactical coherence allows one to either ignore or bypass broader considerations about race and freedom in the United States—or, à la writers such as Twain and Bierce, questions about human nature and the ethics of violence. For all of its emphasis on manhood and warfare, it is a relatively sheltered form of Civil War memory, one that promises to shield us from thinking too hard about the violence that it so lavishly represents.

Recent stories of the tactical war have been heavily influenced by Michael Shaara. A novelist as well as an Army veteran, Shaara updated and popularized the strategic account first developed by the war's officers. His Pulitzer Prize–winning novel, *The Killer Angels* (1974), retells the story of Gettysburg "from the viewpoints of Robert E. Lee and James Longstreet and some of the other men who fought there." Most of the novel recounts various plans being communicated, reconsidered, or carried out. What we find in *The Killer Angels* is not the Battle of Gettysburg but the tactical perspectives of the battle's generals. It features no fewer than seventeen maps, which delineate everything from the prior routes of the armies to the defenses mounted at Little Round Top. The maps' titles are revealing. Here are a few samples: "Situation at 9:00 A.M., July 1: Buford's Defense," "The First Day—11:00 A.M.: Situation after the Death of Reynolds," "The First Day—3:00–4:00 P.M.: Attack of Ewell's Corps on Howard's Flank." Shaara's inclusion of seventeen maps, of course, pales in comparison to Grant's cartophilic memoirs, but the fact that *The Killer Angels* includes all of these maps says a lot about what kind of novel it wishes to be.

Questions regarding the intent of the Confederate assault form the heart of the novel. Is Gettysburg an offensive attack or part of a longer struggle over resources? Is it a concerted strike at the North or an attempt to diminish its forces? Shaara emphasizes the disagreement between Lee and Longstreet on this matter. Prior to the battle, Longstreet studies the geography and then tells Lee, "They're right where we want them. All we have to do is . . . get between them and Lincoln and fight some good high ground, and they'll have to hit us, . . . and we'll have them." Lee will have none of it. "You mean you want me to disengage?" Lee asks. Longstreet replies,

> "Of course . . . You certainly don't mean—sir, I have been under the impression that it would be our strategy to conduct a defensive campaign, wherever possible, in order to keep this army intact."
>
> "Granted. But the situation has changed."
>
> "In what way?"
>
> "We cannot disengage. We have already pushed them back. How can we move off in the face of the enemy?"
>
> Longstreet pointed. "Very simply. Around to the right. He will occupy those heights and wait to see what we are going to do. He always has. Meade is new to the command. He will not move quickly."

Lee put his hand to his face. He looked toward the hill and saw the broken
Union corps falling back up the slope. He felt only one urge: to press on
and get it done.[45]

Shaara's Lee, "an honest man, a gentleman" who never loses "his temper
nor his faith," is very similar to Lost Cause portrayals. Yet *The Killer Angels*
is markedly uninterested in freedom, Southern or otherwise. Instead, the
novel locates the war's meaning in the flow of battle-time information
and decision-making. In *The Killer Angels*, the war consists in military
plans coming into violent and momentous contact with one another.

According to Shaara, the war's meaning is lodged in its battles. This
view of the conflict is expressed by Joshua Lawrence Chamberlain in
response to a soldier who says, "Thing I never will understand. How
can they fight so hard, them Johnnies, and all for slavery?" Provoked by
the soldier's question, Chamberlain realizes that he had "forgotten the
Cause" as soon as "the guns began firing." "It seemed very strange now
to think of morality," Shaara writes, and the only answer Chamberlain
can find—the only response he can muster, silently and to himself—is
that no retrospection was yet possible: "They were not done. . . . They
would fight again, and . . . he was looking forward to it with an incredible eagerness, as you wait for the great music to begin again after the
silence. He shook his head, amazed at himself. He thought: have to come
back to this place when the war is over. Maybe then I'll understand it."[46]
The only understanding we can wrest from the war apparently resides
in its battles. *The Killer Angels* offers readers a chance to "come back to
this place" because the war's meaning is supposedly contained here in
its entirety, inscribed in the armies' shifting movements, which produce
something like a musical score, an opera of death and strategy.

The novel's interpretation of the war is a function of its form. *The Killer
Angels* is a work of military historical fiction, much like the cinematic
war dramas of Tom Clancy, Bernard Cornwell, and Patrick O'Brian. In
contrast with the historical novel (their evolutionary precursor), these
novels say nothing about the shape of history; they are far more interested in maneuvers, technologies, and ideals of manhood. (Think *The*

Red Badge of Courage without any multidimensional characters or philosophical speculations . . . and with a lot more guns, and descriptions of
hardened men making tough decisions while smoking.) *The Killer Angels'*
account of the war is reiterated in *Gettysburg* (1993), the film into which
Shaara's novel was adapted. The music (which swells within and around
the battle's climactic scenes), script (which includes copious exchanges
about attacks and responses), and casting (which features Sam Elliott of
Road House fame as John Buford, and Martin Sheen as Robert E. Lee) all
convey the novel's take on the war, emphasizing military manhood. The
film's take on the Dark and Cruel War is captured by one of Buford's
dialogues, in which he exclaims (in Elliott's knowing, grizzled drawl),

> You know what's going to happen here in the morning? The whole damn
> reb army is going to be here. They'll move through this town, occupy these
> hills . . . [and] Lee will have the high ground. . . . The high ground! Meade
> will come in slowly, cautiously. New to command. . . . And when Lee's army
> is nicely entrenched behind the fat rocks on the high ground, Meade will
> finally attack . . . straight up the hillside, out in the open, in that gorgeous
> field of fire. . . . And afterwards men in tall hats and gold watch fobs will
> thump their chest and say what a brave charge it was.[47]

This vision of the war may seem strange and unfeeling, but it grows
out of a deep and sustained tradition in American culture. In the United
States war has often been grasped not as a moral dilemma but as something that has a technocratic solution. There is a reason for this: the belief
in redemption through violence did not suddenly disappear with the
closing of the American frontier. These stories are the cultural expression
of a violent society that tends to disavow, ignore, or redeem the very
violence that supports it. They are the narratives of an empire—with a
history of almost endless war and, today, more military outposts than any
nation in human history—that does not acknowledge itself as an empire.
These tactical fictions provide that empire with a noble origin story and
suggest that freedom and violence are inextricable from one another.

Michael Shaara's son, Jeffrey Shaara, has depicted the war along similar
lines. In both style and structure, Jeffrey Shaara's books are an homage

Sam Elliott as "John Buford" in *Gettysburg* (New Line Cinema, 1993).

to his father. They not only unfold in the same manner, commencing with brief sketches of the armies and then recounting the battles; their language also echoes that of *The Killer Angels*. Jeffrey Shaara's novels expand—or at least elongate—the Dark and Cruel War by providing a prequel and a sequel to the action at Gettysburg. *The Last Full Measure* (1998) depicts the Battle of the Wilderness in 1864 and Lee's ensuing surrender at Appomattox Courthouse, all of which, Shaara suggests, reveals a single illuminating lesson. "While [Gettysburg was] a tragic defeat for Lee's army," he writes, "there is a greater significance to the *way* that defeat occurs." Until this momentous encounter, the war had been "fought mostly from the old traditions, the Napoleonic method, the massed frontal assault against fortified positions." Gettysburg demonstrated with brutal clarity that the new technologies and strategies had fundamentally transformed warfare. From then on, "the use of shovels become as important as the use of muskets," and the "new methods—strong fortifications, trench warfare—[were] clear signs to all that the war has changed."[48] *The Last Full Measure* actively draws on this lesson, lingering on the entrenched assaults that marked the Battle of the Wilderness.

Gods and Generals (1996) distills related insight from the war's earlier encounters. A prequel to *The Killer Angels*, it follows Lee and Chamberlain, along with leaders such as Stonewall Jackson and Winfield Scott Hancock, in the first years of the conflict. According to *Gods and Generals*, the battles at Bull Run, Chancellorsville, and Antietam divulge a major discovery: that the "old way of fighting a war . . . is becoming dangerously outdated." "One of the great tragedies of the Civil War," he explains, "is that it is a bridge through time. The old clumsy way of fighting, nearly unchanged for centuries, marching troops in long straight lines, advancing slowly into the massed fire of the enemy, . . . collide with the new efficient ways of killing, better rifles, much better cannon."[49] This collision is painstakingly depicted not only in the novel but also in its 2003 film adaptation, the original cut of which ran to nearly six hours because of this fetish for all things tactical.

The Soldiers' perspective has yielded other works, too. In the late nineteenth and early twentieth centuries, several artists tried to record the war's major encounters by creating massive panoramic paintings. The Gettysburg Museum features a giant "cyclorama," or 360-degree painting, that visually narrates the famous battle. Because of its size (42 feet high and 377 feet long), the painting is able to reconstruct the contest on an almost human scale, with lifelike figures populating the various hills, valleys, and ridges. Its chief aesthetic effect, however, lies in the story that it imparts. As the cylindrical work slowly spins around, viewers witness the conflict's key moments, from the assaults at The Angle to Pickett's Charge, and a narrative of tactical movements comes into focus. The Gettysburg cyclorama thereby provides a visual reimagining of *The Killer Angels*, a vision shorn of words but deeply invested in viewing the struggle as a massive, strategic contest carried out by hardened, honorable men. What these works share, what binds them together, is the manner in which they present the Civil War. Again and again, we discover that the conflict was but a sequence of military encounters and its participants a mere assortment of lines, or flanks, whose lives were defined by the Dark and Cruel War in which they were enveloped.

Paul Philippoteaux, *The Battle of Gettysburg* (1883). Oil on canvas. Courtesy of the Gettysburg National Military Park.

Of Worms and Men

If the Soldiers have their inheritors, so do the Philosophers. The tradition inaugurated by writers such as Crane, Twain, and Bierce has also endured, and many of its later versions stridently object to the Dark and Cruel War and the violence it unleashed. Such an objection is implicitly advanced in many nineteenth-century works, from the murdered stranger in "The Private History of a Campaign That Failed" to the abandoned child in "Chickamauga." That latent pacifism is then drawn out and made explicit in the twentieth and twenty-first centuries, and it is recorded in an array of cultural documents.

Both the Soldiers and the Philosophers try to come to terms with the conflict's violation of the human body, with the transformation of people into so much biological material. But they construe that transformation differently, either heralding its tactical import or challenging it on ethical or philosophical grounds. Edmund Wilson, the prolific New York writer and critic, mounted one such challenge. Years after editing

Vanity Fair and composing histories of the Symbolist movement and European socialism, Wilson wrote *Patriotic Gore* (1962), the first literary history of the Civil War. That book provides a lively and perspicacious account of the war and its literature, sparked by Wilson's views on writers such as Melville ("a New Yorker . . . writing versified journalism . . . an anxious middle-aged non-combatant") and Lincoln ("[a man who] believed in laws that imperiously ruled both matter and mind"). Wilson's foremost contribution, though, is his introduction to *Patriotic Gore*, which vigorously critiques the war and everything it uncorked. Wilson is not unmoved by the reasons why the war was fought; he simply does not believe that such reasons ever explain the violence they beget. "Having myself lived through a couple of world wars and having read a certain amount of history," he explains, "I am no longer disposed to take very seriously the professions of 'war aims' that nations make." In 1914, the Germans invaded Belgium and France "on the pretext that they needed *Lebensraum* and had a mission to spread *Kultur*"; and in the early nineteenth century, when Napoleon rampaged across Europe, the French kept bellowing "about *la gloire* as well as about their revolutionary ideals, *Liberté, Egalité, Fraternité.*"[50] The Civil War, Wilson argues, was no different. This time the cant was about *freedom* and *the Union*, but it was propelled by a brute desire for power.

For Wilson, the Civil War anticipated World Wars I and II, as well as the ensuing struggle between the United States and the Soviet Union. The North and the South, he claims, had become so different from one another that they were as distinct "as any two European countries," and they fought as such, using savage methods to project their power, all while singing songs about God and country. The idea that the North sought to emancipate the slaves is now "firmly fixed in the American popular mind," but according to Wilson, it is a myth: although slavery was certainly "embarrassing to many people," many "other people thoroughly approved of it—in the North as well as the South." Even the most fiery abolitionists, Wilson adds, "were handled rather gingerly by the anti-South Republicans, and exploitation of the wickedness of the planters became later a form of propaganda like the alleged German atrocities in

Belgium at the beginning of the first World War. The institution of slavery, which the Northern states had by this time got rid of, thus supplied the militant Union North with the rabble-rousing moral issue which is necessary in every modern war to make the conflict appear as a melodrama." Wilson trashes almost all of the narratives that have shaped Civil War memory, undercutting the idea—so vital to each of the struggle's other narratives—that this war was somehow different, somehow more purposeful than the countless other wars that punctuate human history. *Patriotic Gore* suggests that there is a deep-seated, maybe even ineradicable power drive in human nature, and "the North's determination to preserve the Union was simply the form that the power drive now took."[51]

According to Wilson, the Dark and Cruel War can be understood by looking at basic biology. "In a recent Walt Disney film showing life at the bottom of the sea," he writes, "a primitive organism called a sea slug is seen gobbling up smaller organisms through a large orifice at one end of its body; confronted with another sea slug of an only slightly lesser size, it ingurgitates that, too. Now, the wars fought by human beings are stimulated as a rule primarily by the same instincts as the voracity of the sea slug." That shared voracity reveals a truth we often do not wish to admit: life comes from death and predation. "All animals must prey on some form of life that they can capture, and all will eat as much as they can. The difference in this respect between man and the other forms of life is that man has succeeded in cultivating enough of what he calls 'morality' and 'reason' to justify what he is doing in terms of what he calls 'virtue' and 'civilization.' Hence the self-assertive sounds which he utters when he is fighting and swallowing others: the songs about glory and God, the speeches about national ideals, the demonstrations of logical ideologies." All of us, it seems, are versions of these rapacious slugs, motivated—or biologically compelled—to consume the less powerful. The only difference, Wilson adds (echoing Twain's lament about the human animal's propensity for "that atrocity of atrocities"), is this: we can intellectualize our appetites and console ourselves with grand ideals.[52] To see the Civil War as anything but a manifestation of this principle, Wilson suggests, is to foist on it a false ideology.

Wilson's view of the Dark and Cruel War is complemented by Shelby Foote's. Almost all of the implications of this mythic story, its limitations as well as its allures, are evident in Foote's fiction. Fascinated by Southernness, the power of place, and the lyric potentials of narrative prose, Foote often reads as Faulkner-lite. Nonetheless, his stories about the Civil War—particularly *Shiloh: A Novel* (1952) and *Jordan County: A Landscape in Narrative* (1954)—are some of the most exquisitely rendered versions of the Dark and Cruel War. What matters to Foote is not the cause that brought the soldiers into battle, nor is it the consequences of their fighting; what matters is the web of suffering that emerges within the war, particularly within the minds of the men most directly involved.

One of Foote's best stories, "Pillar of Fire," is narrated by Adam Lundy, a liaison officer newly appointed to the *Starlight*, a Union gunboat making its way down the Mississippi River, heartlessly carrying Sherman's war into the West. Lundy's superior officer, Colonel Frisbie, is a one-eyed Ahab who wants to exact revenge on the people who started this thing and took his eye. So the soldiers steal, burn, and pillage their way through the Mississippi delta. "Where partisan resistance had once been strongest," Foote writes, "soon there was little activity of any kind. It became a bleak region, populated only by women and children and old men and house servants too feeble to join the others gone as 'contraband' with the Union armies." One of these men shoots at the *Starlight*, so Frisbie orders his men to find and kill the would-be assassin. When they enter the suspect's home, all they find is Isaac Jameson, a feeble, 84-year-old man who can barely speak. "His chin, resting upon a high stock, trembled as he spoke. 'Have you brum to run my howl?' he said."[53]

Foote then transports the reader back in time, retracing the old man's life up to this moment. Isaac, we learn, was a restless seeker from his first moments on earth. As a young man, he was always sneaking off to horseraces or cockfights, and he spent his first fifty years "running hard after trouble in any form, first among men—river bullies at Natchez . . . painted Creeks at Burnt Corn, British regulars at New Orleans; he had tried them all—and then against the cat-and snake-infested jungles of the South." All of this restlessness and bellicosity was expunged by the death of his children. When his newborn son died, it concluded "the first phase of his life." At the funeral, he came to a sudden realization: "As he stood beside the small grave, hearing the rector pronounce the service . . . and then the somewhat muffled slither of loose summer earth being dropped on the box, he knew that now, with flesh of his flesh interred in it, he would never leave this land. He was linked to it for life." Isaac Jameson thus remained there, long after the Union's forces had come and everything resembling the Confederacy had begun to collapse, because his soul was tethered to the soil by grief. And that tragic connection was only solidified by his later experiences. His wife had seven more children, six of whom died. Only one little boy, Clive, survived to adulthood, and he was shattered by the war. When Clive finally returns home, living but lifeless, as if "the furnace of war had baked in the flesh," Isaac's wife suffers a stroke and dies. Isaac, distraught and in mourning, also suffers a stroke and then holes up in his house waiting to die. When the soldiers come, he is anticipating death's embrace and thinking about the bond between his life and the land, a "great endless green expanse" now reduced to a bleak wasteland. Then he asks them, or *tries* to ask them, "Have you come to burn my house?"

The implication of Foote's story is that the Dark and Cruel War is lodged in the personal suffering unloosed by the struggle. That link between war and identity, between selfhood and privation, is underscored not only by the life of Isaac Jameson, who dies almost as soon as the soldiers burn down his house, but also by the psychic pain of Colonel Frisbie. "We'll give them war enough," he proclaims, "to last the time of man," and that quenchless desire for revenge originates in Frisbie's own woe. "He'd lost an eye," Lundy explains, "and now [he] . . . wants to lash out at the source of his torment."[54] Everything that happens on the *Starlight*'s southward voyage—all the bloody skirmishes and manhunts, as well as the fiery destruction of Jameson's house—derives from this pain, which Frisbie wants to redirect onto the Confederates left behind in this desolated delta. The story that Foote constructs out of Frisbie's quest for revenge certainly trades on Lost Cause mythology—it's a story, after all, about rapacious Northerners and anguished white Southerners—but its emotional core lies in the experience of suffering. The Civil War is for Foote an immeasurable deluge of loss and pain.

A similar perspective emerges in *Andersonville*, MacKinlay Kantor's 1955 novel about the infamous Confederate prison where nearly 13,000 soldiers died. Kantor recounts the prison's construction, expansion, and dismantlement through an array of characters, such as Ira Claffley, the slaveholder who owns the land and blames the "God damn Yankees" for the death of his sons; Coffee and Pete, two of the enslaved men who build the prison; Eben Dolliver, a Union captive; and Willie Collins, the sadistic leader of a group of imprisoned thugs. Throughout the novel, as the prisoners starve or suffer from theft, disease, and deprivation, Andersonville becomes a place of unspeakable cruelty, a place that makes the nineteenth century almost indistinguishable from the twentieth. Henry Wirz, the camp's vindictive doctor, is cast from the same mold as Nazi physicians. He is cold and rational, convinced of his moral righteousness, and he administers vaccines that produce enormous wounds (provoking rumors that "the vaccine had been adulterated deliberately with blood taken from syphilitic invalids"). Wirz sees the prisoners as subhuman. At one point, he throws carrots at them, and as they scramble on the ground to gather them up, he reflects that these hungry creatures, wrestling in the dirt, are in fact *Bern* ("bears" in German). "*Ja,*" Wirz says to himself, "they are *bears.*"[55]

Kantor depicts the Confederate prison as an early version of a concentration camp. In that regard, Kantor anticipates what later historians and political philosophers have pointed out: the Nazi camps were not anomalies. Similar sites of planned suffering have repeatedly emerged throughout human history. Kantor describes Andersonville as a camp-like site of dehumanizing violence, the effects of which are registered in the novel's language, which repeatedly muddies the distinction between the human and the inhuman. The Raiders, who steal from the weaker prisoners, "had been worms in the outer world," Kantor writes, where "they stood in secret dread of manacles," but here "there was no discipline except such as the Goliaths chose to inflict upon their subordinates." If the Raiders were worms growing fat in this soil of crime, the rest of the men, according to John Winder (another Confederate officer), were "scum," or worse: "a marsh under the scum, pollywogs . . . [they] were too thick, the marsh could not support their life, [and] it was fated that many would die." Winder thinks that the strongest among them might live if they become "sufficiently cannibalistic" and learn to "sustain themselves directly by feasting on dead pollywogs. Or indirectly, as by swallowing fruits to be reared in a forest of growth which the dread creatures had manured."[56] Bears, worms, pollywogs—all of these index the men's inhumanity, which the novel valiantly tries to disprove by offering more than seven hundred pages of personal histories and extended characterization. Nonetheless, the impression left by these pages is that the war's chief legacy—what, more than anything else, marks it as a historical event—is this violent, slug-like reduction of men to animals.

Cruel Wars, Past and Present

Recent glimpses of the Dark and Cruel War have been shaped by the War on Terror. Since 2001, the United States has enlisted the theory of just war to wage battle on "terrorism" broadly defined. The rhetoric that US officials have used to justify these wars—first in Afghanistan, then in Iraq, Yemen, Syria, and other places throughout the world—often revolves around safety, freedom, and security. American society, we repeatedly hear, can only be saved through violence. "Our purpose," in the words of Dick Cheney, "is to end the terrorist threats of the civilized world. We are defending both ourselves and the safety and survival of civilization." Or as Donald Trump asserted in his Inaugural Address, "We do not seek to impose our way of life on anyone, but rather to let it shine as an example for everyone to follow. We will . . . unite the civilized world against Radical Islamic Terrorism, which we will eradicate completely from the face of the earth."[57]

Although pitched as a fight for life and liberty, the War on Terror has firmed up alliances between authoritarian regimes, frayed civil liberties, and caused the deaths of tens of thousands. That gap between rhetoric and reality—that distance between the world as it is talked about and the world as it is actually lived—structures twenty-first-century stories

about the Dark and Cruel War. In these narratives, the Civil War mirrors
the War on Terror in all of its endlessness and all of its absurdity. The
illogic of war is on prominent display in Taylor Brown's *Fallen Land*
(2015). The novel follows Callum, a teenage horse thief fleeing from a
gang of Confederate marauders, and Ava, a 17-year-old girl orphaned
by the war, as they travel together across the desolate wasteland left by
Sherman's army. As they make their way through the war-torn landscape,
everything they see—the pointless violence, greed, and insatiable desire
for revenge—takes on a surreal shape, morphing into the loose feel and
contours of a dream (or nightmare).

At one point, Callum, caught between sleeping and waking, reflects
on the string of events that led to this moment, and as "the layers that
bound him" are slowly "cut away, piece by piece," he conjures up a
wartime world that mirrors his disturbed unconscious. "He floated,"
Brown writes, in the stream of his past, in dreams "fevered" and "dark,"
like "the night of the wreck":

> The men he pushed under, the men who pushed him. Ladders of them,
> limb-conjoined, wanting for air. The spouts of exhalation, gargle-mouthed.
> The groan of the ship sinking beneath them, sucking them under. The
> white jet of expelled air, last of the pockets that saved him, shooting him
> to the surface, white-birthed. Then and now black-whirled. Nightmare and
> memory. The ship gone, the waves high. The pale slit of coast, like snow.
> The beach underneath his feet, his knees, his face. Then the lopsided shack,
> the man called Swinney who nursed him on fish and whiskey, who took
> him in as a father might, and then the Colonel, who took them all. After
> that the land grown mountainous, and meaner, and scarecrow men who
> haunted the ridges, and rib-boned horses beneath them, and always the
> hunger, insatiable, and the wagons raided, and the barns and farmhouses,
> and never so much blood.[58]

His memories shuttle from his earliest moments as an Irish immigrant
("white-birthed" from a sinking ship off the American coast) to his
boyhood (with "the man called Swinney") to the recent outbreak of
violence ("the land grown mountainous, and meaner . . . and never so

much blood"). These moments are only held together—if at all—very loosely. The Civil War emerges as a nightmarish orgy of bloodshed and disorder, an unreal, half-remembered assortment of sounds, textures, and impressions. In *Fallen Land* the war is not a moment when things come together; it is a moment when things become unbound, or perhaps dissolve altogether.

Fallen Land is an altogether appropriate story for an empire in the process of unraveling. It is a novel pitched toward the present as well as the past, illuminating a world seeped in needless violence. In that regard *Fallen Land* is similar to *The Amalgamation Polka* (2006), Stephen Wright's novel about Liberty Fish, the restless son of two prominent abolitionists. As a boy, Liberty wanders endlessly, and his rambles introduce him to strange people: con men in Rochester, circus performers in New York, and a pirate who lives underground. When Fort Sumter is attacked, Liberty, now 17 years old and fueled by his parents' abolitionist zeal, enlists in the Union Army. However, his experiences in the war are clearly an extension of rather than a departure from his earlier life. Soldiering turns out to be wandering in a different form. The novel also plays with the idea that the war itself is wandering writ large—an aimless sojourn for the nation, a boundless "tumbling into a great abyss." That dark, psychological take on the war is voiced by one of the characters, who sees it as an outbreak of national insanity, for "What is war but public madness, the outward manifestation of an unplumbed and tenacious disturbance?"

This link between the war and the mind, between external and internal disturbances, is further explored in Wright's battle scenes. As soon as the fighting starts, Liberty discovers he cannot maintain a sense of individuality. He feels like he is "no longer properly situated inside his body," as though "the thinking, feeling portion of himself was now hovering mysteriously ghostlike above the physical self." He grips the rifle, but his own "hands . . . seemed miles away," and that feeling of disconnection intensifies as Liberty moves, or rather wanders, into the fray. "Think of the bondsmen," his mother had told him in a letter, "Think of their stooped toil, their martyred agony." In battle, the words suddenly felt "cold and distant": all of the impassioned arguments and sermons "he had heard throughout his short life on the wickedness of chained servitude had, for him, come down to this: a mad charge through clouds of dense, choking smoke into the very barrels of the slavocracy." And when "the dread order to advance" was finally given, "his body seemed light, almost weightless, and he floated over the ground like a spirit. Though there was nothing to see, no clear target to fire at, men began toppling out of the ranks like broken dolls, falling soundlessly to the earth." Suddenly, a "riderless horse came charging out of the smoke, a booted human leg dangling from the stirrup. . . . [Liberty] could hardly advance a rod without stepping on a body or a part of one. Heads were lying about like an unharvested crop of grotesque pumpkins. In many places the ground was surprisingly soft, soggy with blood. The wounded groaned and writhed about with an aching slowness, like strange marine animals trapped on the ocean floor."[59]

In war, men become things and animals: unplucked pumpkins, sea life, or soulless dolls that have fallen to the earth. What makes this passage so haunting is the sense of violation imparted by these metaphors. These individuals—or men who, until a mere moment ago, were individuals— have been converted into so much inanimate material, remade into creatures capable of only inhuman acts as they wail and writhe "about with an aching slowness." The Civil War, it would seem, is just a boundless and undirected onslaught of cruelty, an unreasoning rush of violence that unravels mind and body alike.

The Amalgamation Polka plumbs the chasm between war's ideals and war's realities. That is the most biting implication of Liberty Fish's journey: his mother's exhortation ("Think of the bondsmen") is as kind as it is naive. The Civil War, Wright suggests, has nothing to do with freedom or martyrdom; it is just an orgy of cruelty and bloodshed. In the work of another writer, that critique of the war's abolitionist ethos might lend itself to a reclaiming of the Lost Cause. But Wright is making a statement about the Civil War's brutality and the enduring discrepancy between war as a cause and war as a lived experience. Published five years into the War on Terror, after the United States had invaded not one but two countries in an effort to "spread democracy," *The Amalgamation Polka* asks, what if we, like Liberty Fish, are still just wandering into violence?

Wright arrived at these ideas through his own experiences. A veteran of the Vietnam War, he learned from that conflict that warfare, regardless of what principles supposedly justify it, is irredeemably cruel. It is fundamentally hostile to the most fragile parts of us, to the faculties that make us who we are—our memory, our capacity for love, sympathy, and joy. That brutality grounds *Meditations in Green*, Wright's 1983 novel about a veteran's struggle to adjust to civilian life. "A children's breakfast cereal, Crispy Critters, provokes nausea; there is a woman's perfume named Charlie; and the radio sound of 'We Gotta Get Out of This Place' (The Animals, 1965) fills me with a melancholy as petrifying as the metal poured into casts of galloping cavalry, squinting riflemen, proud generals, statues in the park, roosts for pigeons." War's recalcitrant afterlives—its uncanny ability to reemerge in the everyday textures of postwar life—anchors Wright's treatment of the Dark and Cruel War. As one of the characters in *The Amalgamation Polka* declares, "This war, this horrible, evil war, it's never going to end. You do understand that, don't you? Even after it's over it will continue to go on without the flags and the trumpets and the armies."[60]

Wright's suggestion that it will continue to go on in altered forms is born out by the Civil War's literary history. The conflict spawned a whirling array of acts, encounters, and stories of commitment and disillusionment, all of which reenact this struggle that purportedly concluded in 1865, carrying the Civil War into an ever-evolving set of other times and places. The war's extraordinary cultural persistence, however, is not simply a function of its commemorative power. Nor is it merely a consequence of the past being, as William Faulkner famously stated, "not even past."[61] Instead, it is a result of the war's inability to ever be truly settled in American culture, its resolution perpetually deferred either to a fictive past that never occurred or to a future that has not yet arrived. That unsettledness—the fact that the war might still be lost—is troubling. But it also endows Civil War literature with an undeniable power. These works enable us to inhabit this space between the conflict's eruption and resolution, this long present of American history.[62]

The Amalgamation Polka is a case in point. As the Civil War blends into other wars, it becomes clear that American history is essentially a chronicle of unending violence. The tragedies of the Civil War are also the tragedies of the Vietnam War and the War on Terror. Such conflicts are animated by the same slug-like appetite for destruction, and they inevitably yield the same result: suffering upon suffering. "It will continue to go on" indeed. Yet Wright's novel also suggests that the Civil War is a cipher for these other wars—an upheaval that contains the secret of all these other contests. That view of the war's significance pulls together all of these stories. Despite the wild ways in which they differ, offering trenchant critiques as well as militaristic fantasies, providing views of the North and the South and everything in between, these stories point toward a single, simple truth: that the Civil War made us who we are, for better or worse. It revealed—and to this day, continues to reveal—the angels as well as the demons of our nature.

{3} The Lost Cause

BEFORE HE BECAME THE PRIME MINISTER OF ENGLAND, Winston Churchill wrote about the Civil War—and he sided, quite passionately, with the South. After suffering an electoral defeat in 1929, Churchill's political prospects seemed dim, so he turned his attention to the past, chronicling the life and times of prior leaders. Churchill believed wholeheartedly in the great man theory of history, the old-fashioned notion that the course of human events is determined not by economic changes or social movements but by certain leaders who somehow see the shape of things to come and act accordingly. According to Churchill, his own ancestor, the 1st Duke of Marlborough, was one of these great men, and so was the Confederate general Robert E. Lee.

In 1930, Churchill wrote a story in which Lee's strategic acumen and political prowess enable the South to win. In Churchill's retelling, not only does the Confederacy triumph, but the whole world is far better for it. By the mid-twentieth century, peace and order reign supreme, and people have joined together to forge a single, global government. All of this progress, Churchill says, was made possible by Lee, who won the Battle of Gettysburg and then marched on Washington and freed the slaves, thereby setting the stage for the North's defeat and the earth's political unification.[1]

Why would Churchill be drawn to such a fantasy? And why, in writing about the war, would he sympathize so clearly and unabashedly with the South? The answer partly has to do with Churchill's circumstances.

Removed from power but planning a political comeback, Churchill saw in Lee, who "achieved the highest excellence both as a general and as a statesman," an ideal version of himself.[2] However, the answer also has to do with the afterlife of Confederate memory in the wake of the South's defeat. When the Confederate States of America (C.S.A.) collapsed, many of its proponents, instead of abandoning the fight, simply shifted its location, moving from battlefields to books. Stories such as Churchill's, in which Lee becomes an abolitionist and the Confederacy a force for freedom, are striking evidence of the Confederates' success in shaping the Civil War's later interpretation.

It is difficult to overstate the influence that the Confederacy's defenders have exerted on the war's recollection. Perhaps the greatest irony of looking at the Civil War through literature is this: the South, after losing the conflict, largely won the fight over its memory. To this day many people view the war not as an effort to end slavery but as a clash of civilizations—as a battle over sovereignty conducted between an agrarian South and an industrialized North. That view, which is the heart and soul of the Lost Cause narrative, was fashioned out of songs, retold in films, and refined in story after story.

Inventing the Lost Cause

The Lost Cause is rooted in Southern experiences of loss and devastation. The war took place almost exclusively in the South, and it was cataclysmic for those who lived there: nearly one in five Southern men died, and thousands of others suffered from disease or injury. Almost every family in the region was touched by the conflict—a privation that hastened the end of the war itself, as Southern women turned, in their mourning, against the Confederate war machine.[3] That personal grief was compounded by the destruction of Southern homes, schools, bridges, and railroads. Some of this desolation was captured in photographs taken shortly after the North's victory, which reveal hollowed-out buildings and barren landscapes that uncannily anticipate World Wars I and II. What comes in the wake of such bereavement? Left unattended, grief tends to feed upon itself until there is nothing left. White South-

Andrew J. Russell, *Ruins in Richmond* (1865). Courtesy of the Library of Congress, Prints and Photographs Division.

erners desperately needed to provide their loss with purpose—to find some shards of order in the chaos around them—and that is what the Lost Cause promised to provide.

That solace had consequences that continue to be felt. The Lost Cause has supplied many white supremacist movements, from the Ku Klux Klan (KKK) to the American "alt-right," with an emotional architecture and political worldview. To this day, the Lost Cause continues to sway the hearts and minds of many white Americans, anchoring their feelings about race, the federal government, and the symbols of the Confederacy. When Donald Trump tweeted, shortly after the fighting in Charlottesville, "Sad to see the history and culture of our great country being ripped apart with the removal of our beautiful statues and monuments," he echoed sentiments shared by many white Americans whose understanding of history has been anchored by the Lost Cause.[4]

The ideological cornerstones of the Lost Cause can be traced back to two books: Edward Pollard's *The Lost Cause: A New Southern History of the War of the Confederates* (1866) and Jefferson Davis's *The Rise and Fall of the Confederate Government* (1881). Both self-styled historians begin with a single premise: that the sovereignty acquired by the individual states through the American Revolution was never subsequently transferred. States accordingly retained the right, as independent political communities, to secede from the federal government if they so wished. The Constitution, they contend, was a provisional agreement among the states (the "creators, not the creatures, of the General Government") to balance interests and maintain order, in part by recognizing and protecting the system of slavery. For Davis and Pollard alike, the Civil War originated not in an illegal Southern rebellion against the Union but in a Northern coup d'état led by antislavery fanatics who "incited one section to carry fire and sword into the other." Slavery was thus incidental to the war's rationale, a point reiterated by Davis when he recounts his advocacy for the conscription of slaves in the Confederate Army and by Pollard when he says that the divide between the North and the South, instead of centering on slavery, "really went deeper to the very elements of the civilization of each [region]."[5]

Although these books helped establish, as Pollard's subtitle puts it, a "new Southern history" of the war, history can sometimes be a dry affair. For the Lost Cause to truly flourish in American culture, it had to be infused with imaginative life, and Pollard (who coined the term "The Lost Cause") was all too aware of this need. Much of his book reads like an epic tragedy, not dissimilar from Edward Gibbon's *The Decline and Fall of the Roman Empire* (1776). There is astounding pathos in Pollard's description of the "affecting scene" that ensued after Lee's surrender: "Rough and rugged men, familiar with hardship, danger, and death in a thousand shapes, had tears in their eyes, and choked with emotion as they thronged around their old chieftain." That pathos is magnified when the Confederacy craters, revealing "a spectacle of ruin, the greatest of modern times": "There were eleven great States lying prostrate; their capital all absorbed; their fields desolate; their towns and cities ruined; their public works torn to pieces by armies; their system of labour overturned; the fruits of the toil of generations all swept into a chaos of destruction." In the final pages, Pollard switches from tragedy to romance, heralding a coming age in which the South finally wins the war—or, at least, the struggle over its memory: "All that is left the South is 'the war of ideas.' She has thrown down the sword to take up the weapons of argument." The war, he explains, may have ended in defeat, but it also left the South with "its own memories, its own heroes, its own tears, [and] its own dead," which will become fertile ground for future works of literature and history. There "may not be a political South," but, he crows, there will be a *cultural* South as long as people remember and preserve the Confederacy.[6]

It is not difficult to see why the Lost Cause appealed to a war-torn South. It offered an outlet for grief, remaking loss into a story of cultural continuity and civilizational fortitude. It also repackaged the most rotten part of the Southern cause, the Confederacy's armed defense of slavery. Regardless of apologists' statements to the contrary, the C.S.A. was a white supremacist country and would-be empire whose political, economic, and social institutions were based on slaveholding. Alexander Stephens, the Confederacy's vice president, declared, "Our new government is founded upon . . . the great truth that the negro is not equal to the white man; that slavery subordination to the superior race is his natural and normal condition." The Confederate Constitution went so far as to foreclose the possibility of any future emancipation by forbidding all laws "denying or impairing the right of property in negro slaves."[7] The myth of the Lost Cause whitewashes this part of the war, depicting the Confederacy as a doomed defense of noble principles rather than a self-interested fight for racial subjugation and perpetual enslavement. For many Southerners, particularly those with family ties to slavery, that rewriting of the Civil War provided a way around the problem of complicity by presenting the conflict as a defense not of bondage but of an entire way of life.

The Lost Cause enabled the Confederacy to live on immaterially, taking form in word if not in deed. The Charleston-based writer William Gilmore Simms, acting on the idea that a nation's spirit inheres in its songs, reprinted the Confederacy's war poetry, which illuminated, in his words, the South's defining "sentiments, ideas, and opinions—the motives which influenced their actions, and . . . which seemed to them to justify the struggle in which they were engaged."[8] That effort to rehabilitate the Confederacy—to make it abide culturally if not militarily—also spawned anthologies of Southern lyrics and ballads, such as T. C. De Leon's *South Songs* (1866) and Sallie Brock's *The Southern Amaranth* (1869); autobiographies, such as Jubal Early's *A Memoir of the Last Year of the War for Independence* (1866); veterans' organizations, such as the United Confederate Veterans; and Lost Cause periodicals, such as the *Southern Bivouac* and the *Confederate Veteran*, which printed letters, stories, and essays that championed the South's wartime actions.

The Confederacy continued to be a touchstone for Southern writers like Henry Timrod. During the conflict, Timrod spent time near the front, first as a soldier and then, after being discharged for consumption, as a war poet and correspondent. He penned bellicose songs like "A Cry to Arms" (1862), in which he implores Southerners to come "with the weapons at your call— / With musket, pike, or knife," and "brain a tyrant." He also wrote an ode to the Confederacy on the eve of the first meeting of the Southern Congress in 1861. Titled "Ethnogenesis"— that is, the "genesis" (or creation) of a people (or "ethnos")—the poem lauds the formation of a new country blessed by "ample field[s]" yet beleaguered by the North's treachery. In the final lines, Timrod projects a glorious future for the Confederacy, one full of "wealth, and power, and peace" for the slaveholders, as well as "for the distant peoples we shall bless" by giving "labor to the poor, / The whole sad planet o'er."[9] As Timrod envisions it, the Confederacy is not a fledgling nation but an emerging empire whose benevolent force will eventually spread across the entire planet.

When that empire failed to materialize, it was yet another devastating loss in Timrod's life. His father had died when he was only 8 years old, and Timrod's own son, Willie, died in 1865. Despite his reputation as the Confederacy's poet laureate, Timrod was sick and impoverished for much of his career.[10] Before he died of tuberculosis at the age of 38, Timrod composed poems so as to feel and think his way beyond pain. After the South's collapse, he tried to do that for his beloved region, using poetry to discover what part of the cause might be rescued. For the dedication of Magnolia Cemetery in Charleston, where six hundred Confederates were to be buried, Timrod crafted a passionate ode:

> Sleep sweetly in your humble graves,
>   Sleep, martyrs of a fallen cause!—
> Though yet no marble column craves
>   The pilgrim here to pause.
>
> In seeds of laurels in the earth,
>   The garlands of your fame are sown;
> And, somewhere, waiting for its birth,
>   The shaft is in the stone.
>
> Meanwhile, your sisters for the years
>   Which hold in trust your storied tombs,
> Bring all they now can give you—tears,
>   And these memorial blooms.
>
> Small tributes, but your shades will smile
>   As proudly on these wreaths to-day,
> As when some cannon-moulded pile
>   Shall overlook this Bay.
>
> Stoop, angels, hither from the skies!
>   There is no holier spot of ground,
> Than where defeated valor lies
>   By mourning beauty crowned.[11]

Although Timrod mourns the men who died fighting for the C.S.A., he resists fully burying the dead. "Martyrs" of an enduring "cause," these soldiers acquire a kind of life after death, first in the form of memory and then in what that memory produces—hence the language of regeneration ("waiting for its birth") and mining ("The shaft is in the stone"). The Confederate dead, it would seem, may not be dead after all.

The prospect of using poetry to revive the Confederacy also enticed Abram Ryan. The son of Irish immigrants who settled in the South, Ryan was a Catholic priest and Confederate chaplain who saw the world as

an immense spiritual battlefield. In his eyes, the South was on the side
of the angels, fighting for God's divinely sanctioned social hierarchies.
When Ryan took his rites, he joined the Vincentians, a monastic order
that emphasized missionary work. When the war broke out, he threw
himself into it with all the fervor a mission requires, traveling with and
pastoring to the Confederate Army. For Ryan, religion and politics were
one and the same. He took to the Confederacy as a priest would: by
joining the order and dissolving his prior identity into it. As he stated
in 1864, "Remember me to my friends. Whenever *priests* ask about me,
just tell them I am *South*, nothing more."[12]

More than any other writer of the era, Ryan was attuned to the Confederacy's need for a mythology. For the Lost Cause to truly take hold
in people's hearts and minds, it required mystic songs and sacred fables,
and that is what Ryan sought to provide. In his poems the Confederacy morphs into something greater, more sublime, and more righteous than it really was. The war becomes a struggle over God's vision
for humanity, and the Confederates become angels-in-waiting, men
whose

> deeds—proud deeds—shall remain for us,
> And their Names, dear names, without stain for us;
> And the glories they won shall not wane for us,
> In Legend and Lay
> Our heroes in Gray,
> Though dead—shall live over again for us.[13]

Ryan anticipated the insight of later historians: that for the Lost Cause
to succeed, it had to become a "civic religion," a set of beliefs and practices that fused politics to spirituality and told a coherent story about the
evolution of Southern identity.[14] "Souls," he once wrote, "were always
more to [me] than songs," but his songs challenge that very division,
continuously coupling music with mysticism. In "The Sword of Robert
Lee" (1866), the ceremonial scabbard of the Confederate general becomes a sacred object held "high o'er the brave in the cause of Right." In
"The Prayer of the South" (1868), the South's millions, devastated by the

Yankee invasion, mourn in unison, sending up a poem-prayer to relieve their burdened hearts. And in "March of the Deathless Dead" (1879), the Confederacy's soldiers become Christlike martyrs who "fell in a cause, though lost, still just."[15] Collectively, these soul-songs helped make the Lost Cause into what it eventually became, not a mere political agenda or regional philosophy but something deeper and more malleable—a veritable mythology, complete with deified heroes and an origin story about noble men fighting against wickedness itself.

The Georgian writer Joel Chandler Harris helped fashion that mythology. After spending most of the war on a plantation, Harris created the characters Tar Baby, Brer Rabbit, and Grandaddy Cricket, presenting them as authentic figures of black folklore. Underscoring the dangers of leaving home and the risks of stepping out of one's place, Harris's stories repackage slavery as a familial institutional and a normal facet of everyday Southern life. This view of the Old South anchors his famous folktales, which are "told night after night to a little boy by an old Negro who appears to be venerable enough to have lived during the period which he describes—who has nothing but pleasant memories of the discipline of slavery."[16] The lively fables recounted by Uncle Remus— later depicted in Disney's *Song of the South* (1946) as a grinning ex-slave, skipping and singing *"Zip-a-dee-doo-dah, zip-a-dee-ay!"*—not only reinforce the racial politics of the Lost Cause but also vivify its underlying fantasy: that the Old South was a kind of American Eden, gloriously undisturbed before the fall. Such a harmonious South, of course, was no more real than Uncle Remus. But the enduring appeal of that invented place tells us something important about the Lost Cause: its power resides in its ability to make fiction seem real—to make myth feel like memory.

Although that power is on full display in the literature produced by the war, the Lost Cause only truly established itself in the ensuing years, as it spread far and wide, becoming a vital part not only of Southern memory but also of Civil War memory writ large. To this day many people view the Confederate battle flag as a symbol of "heritage" and the C.S.A. as a failed independence movement. That reimagining was the result of a sustained cultural effort, involving a multitude of artists, painters, filmmakers, readers, and audiences.

Myth and Memory

Although they had lost the battle, the Confederates were determined to win the war, as it were, by molding American memory. Lost Causers launched magazines, wrote histories, and published essays designed to transform the Confederacy's white supremacist warmongers into deified heroes. Those efforts culminated in the creation of numerous Lost Cause monuments that continue to be displayed in public parks, town squares, and college campuses. These monuments vary in form and scale but not in intent. They include columns, obelisks, grave markers, and liberty figures, as well as more grandiose memorials, like the ninety-foot-tall Egyptian pyramid that sits in Richmond. Regardless of their size or location, these monuments tell the same story: though the Confederacy may be defeated, its principles—white supremacy above all—will endure.

The racist bent of these monuments is reflected in the timing of their placement. Supporters of the Lost Cause began planting memorials as soon as the war ended, but their efforts spiked in periods of racial tension. Confederate monuments sprang up like wildfire after *Plessy v. Ferguson* (which effectively legalized segregation) and the establishment of the NAACP (National Association for the Advancement of Colored People), and again in the 1950s and 1960s in response to the civil rights movement.[17] Such monuments are not historical artifacts but didactic exercises. They embody a set of values, imparting a lesson for later generations. And the lesson conveyed by Confederate memorials is that white rule can never be stamped out. By laying claim to public space and converting common areas—parks, campuses, cemeteries—into sites of white supremacy, these statues both symbolize and support racism. For that reason, people have sought to remove these memorials either with or without the aid of local governments (efforts we'll revisit in the afterword). Yet a great many of them—by some counts, more than one thousand—continue to stand, preserving the Lost Cause well into the twenty-first century.

The inscriptions that accompany these memorials replay every note on the Lost Cause score. A plaque in Camden, Alabama, states,

THEY GAVE THEIR LIVES FOR US,
FOR THE HONOR OF ALABAMA,
FOR THE RIGHTS OF THE STATES,
AND FOR THE PRINCIPLES OF THE UNION
AS THEY WERE HANDED DOWN TO US
BY THE FATHERS OF OUR COMMON COUNTRY.

The memorial in El Dorado, Arkansas—a soldier with a rifle resting on his shoulder—offers a more menacing declaration:

TRUTH CRUSHED TO EARTH
    SHALL RISE AGAIN.
EVEN DEATH CANNOT SEVER
    THE CHORDS OF MEMORY.[18]

Many memorials lionize the Confederacy's proslavery leaders. Georgia's Stone Mountain, for instance, features a massive carving of Jefferson Davis, Robert E. Lee, and Stonewall Jackson holding their caps to salute the Confederate dead and the cause that united them. (Unfortunately, the recent proposal to chisel Atlanta's greatest rappers, Big Boi and André 3000—i.e., Outkast—into the mountain, riding in a Cadillac beside Jackson, has not yet garnered enough support.[19] But it continues to pick up steam.) The carving tells a story about the war, according to which these leaders ensured the Confederacy's future by being heroic in defeat. As Mildred Rutherford, the historian general of the United Daughters of the Confederacy, put it, Stone Mountain reveals that the cause "for which the Confederate soldier fought was not lost. . . . Time has proven that the cause was a just cause and this memorial vindicates it."[20] Though Rutherford did not explain what that cause may have been, it was no secret: Stone Mountain was the birthplace of the modern KKK, the site where, in 1915, the Klan's new leaders burned a cross and swore an oath to revive the organization.[21] The carving represents nothing less than the KKK's white supremacist ideal made into an image.

Jim Bowen, *Close-up of the Stone Mountain memorial* (2012). Creative Commons Attribution 2.0 Generic.

The only memorial that approaches the audacity of Stone Mountain is Lee's mausoleum. This commemorative space, which includes a capacious crypt (housing the remains of more than two dozen people, including Lee himself) and a grand statue of the Confederate general lying in noble repose, was completed shortly after Lee's death in 1870. Lee's mausoleum is a spectacular example of Lost Cause hero worship, as well as the ardent interest among many Confederates in ancient Rome, Greece, and Egypt—great empires that, after they fell, endured in Western memory, influencing art and politics alike. That is why so many Lost Cause monuments feature Doric columns, and it is why the statue of Lee lies, mummy-like, at the heart of the crypt. Lee's mausoleum is a Southern version of Lenin's tomb or the Taj Mahal. It is designed to do what such mausoleums are always designed to do: to preserve the figurehead of a movement, to fight against death itself and ensure that the movement lives on. As the *Confederate Veteran* stated about this memorial of unequaled "grandeur and sublimity," "Like another Adam fresh from the Creator's hand, Robert E. Lee [seems] . . . to be only waiting for the breath of life to be restored, that he may again stand erect in his greatness and majesty."[22] In Lee's mausoleum, the Confederacy—like the racial hierarchy on which it was based—never really died. It is an indelible principle that cannot cease and cannot be defeated.

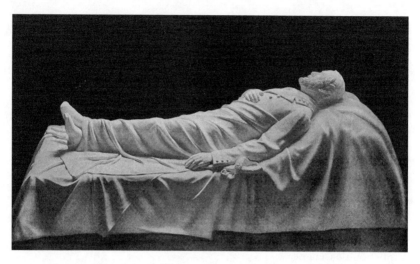

The Recumbent Statue of Robert E. Lee, by Valentine. Postcard (1921).

The sculptor who preserved Lee in this manner was Edward Valentine. Valentine was born in Richmond and raised to be a proud son of the South (his parents gave him the middle name "Virginius"), but he received his aesthetic education in Europe. He studied in France with Thomas Couture (who also mentored Manet), returning home only after the war came to a close. The Confederacy was something he imagined from afar, with all the romantic wistfulness of a pining ex-pat. With his artist's eye and Southern sensibility, Valentine felt that the Confederacy was exquisitely beautiful—an independence movement whose spirit could only be conveyed through art. So he took up his tools and went to work. He created a heroic bronze statue of Stonewall Jackson, immovable above his grave. He made a plaster bust of Matthew Fontaine Maury, a Confederate commander and diplomat. And, years later, he crafted an additional statue of Lee, which to this day (September 5, 2019) is still displayed at the US Capitol.

Valentine's work pulls together one of the most prominent memorials to the Lost Cause: Monument Avenue, a series of massive statues in Richmond that represent the Confederacy's leaders as noble, almost divine heroes. High above those statues stands Valentine's bronze version

Alexa Welch Edmund, *Jefferson Davis Memorial on Monument Avenue*. Photograph, *Richmond Times-Dispatch* (2015).

of Jefferson Davis, poised atop a sixty-seven-foot-tall column (which in recent years has been repeatedly spray-painted by anti-racist activists).

The racist ethos that infuses these memorials also infuses the novels of Thomas Dixon Jr. A pro-segregation, pro-KKK lawyer, writer, and minister, Dixon rhapsodized the Confederacy in book after book, most notably in *The Victim* (1914). Dedicated "To the Brave Who Died for What They Believed to Be Right," *The Victim* is essentially a love letter for Jefferson Davis. Recounting everything from Davis's initial political ascent to his later imprisonment and release, Dixon tries to achieve in fiction what Valentine's statue achieves in commemorative art: to permanently memorialize one of the South's wartime paragons and thereby extend the Confederacy into the future. He fawns over Davis's oratorical prowess and undying fidelity to the Constitution, both of which are on display in *The Victim*'s fictionalized version of the famous "Nullification" speech. After reading from Article IV of the Constitution, Davis, "overcome with emotion," raises "his hand to stay the burst of applause from the galleries" and then excoriates the Northern senators for traducing the nation's most sacred laws. "Your States," he angrily proclaims, "have not only repudiated the Constitution. . . . [Y]our emissaries have [also] invaded the peaceful South and sought to lay it waste with fire and sword"; you "have murdered Southern men who have dared demand their rights"; you have "invaded the borders of Southern States, burned their dwellings and murdered their people"; and you have "proclaimed John Brown, the criminal maniac who sought to murder innocent and helpless men, women and children . . . a hero and a martyr and then denounced *us* . . . as habitual violators of the laws of God and the rights of humanity!"[23]

The Victim contains absurd amounts of historical exposition. This is one of the main generic features of Lost Cause literature: it frequently suspends the plot so as to reframe the war, approaching literature as an opportunity for revisionary history. Narrators interject again and again to explain an event (Reconstruction-era corruption, the devastation wrought by Sherman's army, etc.) that invariably reinforces the South's honor and the North's treachery. Such moments proliferate in Dixon's novel, and these expository sections are some of the most revealing parts of the book. At one point, Dixon states that the "seeds of this tragedy were planted in the foundation structure of the Republic." The country created by the American Revolution and the Constitution, he explains, "was not a democracy. It was from the beginning an aristocratic republic founded squarely on African Slavery. And the degraded position assigned to the man who labored with his hands was recognized in our organic law. The Constitution itself was the work of a rich and powerful group of leaders in each State, and its provisions were a compromise of conflicting sectional property interests." Thus, it was not the South but the *North* that rebelled, "lifting the banner of a mighty revolution" while the South clung "with the desperation of despair to the faith of its fathers."[24]

Dixon arrived at this idea after completing a trilogy of novels: *The Leopard's Spots* (1902), *The Clansman* (1905), and *The Traitor* (1907). These books all focus on Reconstruction, but stories of Reconstruction are almost always stories about the Civil War. Dixon's novels are a case in point. From *The Leopard's Spots* (an updated version of *Uncle Tom's Cabin*) to *The Traitor*, Dixon makes a case for the Confederacy by depicting emancipation as an upheaval that destroyed civil society and reduced the government to a form of "organized crime." That anti-emancipation protest is quite pronounced in the trilogy's second installment, *The Clansman*. Commencing in the final months of the war, it focuses on Lincoln, whom Dixon depicts as a friend of the South and an opponent of black civil rights. In a pivotal scene, Lincoln tells the novel's villain, Austin Stoneman (a radical abolitionist and sadist), that the Emancipation Proclamation was a temporary measure that became defunct as soon as the war concluded. "The Constitution," Lincoln explains, "grants to the National Government no power to regulate suffrage. . . . I have [therefore] urged the colonisation of the negroes, and I shall continue until it is accomplished. . . . We can never attain the ideal Union our fathers dreamed, with millions of an alien, inferior race among us, whose assimilation is neither possible nor desirable. The Nation cannot now exist half white and half black, any more than it could exist half slave and half free."[25] In Dixon's story, Lincoln becomes an entrenched racist and strict Constitutionalist—a kind of Klansman avant la lettre.

When the KKK is established, it is, in Dixon's rendering, a Lincolnite organization dedicated to justice, democracy, and constitutional order. As a matter of historical fact, the KKK was and continues to be a white terrorist organization: the KKK routinely kidnapped, robbed, assaulted, and murdered African Americans, sowing a reign of terror that left a lasting legacy of violence and precipitated the Great Migration. The KKK is nearly the exact opposite of the organization that Dixon describes in *The Clansman*; it has far more in common with the Nazi SS than with Abraham Lincoln. Those are the facts. Yet literature tends to alter and adapt facts in the service of storytelling. In Dixon's reframing, the KKK is a continuation of the nation's most sacred origins, an organization dedicated to the preservation of America's founding ideals.

The novel even features a romanticized origin scene for the KKK, an idealized vision of its primal birth. The would-be Klansmen meet in the forest and don their disguises, long white sheets emblazoned with a "scarlet circle within which shone a white cross" and "three red mystic letters, K.K.K." "At the signal of a whistle," Dixon writes, "the men and horses arrayed in white and scarlet swung into double-file cavalry formation and stood awaiting orders. The moon was now shining brightly, and its light shimmering on the silent horses and men with their tall spiked caps made a picture such as the world had not seen since the Knights of the Middle Ages rode on their Holy Crusades." These clan members, dipped in moonlight and surrounding a flaming cross, are idealized not despite but *because* of their racist opposition to "mulatto citizenship," which, Dixon suggests, carries Lincoln's vision of a white democracy into the future, promising a United States that hews closely to the vision of the Founders.[26]

Dixon's neo-Confederate retelling of the war reached its apex ten years later, when *The Clansman* was remade into *The Birth of a Nation*. Like the novel from which it was adapted, D. W. Griffith's infamous 1915 film blames the war on abolitionist crusaders. It opens with two scenes about the antislavery militants who "plant the seeds of disunion": the first, set ambiguously at some point in the past, features a minister praying over an enslaved man in chains; the second shows an abolitionist meeting, led by a fiery orator who denounces the South and its oppressive regime. The South is thus viewed from the outset as a victim of Northern aggression, a point underscored by the film's war scenes, which reveal Confederates starving on the front lines. Lee's surrender is dubbed "the end of state sovereignty," and later scenes focus on the social anarchy purportedly brought about by that end. At one point, a former slave (played by a white actor in blackface, with bulging eyes) chases a young white woman, who throws herself off a mountain. That suicide becomes the inspiration for the KKK, which is represented as a gallant force for justice that "saved the South from the anarchy of black rule."[27] *The Birth of a Nation* is often remembered for its outrageously racist scenes, but those scenes are rooted in the film's Lost Cause depiction of the Civil War.

The Birth of a Nation may have done more for the Lost Cause than any other story in any other medium. It was a massive commercial and cultural success. Not only was it one of the first films to be granted a private viewing at the White House (a viewing arranged by Dixon, an old college friend of Woodrow Wilson's); it also sparked the revival of the

Theatrical release poster for *The Birth of a Nation* (1915).

KKK. The Klan reached the height of its influence not in the late 1860s, when it was initially formed, but in the decade following *The Birth of a Nation*, as the KKK spread northward and westward, radically expanding its power. Many of the Klan's new rituals, such as the donning of white masks and the lighting of wooden crosses, were lifted directly from *The Birth of a Nation* and Dixon's novels.[28] As strange as it may seem, it was through literature that the Lost Cause became a living mythology, a narrative that was at once imagined and all too real.

Katharine Du Pre Lumpkin, a Southern writer and sociologist, once made a similar point. Years after *The Birth of a Nation* was released, she recalled the electric effect it had on her and her fellow Southerners, indicating just how powerful and ingrained the Lost Cause had become: "Years before I had read the Dixon books. Now they came alive in this famous spectacle. In the South we had heard the motion picture acclaimed, that here at last we had been done justice. . . . Here the Klan rode, white robed. Here were romance and noble white womanhood. Here . . . [were the] noble men the South revered. And through it all the Klan rode. All around me people sighed and shivered, and now and then shouted or wept, in their intensity."[29]

The Agrarian Imagination

After the era of Griffith and Dixon, the Southern Agrarians took up the mantle of the Lost Cause. From the 1920s through the 1950s, this loose-knit group, which included poets, novelists, historians, biographers, and other memory makers, presented the Civil War as a colossal fight between two distinct and irreconcilable types of civilization. From the very beginning of their settlement (the story goes), the North and the South developed in separate and distinct ways. The North, settled by religious communities in the continent's colder reaches, became an industrial society that values innovation and collectivity. The South, settled by planters and farmers in the Sunbelt, became an agrarian society that values localism and individuality. The regions even diverge in how they see history, with the North always looking toward the future and the South always looking toward the past. Such drastically different civilizations, according to the Agrarians, can peacefully coexist only if they do not attempt to remake the other in their image. But that was what happened in the Civil War: the country's industrial half attempted to violently subdue and change its agrarian counterpart.

This was the Lost Cause with a twist. For the Agrarians, the war was no longer just about the U.S.A. It was about the fate of individualism and localism in the Age of Industry. The enduring power of those ideals is conveyed in the Agrarians' 1930 manifesto, *I'll Take My Stand*. In the group's "Statement of Principles," John Crowe Ransom—a poet and professor from Tennessee and de facto Agrarian figurehead—declared that it is only by renewing the South's traditional mode of life that the soul-crushing course of modernization might be resisted. Ransom laments the ways in which capitalism has both sped up and hollowed out everyday life. It has "enslaved our human energies," he writes. Now even the most basic of pleasures—everything from family life to romance and everyday conversations, in essence all of the "social exchanges which reveal and develop sensibility in human affairs"—are either suppressed or debased as business colonizes more and more of the world. The great tragedy that produced this state of affairs, the moment when business truly began its onslaught on everyday life, was the Civil War. For the Agrarians, the Civil War was a vicious War of Northern Aggression that gave birth to all of the ills of our current era.

The Agrarians' romanticization of the Old South was not merely an intellectual enterprise. It was an idea with social consequences. Their essays, poems, screenplays, and other texts provided practices of racial segregation and repression with intellectual cover. The Agrarians created an imaginative space for those practices—a mythic worldview through which white Southerners could view inequality as part of a long cultural tradition, indeed an entire way of life that was now at risk of being stamped out. The Agrarians' declaration that the South should never "surrender its moral, social, and economic autonomy to the victorious principle of Union" was an implicit argument for Jim Crow, only a step or two removed from George Wallace's infamous statement in 1963: "It is very appropriate that from this cradle of the Confederacy . . . that today we sound the drum for freedom as have our generations of forebears before us. . . . Let us rise to the call for freedom-loving blood that is in us and send our answer to the tyranny that clanks its chains upon the South. . . . I draw the line in the dust and . . . I say segregation now, segregation tomorrow, and segregation forever!"[30] That whitewashing of segregation as a Southern tradition has its roots in the mythologization of the Lost Cause.

Agrarian memory reached its crescendo in Gone with the Wind. Though not part of Ransom's circle, Margaret Mitchell was very much a fellow traveler. Raised in Atlanta, Mitchell heard countless stories from the time she was a child about the bravery of the Confederates and the wonders of the Old South. As an adult, she became a journalist, writing for the

Atlanta Journal Sunday Magazine—until she injured her leg and, while recovering at home, started writing the story that became *Gone with the Wind*. In both the 1936 novel and the 1939 film adaptation, the plot is a tempest of doomed desire: Ashley Wilkes, a gentle and mannerly Southern aristocrat, marries Melanie Hamilton but *really* loves the story's beautiful heroine, Scarlett O'Hara, who loves Ashley but falls for Rhett Butler, a rogue who abandons Scarlett during the war and then returns, only to emotionally withdraw, leading to their marriage's dissolution. That love story reflects on its historical setting. Commencing in 1861 and concluding in Reconstruction, *Gone with the Wind* is bracketed on both ends by the Yankee invasion. As the narrative unfolds, it also becomes a kind of commentary *on* that invasion, deploying all of the Lost Cause's major themes. The Confederates are in the right, but they are also cursed by fate and circumstance. (As Rhett Butler—somehow gifted with unheard-of historical perspective—asks, "[Have] any one of you gentlemen ever thought that there's not a cannon factory south of the Mason-Dixon Line? Or how few iron foundries there are in the South? . . . Have you thought that we would not have a single warship and that the Yankee fleet could bottle up our harbors in a week, so that we could not sell our cotton abroad?") Meanwhile, the Yankee troops are cold and vengeful—part of an avaricious horde bent on looting or demolishing everything in their path—and the slaves are both happy and unswervingly loyal: Big Sam defends Scarlett when she is attacked, and Mammy stays on even after emancipation.

As Mitchell depicts it, the Civil War involves nothing less than the violent dismantling of an entire civilization. The Old South—an agrarian paradise of grand plantations, satisfied slaves, and magnificent balls— is obliterated by the cruel, industrial North. Mitchell pays particularly close attention to General Sherman's March to the Sea, which transforms Atlanta into a "hideous place like a plague-stricken city" and the rest of the South into a desolate wasteland. "Behind [Sherman] lay the smoking ruins of Atlanta to which the torch had been set as the blue army tramped out. Before him lay three hundred miles . . . dotted with plantations, sheltering the women and children, the very old and

Publicity photo of Clark Gable and Vivien Leigh as Rhett Butler and
Scarlett O'Hara (1939).

the negroes. In a swath eighty miles wide the Yankees were looting and
burning. There were hundreds of homes in flames, hundreds of homes
resounding with their footsteps." However, for Scarlett—and for Mitchell
too, it seems—this devastation was fundamentally personal, a "malicious
action aimed directly at her and hers." When the Yankees come, they
violate that most sacred of spaces, the Southern home, "dragging furni-
ture onto the front porch, running bayonets and knives into upholstery,"
ripping "open mattresses and feather beds until the air in the hall was
thick with feathers that floated softly down on her head."

"Impotent rage," writes Mitchell, "quelled what little fear was left
in her heart as she stood helpless while they plundered and stole and
ruined."[31] Such rage is all she is left with after the Yankees sack and
steal with abandon. Scarlett is then forced to fend for herself. The film's
most triumphant scene shows her eating a dirty carrot straight from
the ground and then declaring, with tears in her face and with all the
pride her Southern heart can muster, "I will never be hungry again!"

That proclamation taps into the rumors, myths, and memories that had been passed down in the South for generations. With Scarlett's turn from tragedy to triumph, all the South's vast accumulated loss seems to dissipate or give way to a greater and clearer independence. That is part of the reason why *Gone with the Wind* has had such a lasting cultural influence: it channels frustration and defeat—the feelings of love as well as battle—into a tale of resiliency.

As Mitchell presents it, emancipation is the sum of all evils. Most slaves, she writes, wanted no part of it and "refused to avail themselves of the new freedom." There were "hordes of 'trashy free issue niggers,'" though, who "caused most of the trouble," and they were aided by vicious carpetbaggers from the North. "They conducted themselves," she remarks, "as creatures of small intelligence might naturally be expected to do"; like "monkeys or small children turned loose among treasured objects whose value is beyond their comprehension, they ran wild—either from perverse pleasure in destruction or simply because of their ignorance." Recycling nearly every antiblack stereotype that has been passed down in American culture, Mitchell continues:

> Freedom [for them] became a never-ending picnic, a barbecue every day of the week, a carnival of idleness and theft and insolence. . . . Atlanta was crowded with them and still they came by the hundreds, lazy and dangerous. . . . Packed into squalid cabins, smallpox, typhoid and tuberculosis broke out among them. . . . Relying upon their masters in the old days to care for their aged and their babies, they now had no sense of responsibility for their helpless. . . . Abandoned negro children ran like frightened animals about the town until kind-hearted white people took them into their kitchens to raise. Aged country darkies, deserted by their children, bewildered and panic stricken in the bustling town, sat on the curbs and cried to the ladies who passed: "Mistis, please Ma'm, write mah old Marster down in Fayette County dat Ah's up hyah. He'll come tek dis ole nigger home agin. 'Fo' Gawd, Ah done got nuff of dis freedom!"[32]

For Mitchell, slavery was not a system of exploitation but a munificent domestic order, a kind of white man's and white woman's burden. Consequently, the war was the very opposite of, in Lincoln's words, "a new birth of freedom"; it was an anarchic storm that wrecked a once-great civilization. That civilization may no longer exist, but in *Gone with the Wind* and other stories of the Lost Cause, it can certainly be remembered and defended. Mitchell's narrative thus provides what Pollard ardently wished for all the way back in 1866: a literary vindication of the Confederacy.

Mitchell repeatedly blurs the line between the personal and the historical, making the Civil War into a story about Scarlett's social world, and vice versa. That blurring is summarized by Ashley Wilkes, who says that when he contemplates the war he thinks not only of "States' Rights and cotton and the darkies and the Yankees" but also of their life on the plantation. When he asks himself why he is fighting, Wilkes always thinks of "Twelve Oaks . . . and the unearthly way the magnolias look, opening under the moon, and how the climbing roses make the side porch shady even at the hottest noon. And I see Mother, sewing there, as she did when I was a little boy. And I hear the darkies coming home across the fields at dusk, tired and singing and ready for supper. . . . I am fighting for the old days, the old ways I love so much but which, I fear, are now gone forever."[33] Those old ways, Mitchell shows, have been swept away by the gusts of history.

The South depicted in *Gone with the Wind* may be an agrarian fantasy, a dream constructed from Hollywood sets and Lost Cause apocrypha, but it is a dream many people share. *Gone with the Wind* is a cornerstone of American culture. There are now more than 155 editions of the book, and in opinion surveys white Americans continue to rank it as their favorite novel. It has spawned fan fiction like Alexandra Ripley's *Scarlett* (1991), which follows the heroine in her later life, and Alice Randall's *The Wind Done Gone* (2001), which retells the story from the perspective of Cyanara, one of the slaves on Scarlett's plantation. The film has maybe had an even greater impact. After its initial release, MGM reissued it, often to sold-out shows, in 1947, and then again in 1954, 1961, and 1967. Its gross earnings, adjusted for inflation, amount to well over $1 billion. By some estimates, more human beings have watched *Gone with the Wind* than any other film.

Those revenues only hint at the story's broader cultural imprint. In the 1940s, Southern sororities and fraternities started to host Old South Balls in which women wore hoop skirts, men dressed in Confederate uniforms, and the bartenders served mint juleps in rooms decorated with Confederate flags.[34] There are *Gone with the Wind*–inspired perfumes, such as "Scarlett Cologne," which has a bittersweet smell. There are *Gone with the Wind* dolls, figurines, board games, calendars, cups, lockets, neckties, plates, puzzles, playing cards, stamps, sheet music, and nail polish. There is even a *Gone with the Wind* cookbook, as well as Scarlett Chocolates, which has candies named after the iconic characters—Prissy Peppermints, Scarlett Fantasies, Rhett Caramels.

The intensity of white people's affection for the story has to do with the way that it repackages the Civil War. (African American response is another matter altogether. As Malcolm X remarked, "When it played . . . I felt like crawling under the rug.")[35] In *Gone with the Wind*, the Old South is not simply something to admire; it is something that endures. The Old South, the plantation-filled utopia defended by the Confederacy, seems to live on in Scarlett, whose postwar resilience mirrors the region's. Perhaps, *Gone with the Wind* suggests, the war never needed to be fought in the first place: before the violence broke out, the South was a place of happiness and luxury. What has the Lost Cause been from the beginning but a version of that story, retold again and again? *Gone with the Wind* simply took it in a new direction and made it into an elegant, indelible soap opera.

William Faulkner and Southern Memory

With the exception of *Gone with the Wind*, no stories have influenced how people feel about Southern history more than the novels of William Faulkner. The characters, histories, and landscapes of Faulkner's fiction provide the South with a vividly imagined world through which the region continues to be defined. What made Faulkner into the South's preeminent chronicler was not just his verbal artistry, though. It was the way he grasped a fundamental truth about the South and wove it into his fiction: Southernness is not a matter of geography; it is an embodied identity, a felt inheritance that is conveyed through language, memory, and a sense of place.

That inheritance, Faulkner understood all too well, was tied to the Confederacy and everything it left behind. His own great-grandfather, William Clark Falkner (after whom the novelist was named), was an officer in the Confederate Army. Faulkner grew up hearing romantic stories about his heroic namesake, whom the family referred to as the Old Colonel.[36] Faulkner was also surrounded by daily reminders of the Yankee invasion: Oxford, Mississippi, where Faulkner lived, was devastated by the war. It might have been, as one visitor put it, "the most completely demolished town" in all of the South. Many of the buildings were never restored, and the Oxford courthouse—the town's ostensible seat of authority—was, as Faulkner put it, a "blackened shell" of its former self, with its "jagged topless jumble of brick wall enclosing like a ruined jaw."[37]

For Faulkner, the Lost Cause is less of a consciously adopted position than a worldview that shapes Southern culture in a multitude of ways. Southerners, he pointed out, tend to feel the Civil War in their bones. "For every Southern boy fourteen years old," it's "still not yet two o'clock on that July afternoon in 1863, the brigades are in position behind the rail fence, the guns are laid and ready in the woods and the furled flags are already loosened to break out and . . . it's all in the balance, it hasn't happened yet, it hasn't even begun yet." Maybe now, he thinks, "maybe *this* time with all this much to lose and all this much to gain," not just Gettysburg but "Pennsylvania, Maryland, the world, the golden dome of Washington itself to crown with desperate and unbelievable victory the desperate gamble, the cast made two years ago; or to anyone who ever sailed a skiff under a quilt sail, the moment in 1492 when somebody thought This is it: the absolute edge of no return, to turn back now and make home or sail irrevocably on and either find land or plunge over the world's roaring rim."[38]

There is a certain power to the boy's fantasy. Whether one calls it bravery or foolish adventurism, there is some daring feat, or epic "gamble" as Faulkner puts it, which the Confederacy symbolizes. The power of that fantasy, however, also makes one wonder about the consequences of the war's open-endedness. What does it mean if that moment—the instant right before Pickett's Charge on the final day of the Battle of Gettysburg—is, according to Faulkner, still so memorable, and so unaccountably *raw* for many white Southerners? Perhaps it means that the Lost Cause has been so thoroughly and successfully transmitted that it has simply become part of the makeup of white Southern consciousness. To be Southern, Faulkner suggests, is to inherit the Confederacy in one form or another. That inheritance might not take the form of this boy's wistfulness—indeed, it might grow into an antipathy toward the Confederacy and everything it represents—but Southern identity is anchored by an awareness of the Civil War's persistence.

Rather than arguing for or against the Lost Cause, Faulkner explores its cultural and psychological influence. His foremost invention—the fictional Yoknapatawpha County, in which masterpieces like *The Sound and the Fury* (1929) and *Absalom, Absalom!* (1936) take place—is essentially founded by the Civil War. *Sartoris* (1929), which launched the Yoknapatawpha series, starts with a story about a Confederate officer sitting on his porch and waiting for the Yankee troops to arrive. That Confederate turns out to be John Sartoris, a fictional version of Faulkner's great-grandfather. When the Yankees come, they try to kill Sartoris, but to no avail: the bullet misses its mark, he escapes, and his survival jump-starts Faulkner's entire novelistic world. The patriarch for the main family in Faulkner's fiction, Sartoris passes on two different sets of traits: his genes and something more immaterial, a "haughty arrogance which repeated itself generation after generation with a fateful fidelity."[39]

That arrogance dooms his offspring. His sons, Bayard and Johnny, feel compelled to match or outdo their father's wartime service. During WWI, they join the air force, hoping to become dogfighters. That dream quickly turns into a nightmare when Johnny dies in a terrible crash, which Bayard witnesses. In his grief Bayard becomes an alcoholic, and then he dies years later, when his son nearly wrecks their car. When the brothers are laid in the ground, their tombstones are placed next to their father's, whose name, along with his Confederate affiliation, are etched in stone: "Colonel John Sartoris, C.S.A." The spiritual persistence of the Confederacy is symbolized by the colonel's sword. "It was just such an implement," Faulkner writes, "as a Sartoris would consider the proper equipment for raising tobacco in a virgin wilderness. . . . And old Bayard held it upon his two hands, seeing in its stained fine blade and shabby elegant sheath the symbol of his race; that too in the tradition: the thing itself fine and clear enough, only the instrument had become a little tarnished in its very aptitude for shaping circumstance to arrogant ends."[40]

As Faulkner sees it, that desire to shape "circumstance to arrogant ends," passed down from generation to generation, is a crucial feature of white Southern identity. Though it is now worn and tarnished, that desire stretches back to the dawning moments of colonization and forward to the Jim Crow era, entangling the past and the present. Faulkner thus revamps the Lost Cause by showing how the Confederacy has survived not merely by monumentalizing itself in various statues, books, and memorials, but by becoming a basic, almost invisible part of American culture. The Lost Cause certainly persists as a consciously thought-out doctrine, but as we learn from Faulkner, it also persists in more invisible ways, manifesting in attitudes and dispositions, along with everything else the soul unknowingly carries—the flares of sentiment, quiet obligations, and embers of memory.

Faulkner's interest in the less tangible dimensions of the Lost Cause fuels *The Unvanquished*, his 1938 novel about the Sartoris family. The story takes place during the Civil War and is narrated by twelve-year-old Bayard. After shooting at a Yankee soldier, Bayard accompanies his family as they flee (then scam and fleece) the Union Army. Everything the Sartoris clan observes—as the Yankees sack and destroy everything in their path, burning homes, stealing valuables, exploding bridges, and ripping up railroads—illustrates the South's tragic deprivations and the North's depravity, providing a fictional example of Lost Cause memory. The fate of the Sartoris family, which gets absorbed into and partly undone by the war's violence, evokes the fate of the South itself, which loses its harmonious social order to the Yankee invasion. That symbolic association is reinforced by Faulkner's depictions of slavery: the Union

Army is distinctly uninterested in emancipation, either turning away the slaves who seek them out or treating them as contraband, and the novel's most prominent slave, Ringo, is seemingly content with his fate and desirous of neither rebellion nor escape.

One of the foremost fantasies of the Lost Cause—indeed, one of its defining myths—is that slavery in the Old South was relatively mild. Every bit of testimony from formerly enslaved people showed that fantasy to be a figment of the white imagination, but for the defenders of the Lost Cause slavery was a familial institution that involved mutual obligations and fidelity. And Faulkner weaves that fantasy into *The Unvanquished*. Despite their master-slave relationship, Bayard and Ringo cleave to each other as though they were brothers. The novel's first sentences describe Bayard and Ringo's connection as both natural and egalitarian, much like the Southern landscape they inhabit: "Behind the smokehouse that summer, Ringo and I had a living map. Although Vicksburg was just a handful of chips from the woodpile and the River a trench scraped into the packed earth with the point of a hoe, it (river, city, and terrain) lived, . . . the very setting of the stage for conflict a prolonged and well nigh hopeless ordeal in which we ran, panting and interminable, . . . join[ing] forces and spend[ing] ourselves against a common enemy, time."

Faulkner enlists the Lost Cause to craft his story, suggesting that the relation between master and slave was a gentle, organic bond. That view of slavery is further delineated when Bayard and Ringo lay together in the family's wagon:

> That was how he travelled for the next six days—lying on his back in the wagon bed with his hat over his eyes, sleeping, or taking his turn holding the parasol over Granny and keeping me awake by talking of the railroad which he had never seen though which I had seen that Christmas. . . . That's how Ringo and I were. We were almost the same age, and Father always said that Ringo was a little smarter than I was, but that didn't count with us, anymore than the difference in the color of our skins counted. What counted was, what one of us had done or seen that the other had not, and ever since that Christmas I had been ahead of Ringo because I had seen a railroad, a

locomotive. Only I know now it was more than that with Ringo, though neither of us was to see the proof of my belief for some time yet and we were not to recognize it as such even then. It was as if Ringo felt it too and that the railroad, the rushing locomotive which he hoped to see symbolised it—the motion, the impulse to move which had already seethed to a head among his people, darker than themselves, reasonless, following and seeking a delusion, a dream, a bright shape which they could not know since there was nothing in their heritage, nothing in the memory even of the old men to tell the others, "This is what we will find"; he nor they could not have known what it was yet it was there—one of those impulses inexplicable yet invincible which appear among races of people at intervals and drive them to pick up and leave all security and familiarity of earth and home and start out, they dont know where, empty handed, blind to everything but a hope and a doom.[41]

The whole history of the South from the Civil War onward seems to be captured here. This bond between the boys is, unbeknownst to them both, about to dissolve, and Ringo will eventually join his "empty handed" people in their collective attempt to forge a new beginning. For Faulkner, the fate of Bayard and Ringo mirrors the fate of the South itself, as it moved from the antebellum era through Reconstruction. One can detect a great deal of interracial attachment and sympathy in Faulkner's language, but it is also clear that the passage from slavery to freedom is hopeless. It amounts to a passionate and "reasonless" attempt to grasp the ungraspable, a "delusion" that is unsecured by either history or memory. Emancipation, and the Civil War that occasions it, thereby becomes something very different from liberation: it is the tragic destruction of a past—indeed, an entire civilization—recaptured here as a fleeting moment before a train's arrival.

If *The Unvanquished* offers up a Lost Cause vision of the war, it also tests and questions the very ideals in which it is invested. The Sartoris clan is ensnared in Yankee greed and belligerence, but the war, as Faulkner renders it, is fueled and defined by a cycle of violence that extends far beyond the war itself. Granny is eventually killed not by a Union soldier but by an ex-Confederate rogue. The novel's final sequence is also set in motion by violence that begets violence that begets more violence. Colonel Sartoris, wrecked by wartime loss and unyielding in his anger, kills two Northerners in a duel, only to then be murdered by his former partner, whom Bayard, in turn, is expected to hunt down in revenge. Bayard does not wish to perpetuate that seemingly interminable cycle of bloodlust—he allows himself to be shot at and silently watches as the pistol rises, quivers, and releases a "sudden orange bloom and smoke"— but the novel highlights experiences that inexplicably persist: senses of loss that never dissipate, smells that distinguish a particular place, the inexorable memory of a person after he or she has died. As Bayard writes of his father, a paragon of Confederate manhood, "All the pictures we had of him were bad ones because a picture could no more have held him dead than the house could have kept his body. But I didn't need to see him again because he was there, he would always be there; maybe . . . his dream was not something which he possessed but something which he had bequeathed us which we could never forget, which would even assume the corporeal shape of him whenever any of us, black or white, closed our eyes."[42]

That dream is the dream of the Confederacy. As we discover, violence, like grief, is never fully forgotten—and though the South may be defeated, it remains "unvanquished." Throughout his fiction, Faulkner thus enlists the narrative of the Lost Cause, but he also refuses to lapse into simplistic hero worship or monument making. Instead, Faulkner mines the Lost Cause for insights into American culture and the nature of the human mind. Novels like *Sartoris* and *The Unvanquished* reveal the extent to which the Confederacy survived by transforming itself. By the mid-twentieth century, it was no longer a position in which one could simply believe or disbelieve: it was a worldview, an implicit mode of thinking and feeling that, Faulkner suggests, might be coextensive with the South itself.

Robert E. Lee's Emancipation Proclamations

In the 1960s and 1970s, the Lost Cause suffered a blow. The civil rights movement, the women's liberation movement, and the antiwar movement changed not only the nation's politics but also the way that people thought and felt about the Civil War. If the United States is (or should be) a multicultural democracy built on the principle of equality, then it is difficult to find anything redeemable in the Confederacy.

The cultural influence of the Lost Cause began to wane, but it did not expire. That's the not-so-hidden secret of literary and cultural history: nothing ever truly dies; it just gets reborn in new forms. That is what happened, and keeps happening, to the Civil War. It is also what happened to the Lost Cause in the late twentieth century and early twenty-first century, as this narrative found its way into other mediums, expressing itself through school curricula, family lore, and reenactments. The Lost Cause has even experienced a rebirth with the rise of the internet and, more recently, with the resurgence of white supremacy. Numerous websites, threads, and forums promulgate the myth of the noble Confederacy, at once preserving the Lost Cause and radicalizing new generations of neo-Confederates. The Southern Poverty Law Center estimates that there are now nearly three dozen neo-Confederate organizations that are as active as they are dangerous.[43]

In recent decades, defenders of the Lost Cause have increasingly turned to counterfactual fiction, a genre that enables them to write against the grain of history and imaginatively resurrect the Confederacy. Counterfactuals are stories that reenvision the course of human events. Also called "alternative histories," they are fueled by a pressing and feverish *What If?*—What if Lincoln, for instance, had survived his assassination? Or Germany had won World War II? Such stories have an undeniable appeal. They allow us to see history, especially history we take for granted, radically altered before our eyes. For the Confederacy's latter-day sympathizers, the counterfactual provides a rather unique opportunity: it allows them to flip the tables and create a world in which the Lost Cause is never lost, a world in which the South finally *wins*.

In Harry Turtledove's *The Guns of the South* (1992), the tides of history are reversed by advanced weaponry. In 2012, the novel tells us, a group called "America Will Break," led by South African terrorists fanatically devoted to white supremacy, steal a time machine and travel backward

150 years, just in time to aid the Army of Northern Virginia on the eve of the Battle of New Bern (1862). In reality, Lee lost that battle, thereby opening up the Carolina coast to the advancing Union forces, but "America Will Break" changes everything. They bring along thousands of AK-47s, which they present as a gift to Robert E. Lee and disseminate through the ranks. At first, everything goes as planned: the automatic weapons transform the war, as mounted Confederates mow down Union soldiers until the ground is soaked in blood. The Confederates win at New Bern, sack Washington, remove Lincoln from power, and formalize a peace with a prostrate United States. At that point, the terrorists' plan starts to unravel—at first slowly, then with stunning rapidity. Lee grows suspicious of their leader, and the time travelers, in turn, lend their support to Nathan Bedford Forrest, a more hardline white supremacist, in the presidential election. When Lee wins regardless, he immediately pushes through a bill of emancipation, which sparks an all-out battle—a kind of Civil War after the Civil War—between Lee's forces and the South Africans. Eventually the terrorists are defeated, giving way to a new peace, and a new birth for freedom in the Confederate States of America.[44]

That seemingly impossible event, a Confederate victory, lies at the heart of MacKinlay Kantor's aptly titled 1961 novel, *If the South Had Won the Civil War*. In Kantor's tale, the pivotal shift—or *point of divergence* in the language of alternative histories—is the sudden death of Ulysses S. Grant in the spring of 1863. While traveling through the hills of Mississippi, Grant falls off his horse and cracks his skull on a rock, which leads to the disastrous rise of John McClernand, a "pompous" and "unruly" general who responds to the "slightest penetration" of Southern defenses by foolishly sending forth entire brigades. In contrast, the Confederate general, Robert E. Lee, is both tactically and politically brilliant. With his military acumen and uncanny foresight, it seems as though he is playing multidimensional chess. Lee was a "marvel" to everyone around him, Kantor writes, and his superiority to McClernand enables the Confederates to tear apart the Army of the Potomac. Jefferson Davis takes up residence in the White House, and the C.S.A., led by a new Jeffersonian Party founded "in the certainty that liberation must come about," frees the slaves. Sometimes, Kantor writes, great men are guided by a "Divine light" that "reveals the errors of humanity as assuredly [as] it illuminates the pathway forward." That is what happens with Lee in Kantor's story: the former Confederate general leads the country into a new, post-emancipation future and helps Congress pass a law prohibiting slavery (and providing slaveholders with financial restitution).[45]

Other stories imagine different routes to Southern victory. In one novel, *Lee's Special Order No. 191*, the note detailing Southern troop movements that accidentally fell into Northern hands before the Battle of Antietam (1862) is recovered by the Confederates. That seemingly small turn of events alters everything: the South wins, Lincoln goes into exile, and the C.S.A. grants emancipation. In another novel, Lee defeats the Union Army by heeding James Longstreet's counsel and engaging in WWI-style trench warfare. In yet another, written by Newt Gingrich (yes, that Newt Gingrich), Pickett's Charge works like a charm and the Confederates take Gettysburg. There are scores of these narratives that try to imagine what might have happened, what *could* have happened, if the South had won. But no matter what changes—no matter who wins, or why, or how—slavery always seems to be abolished, often at the urging of Lee himself.

The fact that these Southern victories tend to involve emancipation tells us a great deal about what these stories are doing with the war's cultural materials. These counterfactuals reinforce the belief, which has fueled the Lost Cause myth from its inception, that slavery was merely a secondary consideration for the Confederates, whose principal goal was preserving state sovereignty. If the South rather than the North abolishes slavery, it means that the war really *was* about regional independence, Southern honor, and the incompatibility of agrarianism and industrialism. It means that all of the defenders of the Lost Cause, everyone from Edward Pollard to Thomas Dixon and John Crowe Ransom, had been right all along. It means that the South really *should* have won, and if they had—if this or that battle had just gone a bit differently, or this or that event had not occurred—the world today would be much better off.

These counterfactuals also grow out of a deep-seated desire to believe that the Civil War never needed to occur in the first place. The idea that the war was somehow avoidable has buttressed a great deal of white American memory. And that idea is premised on a single conviction, as powerful as it is fanciful—namely, that slavery would have ended one way or another; indeed, it was already dying out when the war occurred. One of the more recent statements to this effect was made by Ron Paul. A few years ago, in an interview on *Meet the Press*, Paul said that Lincoln "shouldn't have gone" into a "senseless Civil War." When Tim Russert objected, saying, "We'd still have slavery," Paul replied, "Oh, come on, Tim. Oh, come on. Slavery was phased out in every other country in the world. And the way I'm advising it should have been done is what the British Empire did. You buy the slaves, then release them. How much would that cost compared to killing 600,000 Americans, and where it lingered for 100 years? . . . Every other major country in the world got rid of slavery without a civil war."[46]

For Paul, as for many neo-Confederates, slavery was going to be stamped out one way or another. The problem, of course, is that it's simply not true. In Cuba, enslaved people were not emancipated until 1886; in Brazil, not until 1888. The multinational agreement to outlaw the slave trade, the Brussels Conference Act, was not passed until 1890, and slavery continued even after that, enduring in Morocco, Nepal, and other countries well into the twentieth century. The prospect of a Confederate emancipation proclamation is also belied by the history of American slavery. The institution was a vital feature of rather than an aberration within modern capitalism. By some estimates, slavery was actually becoming *more* profitable by the eve of the war owing to the ways in which enslaved people were treated as collateralized capital.[47]

Stories in which the Confederacy frees the slaves, frequently on its own accord or through the goodwill of Robert E. Lee, imaginatively resolve the racial tensions that have haunted the United States ever since its inception. They present the United States as a nation of innate enlightenment and slavery as a kind of accident or anomaly within this city upon a hill. The allure of these counterfactuals, however, has as much to do with their sense of history as with their racial politics. If the South instead of the North enacts abolition, then the history of the United States really is a story of uninterrupted progress. Counterfactuals buttress the idea, the collective wish to believe, that history is a continuous advance toward greater freedom—that slavery inevitably dissolves, racism recedes, and the world slowly but surely becomes happier, more liberated, more connected.

These counterfactuals are tied to other contemporary efforts to preserve and advance the Lost Cause. This mythology continues to snake its way into school textbooks and inform museum exhibits, providing an ideological "safe space" for white supremacists and anchoring the historical perspectives of many white Americans. These current revivals all draw on a long tradition of Lost Cause art and literature, which has lived on not despite but because of the South's defeat, taking form as a way to remember history against the grain. It has lived on because it is highly elastic, adapting to different moments and different mediums. It has lived on because it is politically resonant, structuring ongoing debates about race, region, and nation. And it has lived on because politicians like Churchill, filmmakers like D. W. Griffith, novelists like Margaret Mitchell, poets like Abram Ryan, and sculptors like Edward Valentine have all retold a version of the same, utterly wishful story: that the South fought not for slavery but for freedom—that its righteous cause, all along, was liberty.

||||||||||||||||||||||||||||||||||||||||||||||||||||||||||||||||||||||||||||||||||||||||||||||||||||||||||||||||||||

{4} The Great Emancipation

THE SAILORS HAD NEVER SEEN ANYTHING LIKE THIS before. There, speeding across the waves, was a lone Confederate gunship headed straight for the Union blockade. Surely wondering what this one vessel hoped to achieve against an entire line of heavily armed warships, the men aimed their cannons at the ship and waited for the inevitable, deadly exchange. But that exchange never occurred. The Confederates hoisted a white flag, a bedsheet that fluttered in the wind. The Northerners then boarded the ship and discovered that the Confederates were not, in fact, Confederates at all. They were escaped slaves: seventeen men, women, and children who had commandeered the ship and sailed their way to freedom.

The vessel was captained by Robert Smalls, a 23-year-old enslaved father, husband, and seasoned pilot, who had spent the past ten years working on Charleston's wharves. That morning, in the predawn darkness, he and his compatriots carried out a plan they had been hatching for the past several weeks. While the white crew was away onshore, they slipped aboard, fired up the ship, picked up their families, and lit out for the North on a steam-powered gunner. Their plan was a perilous one: they needed to pass by several Confederate forts, each of which was easily capable of destroying the ship and everyone inside of it. Smalls, however, had memorized the code used at the checkpoints—two long whistles, then a shorter burst—and, to complete the deception, donned the Confederate captain's gray suit and straw hat. When they finally reached Union waters, the escaped slaves celebrated, and Smalls told the commanding officer, "I thought this ship might be of some use to Uncle Abe." The officer responded, "I don't know exactly what you are now . . . but you're certainly not slaves, not after what you have gone through tonight for your freedom."[1]

The story traveled quickly, spreading at the speed of print. Numerous mariners, writers, editors, slaves, and abolitionists retold the narrative of Smalls's great escape. The *New York Herald* called it "one of the most daring and heroic adventures since the war commenced." Samuel Dupont, the admiral in charge of the Union blockade, praised the "intelligent slave" who "performed this bold feat so skillfully."[2] The story has also continued to resonate, appearing in novels, poems, children's stories, and several nonfiction histories. In 2012, it was even reenacted off the South Carolina coast to mark the 150th anniversary of the *Planter's* northern trip. The power of Smalls's story is richly illustrated by Josephine Henderson Heard's 1890 poem "General Robert Smalls":

His deeds of valor we will tell to Nations yet with pride,
To Afric's sons and daughters we'll leave it as no mystery,
But hand them down on blocks of stone, and they shall
  live in history.

With Touissant L'Ouverture and Crispus Attuck brave,
John Brown and Abraham Lincoln, who died to free the
  slave—
They, the nation's martyrs, and each loyal negro's walls
Should be adorned with portraits of these and Robert
  Smalls.

The poem, too, is a portrait of Smalls—a verbal sketch of his historical and political importance. The ingenious pilot of the *Planter* follows in a distinguished line of warriors who fought "to free the slave," a lineage that stretches backward to the Age of Revolution and forward to the Age of Emancipation. (Crispus Attucks was a black dockworker killed in the Boston Massacre; Toussaint L'Ouverture was a slave turned general who led the Haitian Revolution.) By making such connections, the poem morphs into a verbal portrait not only of Smalls but also of the Civil War, which Heard suggests is nothing less than a grand struggle for liberation, a battle to crush the South's "peculiar institution" and free the slaves.

That battle is imagined in different ways by different writers. For some, the war involves divine intervention: it is a scourge guided by the hand of God to clear the land of injustice and bring about Jubilee. For others, the war originates in a global struggle for emancipation, an international and interracial fight that ties the United States to South America, Europe, and Russia. For still others, the war's deliverance arrives very slowly, or only by way of arms or art. But throughout this literature, the war takes shape as a grand overturning—a liberation that remakes history and literature alike.

The Abolition War

During and shortly after the war, a furious debate emerged about what it should be called. In both the North and the South, many people referred to it as "the Rebellion," a term that foregrounded issues of constitutional interpretation and national belonging. Others enlisted different monikers, from "The Secession War" to "Lincoln's War," to name the struggle that had swept up the American people and swept away the polity that previously held them together. Antislavery advocates, who viewed the conflict as a struggle to liberate the slaves and annihilate the institution that held them in bondage, adopted a different term (which has largely faded from public memory): the Abolition War. As Frederick Douglass—the former slave turned writer, orator, and editor—put it, "This war is, and of right ought to be, an Abolition War": "The Abolition of Slavery is the comprehensive and logical object of the war, for it includes everything else which the struggle involves. It is a war for the Union, a war for the Constitution, I admit; but it is logically such a war only in the sense that the greater includes the lesser. . . . What we want now is a country . . . not saddened by the footprints of a single slave—and nowhere cursed by the presence of a slaveholder."[3]

This was a minority viewpoint during much of the conflict. In the North, Unionism repeatedly trumped emancipation as a rationale for the war. As Lincoln proclaimed, "If I could save the Union without freeing *any* slave, I would do it; and if I could save it by freeing *all* the slaves, I would do it. . . . What I do about Slavery, and the colored race, I do because I believe it helps to save the Union." Nonetheless, the rumor of freedom sped throughout the South, and countless slaves made their way to the Union lines, hazarding life and limb in search of liberty—or, at least, some respite from bondage. Many of these escapees were classified by the Union Army as "contraband" (a designation of smuggled property) and put to work digging, cooking, and cleaning for the North. Day after day, more fugitive slaves joined the camps and their ranks swelled, mounting what W. E. B. Du Bois would later call a general strike against slavery itself. That strike, through which the slave "transferred his labor from the Confederate planter to the Northern invader," then became armed when the Union created black regiments and put them into pitched battles against the Confederates.[4] For many slaves, those battles were a direct extension of the Emancipation Proclamation and its allied measures, all of which helped transform the Union War, slowly but surely, into the Abolition War.

That transformation is both recorded and recast in literary history: recorded, because literature is a piebald archive of history's otherwise ineffable moments; recast, because literature often unfolds against the grain of history, offering up alternative memories for the past and its connection to the present. This tension is particularly evident in the literature of emancipation, which simultaneously registers the hopes, dreams, and anxieties occasioned by liberation and reveals just how partial and curtailed that liberation was. From the nineteenth century to the twenty-first, this literature reassesses American history by imaginatively returning to emancipation's origin point and inhabiting the foundational moments of slavery's dissolution.

During the war, much of this literature focused on the black soldiers who rose up in armed opposition against the Confederacy. Almost as soon as these regiments were assembled, their feats were conveyed in poems, stories, and engravings. Some of those representations were derogatory: many whites were terrified by the prospect of black men trained to kill, and that terror inspired racist caricatures and dismissals. For many abolitionists, however, these soldiers were living symbols of emancipation. James Madison Bell, a free black poet from Ohio, likened the Battle of Milliken's Bend (1863), in which Iowa's "African Brigades" defended the Union supply line against a surprise attack, to the famous battle that inspired Alfred Lord Tennyson's "The Charge of the Light Brigade." Though "the poet king," Bell writes, "has sung" of that fateful charge,

> The pleasing duty still remains
> To sing a people from their chains—
> To sing what none have yet assay'd,
> The wonders of the Black Brigade.

There, in the midst of a Mississippi summer, the "war waxed hot, and bullets flew,"

> But they were there to dare and do,
> E'en to the last, to save the land.
> And when the leaders of their corps
> Grew wild with fear, and quit the field,
> The dark remembrance of their scars
> Before them rose, they could not yield:
> And, sounding o'er the battle din,
> They heard their standard-bearer cry—
> "Rally! Prove that ye are men!"[5]

Sarah Shuften cultivated an even wider view of emancipation. While living in Georgia in 1865, Shuften wrote a eulogy for all of the war's fallen black soldiers. The remains of these warrior-martyrs, she writes, are now inhumed in America's hills and plains, consecrating the land:

> The land is holy where they fought,
> And holy where they fell;
> For by their blood, that land was bought
> That land they loved so well—

Then glory to the valiant band,
The honored saviors of the land.

. . . .

Fair Afric's *free* and valiant sons,
Shall join with Europe's band
To celebrate in varied tongues,
Our *free* and happy land

Till freedom's golden fingers trace,
A line that knows no end,
And man shall meet in every face,
A brother and a friend.[6]

This poem seems to join the very celebration of interracial freedom that it invites. As Shuften imagines it, the war is something very different from a struggle over regional sovereignty or national unity. It is part of emancipation's inexorable march forward, which shall proceed until "freedom's golden fingers trace" a limitless line around the world.

Black soldiers faced an unusually brutal set of circumstances. The Confederates sometimes executed them rather than taking them prisoner, a policy that culminated in the brutal slaughter at Fort Pillow, led by Confederate general (and future Grand Wizard of the Ku Klux Klan) Nathan Bedford Forrest. The Union generals also placed them in some of the most desperate battles, such as the raid on Fort Wagner in July of 1863.[7] The 54th Massachusetts led that assault, storming the heavily armed fort and suffering major casualties: nearly half of the regiment was killed, along with their colonel, Robert Gould Shaw. Although the attack ultimately failed, the soldiers' daring charge was channeled into drawings, songs, stories, and speeches. Paul Laurence Dunbar reflected on "this hot terror of a hopeless fight" carried out by "unlettered and despised droves." William James, the Bostonian philosopher and brother of both Henry James (the novelist) and Wilkie James (a white officer in the 54th), commented that the historical importance of the assault "is measured neither by its material magnitude, nor by its immediate success": "Thermopylae was a defeat; but to the Greek imagination,

Leonidas and his few Spartans stood for the whole worth of Grecian life.
... And so here." The war, James declared, has "but one meaning in the
eye of history": it "freed the country from slavery," and "nowhere was
that meaning better symbolized and embodied than in the constitution
of this first Northern negro regiment." Harriet Jacobs, a former slave
turned autobiographer and activist, similarly celebrated "the colored
soldiers fighting and dying in the cause of Freedom," adding, "Look at
the Massachusetts Fifty-fourth! Every man of them a hero! marching
so boldly and steadily to victory or death, for the freedom of their race,
and the salvation of their country! *Their* country! . . . A Power mightier
than man is guiding this revolution; and though justice moves slowly, it
will come at last."[8]

The transition that Jacobs announces, the metamorphosis of a slave
into a soldier, was visually articulated in a set of images that appeared in
Harper's Weekly in 1864. Entitled "The Escaped Slave," the engravings—
each based on photographs of a man from Alabama who fled from
slavery and joined a black regiment—form a diptych, showing the man
on the plantation and then draped in Union blue. Between these images
a story unfolds, a story of release and becoming, of peril and freedom.
The column that accompanied the sketches in *Harper's* described that
story in national terms, stating that this man made his way north from
Montgomery "for the express purpose of enlisting in the army of the
Union" and "fighting for the nation which is hereafter pledged to protect
him."[9] However, the images impart a slightly different narrative, one that
centers on *attaining* rather than receiving freedom, one less concerned
with the Union than with abolition writ large.

The transformation of soldiers into slaves was deftly recounted by
William Wells Brown. Born a slave in Kentucky, Brown quickly learned
that life consists in constant change. Fathered by one of his master's
relatives, Brown was repeatedly sold while growing up, but he finally
escaped—not to freedom but to fugitivity—as a young man, when a
steamboat he worked on docked in Ohio, a free state. Shortly afterward,
he met his first wife, Elizabeth Spooner, with whom he started a family.
Brown then got involved in the burgeoning abolitionist movement, de-

T. B. Bishop, *The Escaped Slave* (1864). *Harper's Weekly*, July 2, 1864.

livering speeches, participating in antislavery conferences, and helping conduct the Underground Railroad. His fervent belief in the power of moral suasion and social reform led him to wear many hats. He was (among other things) a passionate advocate for women's suffrage and a diehard opponent of alcohol; a seasoned orator and traveler; an antiwar activist; and, toward the end of his life, a homeopathic doctor.

Brown was also an incredibly talented writer. Before the war, he published versions of his autobiography, which were met with acclaim by abolitionists. He also wrote one of the earliest African American novels, *Clotel; or, The President's Daughter* (1853), a book that interlaces history with fiction to tell a tragic story about race and liberty. Thomas Jefferson's mixed-race daughters are sold as slaves and subjected to untold indignities. In the novel's climactic scene, Clotel—"the daughter of Thomas Jefferson, a president of the United States . . . [and] author of the Declaration of American Independence"—escapes from her master, is chased onto a bridge, and then propels herself over the railings, sinking "for ever beneath the waves of the river."[10]

When the Abolition War broke out, Brown used his pen to document the role played by black soldiers before, during, and after the conflict. His book *The Negro in the American Rebellion* (1867) is a compelling and faithful historical chronicle. But it also bears the traces of its author's restless, creative mind. It is one of the most multifaceted books about the Civil War ever produced, weaving together interviews, poems, government reports, telegraphs, songs, legal documents, newspaper articles, regimental musters, and quotes from histories, diaries, letters, and travel narratives. And Brown enlists—or more accurately, remixes—all of these texts to construct a multifaceted story about the Great Emancipation.

Brown devotes most of his attention to individuals who symbolize the war. He lauds John Brown, who "struck a blow that rang on the fetters of the enslaved" and "caused the oppressor to tremble," as well as his revolutionary precursors: Denmark Vesey, Nat Turner, and Madison Washington. He narrates the exploits of Robert Smalls, who boldly piloted *The Planter*, as well as Big Bob, an as-yet-unidentified preacher who worked as a spy and saboteur by disguising himself in Confederate uniforms. One of the most affecting passages focuses on William Tillman, a free black sailor from Delaware. Tillman was working as a cook on board the *S. J. Waring*, a Northern schooner, when it was suddenly commandeered by Confederate privateers. After taking control of the vessel, the Confederates set sail for Charleston, where they planned to sell Tillman as a slave. In the middle of the night, after the Confederates retired to their cabins and fell asleep, Tillman grabbed a large club, entered the captain's quarters, and killed him. Tillman then proceeded to the next room and killed the first mate. "Cautiously," Brown writes, switching to the present tense to heighten the sense of action, "he ascends to the deck, strikes the mate [and] . . . seizes the revolver, . . . puts the enemy in irons, and proclaims himself master of the vessel."[11]

Brown also witnessed some of the more joyful experiences of emancipation. With verve and grace, he describes the jubilant proceedings at the contraband camp in Washington, DC, on the eve of the Emancipation Proclamation. Men, women, and children sang and prayed together, lifting up their hearts and voices for manumission. Throughout the night

they recounted stories, delivered speeches, and read scripture—especially
the story of Exodus, in which Moses leads the Israelites out of bondage
and into Canaan. That story acquires an American twist in the sorrow
song, "Go Down, Moses," which was sung at the camp several times over:

> Oh, go down, Moses,
> Way down in Egypt's land;
> Tell king Pharaoh
> To let my people go.
>
> Oh, Pharaoh said he would go cross,
> Let my people go.
> But Pharaoh and his host was lost,
> Let my people go.
>   *Chorus*—Oh, go down, Moses, &c.

Though the song was rooted in slavery, it attained its full force and meaning in the Civil War. The moment of release, of Pharaoh's relinquished
grip, seemed to have finally arrived.

Shortly before midnight, silence enveloped the camp. Then, when
the clock struck twelve, announcing emancipation's dawn, "every heart
seemed to leap for joy: some were singing, some praying, some weeping,
some dancing, husbands embracing wives, friends shaking hands, and
appearing to feel that the Day of Jubilee had come." Almost immediately, Brown writes, a "sister broke out in the following strain, which
was heartily joined in by the vast assembly":

> Go down, Abraham, away down in Dixie's land,
>   Tell Jeff. Davis to let my people go.
> Our bitter tasks are ended, all our unpaid labor done;
> Our galling chains are broken, and our onward march begun:
>   Go down, Abraham, away down in Dixie's land,
>   Tell Jeff. Davis to let my people go.
>   .   .   .   .
>
> Not vainly have we waited through the long and darkened years;
> Not vain the patient watching, 'mid our sweat and blood and tears:

Go down, Abraham, away down in Dixie's land,
Tell Jeff. Davis to let my people go.[12]

The song's power derives from its revisionary spirit. It is an improvised rewriting of "Go Down, Moses," replacing Exodus's hero with President Lincoln, Egypt with America, and Ramses with Jefferson Davis. This song, which at once declares emancipation and provides it with a collective voice, also rewrites that most famous Southern tune, "Dixie." That song's nostalgia for a pre-emancipation past ("Oh I wish I was in the land of cotton, / Old times there are not forgotten") gives way here to a post-emancipation future ("Not vainly have we waited") while retaining the same, melodic injunction: to turn away, or down, to Dixie.[13] All of this revisionary energy imparts a distinct narrative for the Civil War, according to which the historical, political, and military purpose of this struggle—indeed, its entire rationale—is the emancipation of the slaves, now and forever.

The sorrow songs floated up in public and in private, at numerous camps, churches, and other gatherings. They also attracted the attention of white abolitionists, several of whom transcribed the songs and provided them with musical notation. The resulting collection, *Slave Songs of the United States* (1867), contains 136 songs that shuttle between joy and sorrow, wresting melody from affliction. As Du Bois later remarked, this is the music "of an unhappy people, of the children of disappointment," yet through all their sorrow "there breathes a hope—a faith in the ultimate justice of things."[14] That raucous mixture of emotions and expectations was intensified by the conflict. When formerly enslaved people sang these songs, from the Sea Islands to the contraband camps, the war seemed to be ushering in much of what they describe: the arrival of Canaan and a long-deferred release from bondage. One of the more recent songs (perhaps even coterminous with the war) cheered this burgeoning freedom:

No more peck o' corn for me,
No more, no more;
No more peck o' corn for me,
Many thousand go.

No more driver's lash for me, (*Twice.*)
No more, etc.

   .   .   .   .   .

No more mistress call for me,
No more, no more;
No more mistress' call for me,
   Many thousand go.[15]

Such songs provide an inclusive view of emancipation, one that surpasses the stories of martial heroism—impressive as they are—by drawing attention to the experiences of people who either could not fight or did not wish to, finding instead other paths toward liberation.

That liberation turned out to be more circumscribed than many freedpeople had hoped. After the war, emancipation became a largely abstract political principle, a theory gloriously enshrined in the Thirteenth, Fourteenth, and Fifteenth Amendments but cruelly undercut by the conditions in which many former slaves lived. The spread of Jim Crow, the return of the Black Codes, and the formation of the convict lease system all created a post-emancipation world that was not all that measurably different from the pre-emancipation world that preceded it.[16] That paradoxical condition of being at once liberated and subjugated, at once free and unfree, is the subject of a great deal of the emancipationist literature produced in the late nineteenth and early twentieth centuries. These texts tend to highlight the fragility of black freedom and the continuation of the Confederacy—as a social entity, political force, and commemorative ideal—while returning to the war, again and again, as the violent crucible out of which emancipation ever so tenuously emerged.

Frederick Douglass's Civil War

Frederick Douglass masterfully articulated this bifocal view of the war. Born a slave in Maryland, Douglass eventually escaped from bondage, at the age of 20, by disguising himself as a sailor and slipping aboard a train bound for New York City. That escape released him from the "blight and mildew" of slavery, the "hottest hell of horrors" that he later

Frederick Douglass in 1870. Courtesy of the Library of Congress,
Prints and Photographs Division.

documented in his autobiographies. While enslaved, his masters tortured
him both physically and psychologically, and he desperately desired to
be free. When he was a child, he sometimes went to Chesapeake Bay,
looked out at the boats gliding along the water, and felt envy swell up
in his heart. "[I often] stood alone," he recalled, "upon the banks of that
noble bay, and . . . pour[ed] out my soul's complaint . . . to the moving
multitude of ships," declaring, "You are loosed from your moorings, and
free; I am fast in my chains, and am a slave! You move merrily before the
gentle gale, and I sadly before the bloody whip! . . . O, why was I born
a man, of whom to make a brute!"[17] He even tried—and failed—to flee
once before, a crime for which he was imprisoned.

   When Douglass finally escaped, he felt an overwhelming elation—"a
joyous excitement," in his words, "which no words can describe." But

he quickly discovered that freedom was very different from what he had imagined:

> A sense of my loneliness and helplessness crept over me, and covered me with something bordering on despair. In the midst of thousands of my fellow-men, and yet a perfect stranger! . . . I was without home, without friends, without work, without money, and without any definite knowledge of which way to go, or where to look for succor. Some apology can easily be made for the few slaves who have, after making good their escape, turned back to slavery, preferring the actual rule of their masters, to the life of loneliness, apprehension, hunger, and anxiety, which meets them on their first arrival in a free state. . . . It takes stout nerves to stand up, in such circumstances. A man, homeless, shelterless, breadless, friendless, and moneyless, is not in a condition to assume a very proud or joyous tone; and in just this condition was I, while wandering about the streets of New York city and lodging, at least one night, among the barrels on one of its wharves. I was not only free from slavery, but I was free from home, as well.[18]

Is one truly free if one is simply free to starve? Through his personal experiences, Douglass landed on a vital truth: freedom does not simply entail being removed from someone or something else—what political philosophers dub "negative liberty."[19] Real freedom, living as one sees fit and making meaningful choices, requires certain material and institutional conditions.

That realization shaped Douglass's response to the Abolition War. On the one hand, he saw the conflict as a mighty revolution against slavery itself, as an institution as well as an idea. For Douglass, the war recalled and revived the American, French, and Haitian Revolutions, as well as the European rebellions of 1848.[20] As he asserted in 1864, the "world has witnessed many wars," and "history records and perpetuates their memory," but no one has witnessed a "grander war than that which the loyal people of this country are now waging against the slaveholding Rebels. The blow we strike is not merely to free a country or continent—but the whole world from Slavery."[21] On the other hand, Douglass was keenly aware of the fact that the United States never provided the material conditions that former slaves required to live free and equal lives. Although the Reconstruction Amendments guaranteed access to basic civic acts, such as voting and legal representation, they offered nothing in the way of redistributed land, money, or property. Even the civic rights formally guaranteed to African Americans were violently challenged by white supremacists, leading Douglass, later in life, to "denounce the so-called emancipation as a stupendous fraud."

While the war raged, it was unclear how it would turn out—whether it would lead to a revolution or end up a disappointment. To help "strike the blow," he worked long and hard in all the ways that he could, writing letters and essays, delivering lectures around the country, and reporting on it in his newspaper, *Douglass' Monthly*. After the Emancipation Proclamation, he helped recruit soldiers for the North's black regiments and even encouraged his own sons to enlist. His eldest and youngest sons, Lewis and Charles Douglass, both joined the 54th Massachusetts: Charles fell ill and spent most of the war in camp, while Lewis fought in some of the regiment's major battles. To his sons, Douglass might have made a pitch similar to the one he made to many other young black men:

> You should enlist because the war for the Union, whether men so call it or not, is a war for Emancipation. The salvation of the country, by the inexorable relation of cause and effect, can be secured only by the complete abolition of slavery. . . . Can you ask for a more inviting, ennobling, and soul enlarging work, than that of making one of the glorious Band who shall carry Liberty to your enslaved people? . . . One black Brigade will, for this work, be worth more than two white ones. Enlist, therefore, enlist without delay, enlist now, and forever put an end to the human barter and butchery which have stained the whole South with the warm blood of your people, and loaded its air with their groans.[22]

Douglass hoped the war would result in the total destruction of the slave system and everything that supported it. That destruction never quite occurred, so Douglass devoted much of his later life to preserving the memory of the Abolition War and using that memory to challenge subsequent restrictions on black freedom. At an 1871 gathering in Arlington National Cemetery, he chastised the whitewashed memories that had already begun to color people's view of the conflict. "We are sometimes asked," he said, "in the name of patriotism . . . [to remember] with equal admiration . . . those who fought for slavery and those who fought for liberty and justice." But such ecumenicalism does an injustice to the war's causes and consequences. "Manly courage," he explained, only matters to the degree to which "it has been displayed in a noble cause," and "we must never forget that victory to the rebellion meant death to the republic" and the perpetuation of "the hell-black system of human bondage."

Douglass continued to advocate partisan remembrance years later, after Reconstruction had been broken up and the narratives of the Family Squabble and the Lost Cause had largely won the day. In 1878, Jefferson Davis, the former Confederate president, declared that Southerners should not feel any shame or regret for their role in the rebellion: "Let not any of the survivors impugn their faith by offering the penitential plea that they believed they were right." To which Douglas replied: Jefferson Davis may very well "speak out of the fullness of the heart," but that does not mean that justice is on his side. The South, of course, believed that it was right, but "the nature of things is not changed by belief. The Inquisition was not less a crime against humanity because it was believed right by the Holy Fathers. . . . I admit further, that viewed merely as a physical contest, it left very little for self-righteousness or glory on either side." Yet the war must not and cannot be seen simply as "a physical contest." After all, "it was not a fight between rapacious birds and ferocious beasts, a mere display of brute courage and endurance." Rather, "it was a war between men, men of thought as well as action, and in dead earnest for something beyond the battle-field. It was not even a war of geography . . . or of race. . . . It was a war of ideas, a battle of principles . . . between the old and the new, [between] slavery and freedom."[23] The war was not a contest between two equal, and equally justified, forces; nor was it a struggle over geography, law, or economics. As Douglass views it, the war was a momentous fight over the scope and definition of liberty in the modern world—a violent but altogether necessary struggle to radically expand the realm of freedom.

Properly remembering the Abolition War therefore requires acknowl-

edging the ways in which that struggle endures, long after the cessation
of hostilities in 1865. As Douglass stated, the contest's "great work" is
"still incomplete," and it will remain so as long as the legacies of slavery
plague the United States and the Confederate ethos endures. He later
reiterated that same idea in his final autobiography, *The Life and Times of
Frederick Douglass* (1881/1892). Emancipation, he wrote, *seemed* to break
up "the gigantic system of American slavery" and establish freedom as
"the organic law of the land." But as soon as the war concluded, the
North and South began to reconcile, and since then, the "malign elements of the country [arrayed] against equal rights" have only gained
in power.[24]

Emancipation and the Art of Memory

Douglass's reflections were part of a broader culture of countercom-
memoration. Freedmen and freedwomen composed autobiographies,
as well as emancipationist poems, letters, essays, and works of art, that
depicted the war as a transformative upheaval. These works challenged
white memories of the conflict, which tended to prioritize considerations
of "law" and the "Union," in order to highlight black people's wartime
acts of liberation. This ethos of active remembrance recasts the Abolition
War as an enduring struggle—an event coextensive with the present.
As the African American writer and activist F. E. W. Harper asserted,
"It is no time / To quit the battle-field" simply because the armies have
gone home:

> The minions of a baffled wrong
> Are marshaling their clan,
> Rise up! rise up, enchanted north!
> And strike for God and man.
>   .   .   .   .
> 'Tis yours to banish from the land
> Oppression's iron rule;
> And o'er the ruin'd auction-block
> Erect the common school.[25]

Abolitionism, Harper suggests, must subsist as long as oppression does. Memory requires action—or, as Harper puts it later in the poem, recollecting so as to "build on Justice, as a rock, / The future of the land."

This emancipationist narrative is visually articulated—or, as Harper would have it, built—in the sculptures of Edmonia Lewis, which provide a striking contrast to the Lost Cause sculptures we saw in chapter 3. Lewis's art, like her life, was defined by mixture. The daughter of an Afro-Haitian father and Native American mother, Lewis created war-related statues in a neoclassical style. Out of clay, she made a medallion of the fiery abolitionist Wendell Phillips with his face lifted toward the heavens. She crafted a plaster bust of Ulysses S. Grant, whose flowing beard and noble brow make him look more like an ancient Greek philosopher than an American general. And she constructed related sculptures of John Brown, Abraham Lincoln, and Robert Gould Shaw. Her Civil War studies were all Northern, but the perspective cultivated by these sculptures emphasizes the struggle's liberationist spirit. These men, as Lewis represents them, are historic participants in a momentous fight against slavery—a fight whose significance is symbolically registered in their classic, chiseled forms. The emancipation brought about by the war is similarly evoked in *Forever Free* (1867). What could be further afield from the Lost Cause statues that still cover so much of the country? Here, the slave's chains are broken. The resulting sensations of unloosed hope and wonder, of release and anticipation, are communicated by the couple as they gaze upward, away from the past. (In drawing attention to the different conditions of the man and the woman—standing versus kneeling, lifting an arm versus praying—Lewis also highlights the gendered exclusivity of official emancipation.)

Emancipation is similarly imbued in the works of Meta Vaux Warrick Fuller. Born in 1877, the year of "Redemption" (i.e., when the Democrats finally ended federal Reconstruction), Fuller was one of the first African American artists to gain international renown. Her sculptures have a conceptual bent redolent of Auguste Rodin, but Fuller, unlike Rodin, draws upon the felt histories of African American experience, turning ineffable sentiments into chiseled forms. *The Wretched* (1902) shows writh-

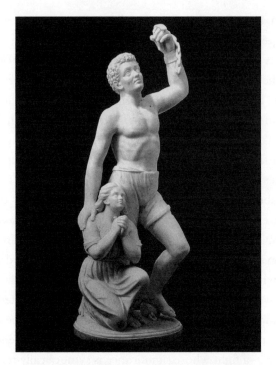

Edmonia Lewis, *Forever Free* (1867). Courtesy of the
Howard University Gallery of Art.

ing bodies and twisted faces that seem to converge and become a single,
multilimbed mass of pain. *Talking Skull* (1937) shows a young man staring
inquisitively at a hollowed skull, as if he hopes that it might speak—that
the dead indeed might live again (or at least tell us their secrets).

Other sculptures are more ennobled, such as the African queen poised
like an Egyptian goddess in *Ethiopia Awakening* (1910), as well as the freedpeople of *Emancipation*, which Fuller initially cast in 1913. The sculpture
retells the story of Genesis through the Civil War. This freedman and
freedwoman are black Adam and Eve, creatures of God perfect in body
and spirit.[26] But Eden would not be Eden without a serpent and a curse.
As Fuller stated, "The Negro has been emancipated from slavery but not
from the curse of race hatred and prejudice." That is why the sculpture
shows "Humanity weeping over her suddenly freed children, who, beneath the gnarled fingers of Fate, step forth into the world, unafraid."[27]

Meta Vaux Warrick Fuller, *Talking Skull* (1937). Courtesy of the
Museum of African American History.

Meta Vaux Warrick Fuller, *Emancipation*. Photograph (2013).

Emancipation anchored African American autobiography as well. Up through the early twentieth century, many former slaves transferred their stories into written form, crafting memoirs and diaries that revolved around abolition. John Quincy Adams, an enslaved man from Virginia, recalled the date that everything changed: "On Saturday, June 27, 1862, we left old mistress, and young miss, and every other kind of miss." He added, "I am told that when old mistress got up in the morning, [and] found all the negroes gone, they thought that the devil had got into them negroes last night. *Every one is gone, and where are they gone to? I suppose they have gone with them devilish Yankees.*" Evidently, his former master promised to set them free if they returned, but Adams was not convinced: "I had heard that [promise] too often, so I did not listen to that kind of talk. I thought that they had had their time, and this was my time. So off we went."[28] They made their way up to Pennsylvania, into General Geary's division, and eventually settled in Harrisburg, where Adams worked at a hotel, learned how to read, and composed a narrative of his life.

The escape from slavery looked very different for Elizabeth Keckley, who lived and worked in the Lincoln White House. Keckley's autobiography, *Behind the Scenes; or, Thirty Years a Slave, and Four Years in the White House* (1868), is in many ways a feminine corrective to the more well-known memoirs of male ex-slaves. She sewed rather than fought her way to freedom, purchasing her liberty through dressmaking. After moving to Washington, DC, she worked for the family of Jefferson Davis, and then, after Secession, she became a friend and employee of Mary Todd Lincoln. Her memoir provides a multisided account of life with the Lincolns during the Civil War—and it is for this that she is often remembered—yet in between those domestic scenes Keckley sketches a vibrant account of the world outside, as emancipation takes hold. She describes the influx of freedmen and freedwomen, fresh from the plantations and full of "hope in their hearts," as well as the cold reception they receive in the capitol: "Many good friends reached forth kind hands, but the North is not warm and impulsive . . . there was something repelling in the atmosphere, and the bright joyous dreams of freedom to the slave faded." The Lincolns' grief—especially after the death of their son, Willie, in 1862—is mirrored by Keckley's anxieties about the prospects for black freedom. Those anxieties do not entirely curb her hope, however. As she witnesses "the sanguinary struggle," the "people of my race," she writes, look "Zionward," as if to "catch a glimpse of the Promised Land beyond the sulphureous clouds of smoke."[29]

Harriet Tubman looked Zionward too. Tubman played a crucial role in the Underground Railroad, ferrying numerous slaves to freedom, and she was equally instrumental to the Union's war effort. "General Tubman," as John Brown called her, acquired intelligence on Confederate forces, led troops through the swamps, created maps, and aided the wounded. For many soldiers and slaves, Tubman was both an agent and an icon of emancipation. In the summer of 1863, after the Emancipation Proclamation had taken effect, she led a raid in the Combahee River Valley, in South Carolina, to liberate several plantations. As word spread among the slaves that the Northerners were there to guide them to freedom, first dozens and then hundreds of men, women, and children flocked to them.

As Tubman later told Sarah Bradford, a white writer and admirer who recorded Tubman's story, many of the slaves were now refugees seeking freedom in another land. When Tubman arrived, she saw a young mother holding several children by the hand, carrying a pig over her shoulder and balancing a pot of hot rice on her head, which another child—strapped to her back—eagerly ate. Another woman brought along a white pig, which they named "Beauregard," and a black pig, which they named "Jeff Davis." "Sometimes," added Tubman, the "women would come twins hangin' roun' der necks," "baskets on der heads, and young ones taggin' behin', all loaded; pigs squealin', chickens screamin', young ones squallin'."

In the midst of this uproar, one of the Union soldiers called out, "Moses, you'll have to give 'em a song." And so she did. She sang about the free place where they were headed, where there were no masters

and plenty of land and food—a place rich enough to give every freedman a farm—to which the slaves responded by raising their hands and
shouting, "Glory! Glory!"[30]

W. E. B. Du Bois: The Abolition War
in the Era of Jim Crow

This movement to not simply preserve but *extend* emancipation—to
see it as a living principle rather than accomplished deed—was kept
alive in the twentieth century by W. E. B. Du Bois. The first African
American to receive a PhD from Harvard, Du Bois became a prolific
historian, sociologist, novelist, memoirist, artist, and activist, producing
more than two dozen books, as well as numerous essays, speeches, and
editorials. Across his career, from his earliest writings about the slave
trade to his final reflections on Pan-African Revolution, he turned back
to the Abolition War as a touchstone for the modern world.

In *The Souls of Black Folk* (1903), Du Bois famously remarked, "The
problem of the twentieth century is the problem of the color-line,—the
relation of the darker races to the lighter races." Less famous though no
less important is the sentence that follows: "It was a phase of this problem
that caused the Civil War; and however much they who marched South
and North in 1861 may have fixed on the technical points, of union and
local autonomy as a shibboleth, all nevertheless knew, as we know, that
the question of Negro slavery was the real cause of the conflict." Nor, he
adds, was that question entirely resolved: "No sooner had Northern armies touched Southern soil than this old question, newly guised, sprang
from the earth,—What shall be done with the Negroes? Peremptory
military commands . . . could not answer the query; the Emancipation
Proclamation seemed but to broaden and intensify the difficulties; and
the War Amendments made the Negro problems of today."

Du Bois's point is far-reaching. If nearly all of the "problems of today,"
from segregation at home to colonization abroad, can be traced back to
the Civil War, then it wasn't really a war at all: it was a failed social revolution, a grand effort to create a truly democratic society. That revolution,
Du Bois says, was never allowed to complete itself. The forces of white

W. E. B. Du Bois (ca. 1911). Courtesy of the Library of Congress,
Prints and Photographs Division.

supremacy returned to power and have reigned ever since, maintaining
control through prisons and policing, banking and economics, and the
segregation of public spaces. Du Bois also has in mind European imperi-
alism, which by that point had enveloped much of the globe. When he
wrote *The Souls of Black Folk*, a majority of the world was controlled by
a small number of white empires. That the twentieth century was defined by "the color line" reveals an important historical lesson: the Civil
War was an opportunity to *erase* that line once and for all, a chance to
deal racial oppression, as well as the practices and institutions on which
it depends, a fatal blow.

Du Bois wrote about the war often and in a variety of mediums—
in essays and historical studies, in plays and autobiographies. It is one
of the major themes running through nearly all of his works. Born in
1868, in the middle of Reconstruction, he lived to the age of 93, dying in
1963 after he had moved to Ghana (partly in response to the draconian

McCarran Act, which required communists to register with the US government).[31] As he wrote in 1940, the years in which he lived were "years of cosmic significance, when one remembers that they rush from the American Civil War to the reign of the second Roosevelt; from . . . the Franco-Prussian to the two World Wars. They contain . . . the shadowy emergence, magnificence, and miracle of Russia; the turmoil of Asia in China, India and Japan, and the world-wide domination of white Europe."[32] To "rush from" is to flow, like a stream from a river. The Civil War, Du Bois felt, did not merely precede these later events; it kicked them into motion.

The war's importance is dramatically conveyed in *The Star of Ethiopia*, Du Bois's 1911 play about the arc of black history. Instead of traditional acts, the play is divided into six parts, each corresponding to a progressive series of gifts given to the world by its "eldest" race. It begins with the invention of iron and then moves through the flowering of Egyptian civilization, the rise of Islam, the emergence of Ethiopia, and the resistance to the Atlantic slave trade—all of which is exemplified by representative heroes like Nat Turner and Alonzo the pilot. The Civil War then erupts as part of the sixth and final part, the "Gift of Freedom for the workers." To demonstrate how "the freedom of black slaves meant freedom for the world," the play marches out John Brown (accompanied by the sound of tom-toms), who reenacts his rebellion only to be arrested and executed, prompting Frederick Douglass to declare, "Slavery must end in blood." That blood is spilled by the black soldiers of the 54th Massachusetts, led by Robert Gould Shaw mounted on horseback. Then, to the tune of "O Freedom," dozens of children flood the stage dressed as symbolic figures—the Laborer, the Artisan, the Musician, the Actor—all of whom are set free by the Abolition War.[33]

Because that liberation was violently opposed by the Confederates, Du Bois had little patience for defenders of the Lost Cause. In one of his most incisive and devastating essays, he took aim at the Confederates' sacred cow, the myth of noble Robert E. Lee. The Confederacy's postwar defenders canonized Lee as a kind of American saint, a man of honor who fought not to defend slavery but to protect his beloved state of Virginia. That myth, Du Bois wrote, overlooks one "terrible fact," and "that is the inescapable truth that Robert E. Lee led a bloody war to perpetuate slavery." Apologists say otherwise, but one must ask, "For what did he fight? State rights? Nonsense. The South cared only for State Rights as a weapon to defend slavery. . . . People do not go to war for abstract theories of government. They fight for property and privilege and that was what Virginia fought for in the Civil War. And Lee followed Virginia."

Robert E. Lee was the very opposite of a noble leader. He fought not "because he particularly loved slavery (although he certainly did not hate it), but because he did not have the moral courage to stand against his family and his clan. Lee hesitated and hung his head in shame because he was asked to lead armies against human progress and Christian decency and did not dare refuse." Lee, in other words, was a coward. More importantly, his cowardice continued to plague the South long after Lee's death: "What Lee did in 1861, other Lees are doing in 1928. They lack the moral courage to stand up for justice to the Negro because of the overwhelming public opinion of their social environment. Their fathers in the past have condoned lynching and mob violence, just as today they acquiesce in the disfranchisement of educated and worthy black citizens, provide wretchedly inadequate public schools for Negro children and endorse a public treatment of sickness, poverty and crime which disgraces civilization."[34]

In his takedown of Lee, Du Bois lands on a crucial insight: Civil War memory is always a memory of the present—a way to understand how we arrived where we are now. Few people were more attuned to that relationship between then and now than Du Bois. As the editor of the *Crisis*, the magazine for the NAACP (National Association for the Advancement of Colored People), he tirelessly documented injustices carried out by other, modern-day Robert E. Lees. He reported on poll taxes, lynchings by white mobs, and restrictions on interracial marriage, along with the variety of other measures undertaken to maintain white supremacy: local ordinances that segregated everything from drinking fountains to carnivals, racist districting policies for schools and neighborhoods, and laws forbidding racial mixing in buses, trains, pools, bathrooms, bars, restaurants, and sports facilities.[35]

America's racially segregated society inspired the Nazis when they came to power in the 1930s. When the Nazi leaders met at Nuremberg in 1934 to create a legal framework for the Aryan state, they studied (and greatly admired) American race law. Roland Freisler, the Nazi judge who became the president of the *Volksgerichtshof*, or "People's Court," summed up this fixation when he stated, "This jurisprudence would suit us perfectly."[36] Some of the Nazis, though, feared that the American laws were too extreme. As the historian James Whitman notes, "The ironic truth is that when Nazis rejected the American example, it was sometimes because they thought that American practices were overly harsh: for Nazis of the early 1930s, even radical ones, American race law sometimes looked *too* racist." Hitler did not share those concerns. In *Mein Kampf* (1925), he praised America as "the one state" where white supremacy had fully established itself and could be expected to rule in perpetuity. "The racially pure and still unmixed German," Hitler marveled, "has risen to become master of the American continent, and he will remain the master, as long as he does not fall victim to racial pollution."[37]

As the color line became more firmly and vividly established across the globe, Du Bois found hope in antifascist politics. His interest in the Abolition War played an important role in Du Bois's turn toward Marxism. The events of the 1920s and 1930s radicalized him. With the spread of fascism and segregation, he carefully studied Marx and did a deep dive into Civil War history. The resulting seven-hundred-page tome, *Black Reconstruction in America: An Essay toward a History of the Part Which Black Folk Played in the Attempt to Reconstruct Democracy in America, 1860–1880* (1935), continues to be one of the best books about the Civil War ever written.

In *Black Reconstruction*, Du Bois challenged prevailing historical approaches by portraying the Abolition War as part of a longer story about labor, capital, and the social dimensions of freedom. "The most magnificent drama in the last thousand years of human history," he posited, "is the transportation of ten million human beings out of the dark beauty of their mother continent into [the New World]," their descent "into Hell," and subsequent resurrection through the Civil War, which ushered in "the finest effort to achieve democracy for the working millions [that] this world has ever seen." The slaves themselves played an indispensable part in this upheaval by abandoning the plantations, joining the Union lines, and dismantling the cotton kingdom. "This was," Du Bois writes, "not merely the desire to stop work." It was a "strike on a wide basis against the *conditions* of work," which provided a glorious flash of "reason in all this mad orgy" of death.[38]

For Du Bois, it could not be more important that this general strike occurred. It means that the slaves seized rather than received freedom, acquiring emancipation through their own will and courage. It also means that the Abolition War had both negative and positive political purposes: it was not merely about *eliminating* slavery but about *creating* a real democracy, as well as a more just world. Du Bois devoted his life and writing to helping build that world. That is why, in the 1940s, he joined the Civil Rights Congress (CRC), a human rights organization that fought against racism and anticommunism. In 1951, the CRC tried—unsuccessfully, it turned out—to convince the United Nations to condemn the United States for carrying out genocide against its black citizens. It was Du Bois who presented their 237-page petition, titled "We Charge Genocide," to the UN's General Assembly.[39]

"Out of the inhuman black ghettos," the CRC decried, "out of the cotton plantations of the South, comes this record of mass slayings on the basis of race, of lives deliberately warped . . . by the willful creation of conditions making for premature death, poverty, and disease." Those conditions, they asserted, derived from the country's failure to enforce the social revolution started by emancipation:

> The genocide that was American slavery, the killing of part of the group so that the remainder could more readily be exploited for profit, resulted in . . . the Civil War of the states. The American Civil War . . . was a revolutionary war in which the American people destroyed the slaveocracy, that minority of slaveholders who had controlled the country and its government for

generations. In the wake of this conflict, . . . four million liberated slaves and the poor whites of the South [sought to] impose its democracy on the former slaveocracy. . . . It was during this progressive period . . . that the Fourteenth and Fifteenth Amendments [were passed]. . . . If these constitutional safeguards were enforced, instead of being effectively abrogated by administrative and legislative action and inaction, . . . it is unlikely that this petition would [even] be necessary.[40]

What we find here, in the midst of this vehement condemnation, is a glimmer of hope. The new democracy unleashed by the Abolition War, if only it had been allowed to grow, could have prevented all of the atrocities that followed, all of the horrors exhaustively documented by the petition. In that regard the CRC was merely extending *Black Reconstruction*, effectively updating Du Bois's account of the Abolition War to shed a light on Jim Crow America.

Du Bois's perspective on the war also comes into sharp focus in his biography of John Brown—or, I should say, his biographies, the first published in 1909 shortly after the establishment of the NAACP, and the second published in 1962 when Du Bois was 94 years old and living in Africa. In both versions Du Bois is fascinated by the disparity between Brown's plain character and his massive historical importance. On the one hand, Brown was homely, uncultured, and "simple, exasperatingly simple." On the other hand, his soul was fueled by a white-hot abolitionist zeal that enabled him to envision a multiracial democracy and launch a war against the planter class. For Du Bois, the significance of Brown's failed revolution extends not simply through the Civil War and Reconstruction but through the entirety of the twentieth century, illuminating an important principle: Brown not only felt in his very bones "the wrong and danger" of repression; he also took direct, militant action against it. For that reason, Du Bois contends, his memory still stands "as a mighty warning," bearing on "the exploitation of Africa, the problem of the unemployed, [and] the curbing of the corporations."

In the book's final chapter—which he added more than fifty years later—Du Bois clarifies this point by bending his vision forward. He wonders, *What might John Brown do and say if he were still alive?* Most likely, Brown would marvel at socialism's success in fighting injustice and inequality. "One could wish that John Brown could see the new world of Socialism and Communism expanding until it . . . comprises the majority of mankind; until it has conquered the problem of poverty, made vast inroads on the problem of ignorance and even begun to put to flight the problem of avoidable disease." Brown, he admits, "never read the *Communist Manifesto*," but all of his actions were in the service of this greater, worldwide liberation. He "realize[d] that a suppressed and exploited part of the laboring class in America—the Negroes—had been deprived by capitalists and land monopolists of the freedom to earn a living and to direct their lives which was vital in John Brown's mind to a human being. He espoused therefore the freedom of the slave knowing well that freedom alone was not the settlement of the Negro problem; that this must be followed by education, the right to vote, and treatment as human beings."[41]

There was a reason why Du Bois returned, again and again, to the Abolition War. For Du Bois the war was the birth moment for the modern world, the instance in which all of the hope and doom that surround us—all of the cruelty, sympathy, and potential—were suddenly, violently hatched. The Abolition War, in short, presented a moment of radical possibility, for both good and ill, which we have *still* not fully capitalized on. Yet, as we will see, Du Bois was hardly alone in sensing the possibility unloosed by emancipation. During and after the era of Jim Crow, many people turned back to emancipation to better understand the present, as well as the prospects for the future.

"We Carry It within Us": Emancipationist Memory in the Civil Rights Era

For Du Bois, emancipation was a cipher for understanding later political events. Throughout the twentieth century, scores of other artists, writers, and activists shared that view. The nineteenth century, it would seem, set the stage for the defining struggles of the twentieth century, from the fight against fascism in the 1940s to the civil rights movement that flowered in the 1960s.

According to Howard Fast, the Abolition War was nothing short of an antifascist revolution. Fueled by a lifelong commitment to social equality and radical democracy, Fast joined the Communist Party at the height of the Red Scare and suffered the consequences: after refusing to divulge sensitive information to the House Un-American Activities Committee, he was imprisoned. It was there, in jail, that he began writing *Spartacus* (1951), his novel about a slave revolt in ancient Rome (which he was forced to self-publish after getting blacklisted by publishers).[42] Fast's literary and political investment in human liberty similarly shines through in his novel *Freedom Road*. First published in 1944 (and then, in the late 1970s, made into a film starring Mohammed Ali), *Freedom Road* follows Gideon Jackson, an enslaved man from the backwoods of South Carolina who travels to Charleston in 1865, learns how to read, and serves as a delegate in the new Constitutional Convention. The Constitution that he helps draft turns out to be one of the most progressive political compacts ever produced, guaranteeing universal education, equal protection under the law, and provisions for divorce (universal suffrage was hotly debated and vociferously supported by Jackson, but it failed to acquire enough votes). Interlacing fact with fiction, *Freedom Road* celebrates multicultural democracy and black self-governance, effectively depicting the Civil War and Reconstruction as—in Fast's words—an "incredible revolution," a kind of "pause in history" or "hole scooped in the developmental stream of America by Union bayonets." Du Bois even wrote a glowing preface for the novel in which he asserts that although the "story is fiction," its "basic historical accuracy is indisputable"; indeed, "I am glad to commend it to all people who want to know the Truth and be free."

Revolutions, however, often give way to counterrevolutions, and that is exactly what happens in *Freedom Road*. All of the democratic efforts of Jackson and his fellow delegates are met with resistance, as the planter class regroups under the banner of the KKK. This narrative of freedom's long road, as it were, is ostensibly a retelling of the Civil War, Reconstruction, and the latter's dismantling in the 1870s, but the story's historical scope and political vision are much wider and more capacious than that. Fast dedicates the novel to "the men and women, black and white, yellow and brown, who have laid down their lives in the struggle against fascism," and that sense of transhistorical solidarity shapes the novel's representations of the Klan, who seem to be fascists avant la lettre. Their "one purpose," Fast writes, was to "destroy democracy" by dividing "the black man from the white man" and further entrenching "poverty, hunger, [and] hatred." In fact, their racial animus is but a corollary to their political project of demolishing democracy altogether. The struggle over emancipation and its legacy thereby becomes part of a protracted conflict that continues to unfold long after the nineteenth century. As Jackson, who is eventually murdered by the Klan, tells President Grant, "There are *still* battles. . . . Reconstruction was [only] the beginning."[43]

The tie between emancipation's past and present became particularly important during the civil rights era. Numerous writers and activists turned back to the 1860s to understand the 1960s, either by invoking the rhetoric and promise of emancipation or by reclaiming that era's documents. The movement's most iconic text, Martin Luther King Jr.'s "I Have a Dream" speech, was not only delivered in front of the Lincoln Memorial; it also revolved, rhetorically and imaginatively, around the Civil War. "Five score years ago," King declared (drawing on Lincoln's own language), "a great American, in whose symbolic shadow we stand today, signed the Emancipation Proclamation. This momentous decree came as a beacon light of hope to millions of Negro slaves who had been seared in the flames of withering injustice." But this "joyous daybreak," he adds, did not fully "end the long night of their captivity": "One hundred years later, the Negro is still not free. One hundred years later, the life of the Negro is still sadly crippled by the manacles of segregation and the chains of discrimination. One hundred years later, the Negro lives on a lonely island of poverty in the midst of a vast ocean of material prosperity. One hundred years later, the Negro is still languishing in the corners of American society and finds himself an exile in his own land." The civil rights movement, as King presents it, is an act of historical recuperation, an attempt to both revive and expand emancipation. The work of the Civil War still needs to be completed, and it will remain incomplete until people "from every village and every hamlet, from every state and every city"—"all of God's children"—will "be able to join hands" and form a fully democratic polity.[44]

The moral and political lessons of the Abolition War inform King's "Letter from Birmingham Jail" (1963). The racial segregation and police brutality in Birmingham stood out even by the standards of the Jim Crow South. When King and the Southern Christian Leadership Conference marched there in protest, the police imprisoned several of the activists, including King, and a group of white clergymen implored him to quiet down and leave. King's letter, penned in response, is a glorious refusal. To the clergymen's objection that he is an extremist, King says, "Was not Jesus an extremist in love? . . . Was not Abraham Lincoln an extremist?—'This nation cannot survive half slave and half free.'" To their objection that the protests were illegal, King uses the legal philosophy popularized by the abolitionists, arguing that there are "two types of laws: there are just laws, and there are unjust laws," and any law that supports racial repression violates the law of God. To their objection that black citizens needed to wait just a little longer and let the courts resolve everything, King says, "When you have seen vicious mobs lynch your mothers and fathers at will and drown your sisters and brothers at whim; when you have seen hate-filled policemen curse, kick, brutalize, and even kill your black brothers and sisters with impunity; when you see the vast majority of your . . . brothers smothering in an airtight cage of poverty in the midst of an affluent society," only then "you will understand why we find it difficult to wait." Eventually there "comes a time when the cup of endurance runs over and men are no longer willing to be plunged into any abyss of injustice."[45]

What was the Abolition War but a similar point in history—another moment in which people, "no longer willing to be plunged into an abyss of injustice," took action? King made a related point in a speech he delivered in 1962 to the New York State Civil War Centennial Commission. When King addressed the commission, he emphasized the great historical significance not of the war itself but of the war's defining statement, the Emancipation Proclamation. That document, like the Declaration of Independence, is a resounding warning, King declared, to "all tyrants, past, present and future," telling them they cannot repress the truth of human equality, "no matter how extensive their legions, [no matter] how vast their power or malignant their evil."

Yet repressed it was. As King put it, "What the Emancipation Proclamation proscribed in a legal and formal sense has never been eliminated in human terms. . . . Negroes, north and south, still live in segregation, . . . eat in segregation, pray in segregation and die in segregation." There has always been a breach between abstract rights and the concrete conditions of black life, but the Civil War was a rare opportunity to change that and usher in a real revolution. King believed that human events have certain inflection points: crises in which everything can suddenly be changed, leading us to either progress or destruction. He believed that the Civil War was one of those rare, transitional moments—and so is our modern age: "We are at one of history's awesome crossroads. Our technological creativity is almost boundless. We can build machines that think. We can dot the landscape with houses and super-highways teeming with cars. We can now even destroy our whole planet . . . nuclear weapons. . . . And our guided ballistic missiles have carved highways through the stratosphere. In short we have the capacity to re-build the whole planet, filling it with luxury—or we are capable of destroying it totally. The shocking issue of our age is that no one can confident[ly] say which we will do."[46]

King's writings reveal the degree to which the Civil War endures as an unfinished conflict in American civilization. James Baldwin provocatively summarized this perspective in 1965, when he wrote, "History, as nearly no one seems to know, is not merely something to be read"; nor does it "refer merely, or even principally to the past. On the contrary, the great force of history comes from the fact that we carry it within us, are unconsciously controlled by it in many ways, and history is literally *present* in all we do. It could scarcely be otherwise, since it is to history that we owe our frames of reference, our identities, and our aspirations."[47] During and after the civil rights era, emancipation was that living history. As the movement unfolded, African American writers and artists reimagined emancipation through a variety of media. In the visual arts, works were produced such as R. Furan's *Harriet Tubman* (1963), a fresh portrait of the abolitionist leader turbaned and indefatigable, and Sophie Wessel's *Contraband on Cairo Levee* (1963), a painting of freedmen and freedwomen waiting for a Union steamboat to carry them northward. These images were accompanied by poems, novels, histories, and TV programs that retold the story of emancipation, from Robert Lowell's "For the Union Dead" (1964) to Ishmael Reed's *Flight to Canada* (1976) and the epic novel and television series *Roots*, which concludes with the return of Chicken George, Kunta Kinte's grandson, in the war's aftermath.

The story about the Abolition War imparted by these narratives is not a simple one. Raven Quickskill, the protagonist of *Flight to Canada*, is removed from emancipation in multiple senses: he lit out for Canada when the war broke out, and now that he has inherited the property of his Uncle Robin (who manipulated his late master's will, thereby acquiring the plantation on which he used to work), he finds that this legacy is both a blessing and a curse. Similarly, *Roots: The Next Generations* (1979), a sequel to the original series that takes Kunte's descendants into the twentieth century, makes it clear that Chicken George's return is only a prelude to other struggles, from social discrimination to educational inequality. And in Lowell's poem, the past and the present commingle in ways that question the arc of progress. Lowell moves from Boston Common, where "yellow dinosaur steamshovels" cleave the earth and "Colonel Shaw / and his bell-cheeked Negro infantry" stand in perpetuity, to Boylston Street, where "a commercial photograph / shows Hiroshima boiling." Although the Civil War was inarguably a war for emancipation, Lowell suggests that history does not consist in a steady march forward. In fact, the monument of the 54th Massachusetts now

> sticks like a fishbone
> in the city's throat.
> Its Colonel is as lean
> As a compass-needle.[48]

In the late twentieth century, that compass-like sense of direction can certainly be felt (or, to follow Lowell's metaphor, choked on), but it cannot be recaptured.

Margaret Walker, who lived in Mississippi throughout the 1960s, was similarly inspired by the past but skeptical about the future. Her 1966 novel *Jubilee* registers the simultaneous hope and despair of the civil rights era by turning back to the Civil War. On the one hand, the novel fundamentally reimagines *Gone with the Wind*: Walker uses the same historical framework—beginning shortly before the war, and then migrating through its violence and aftermath—and *Jubilee* likewise focuses on a Southern heroine. But Walker flips the story. The Civil War is a war of liberation, and the heroine, Vyry, is black. In one of the novel's most compelling scenes, a Union soldier reads the Emancipation Proclamation out loud. Vyry, Walker writes, "would never forget the scene . . . as long as she lived": her son Jim was so restless that "he wanted to dance a jig before the reading was over"; her daughter Minna "stood quietly beside her . . . holding a corner of Vyry's apron in her hand"; and it is only after the officer concluded, placing the proclamation back in his pocket, that Vyry suddenly realized that "tears were running down her face."[49]

But the 1860s turn out to be just as complicated as the 1960s. The Union soldiers who liberate the plantation are more interested in pillaging than in spreading freedom: they steal and consume most of the food and rape Vyry's white half-sister. Even Vyry's tearful liberation quickly gives way to yet more unremunerated labor, as she returns to working in the kitchen, cooking now for white Northerners rather than white Southerners. When Walker was writing the novel, civil rights activists had secured crucial victories—most notably, with the Civil Rights Act of 1964—but had not yet made significant gains in addressing poverty, housing laws, or police violence. As King declared, the "essential texture of freedom . . . for the Negro one hundred years after the Emancipation Proclamation" is marked by an inequality "so pervasive . . . that its detailing is impossible."[50] The year after *Jubilee* was published, riots sprang up in over one hundred cities, as African Americans protested the racist practices that, regardless of federal laws, continued unabated, rendering black life both fragile and devalued. *Jubilee* fully partakes in this spirit of the times. For Walker, the 1960s and 1860s share a historical lesson: no matter what progress may be made, in a country founded on white supremacy the past always has a way of returning. The persistence of past violence is symbolized by the scars on Vyry's back. On the eve of the war she was brutally whipped and then overcome by a fever that "ran through her brutalized flesh." After three days of rest, the fever cleared, but she discovered that "one of the lashes had left a loose flap of flesh over her breast like a tuck in a dress." Walker adds, "It healed that way," providing a permanent reminder of her enslaved condition—right over her heart.[51]

The Great Emancipation in the Twenty-First Century

The reimagining of emancipation carried out during the civil rights era has been complemented, in recent years, by numerous artists, writers, and historians. The late twentieth and early twenty-first centuries have witnessed an unprecedented flowering of emancipation-centered histories of the Civil War, yielding books such as Eric Foner's *Reconstruction* (1988) and David Blight's *Race and Reunion* (2001). This interest in the Abolition War has inspired numerous reprintings of African American memoirs, letters, and narratives from the Civil War era, as well as films like *Glory* (1989), which retells the story of the 54th Massachusetts, and the 2013 inscription for Meta Vaux Warrick Fuller's *Emancipation* (1913). Even political commentaries—on policing, voting rights, mass incarceration, and economic inequality in the United States—tend to draw on the history of the Civil War and the legacies of emancipation. Ta-Nehisi Coates's influential essay "The Case for Reparations" (2014), for instance, grounds much of its argument in the Abolition War, from the opening quotations (one of which is from an anonymous slave in 1861: "By our unpaid labor and suffering, we have earned the right to the soil, many times over and over") to the trenchant discussion of Jim Crow, which, Coates demonstrates, created a massive kleptocracy that erased nearly all the gains made by emancipation and Reconstruction.[52]

The most illuminating recent poetry about the Abolition War comes from Natasha Trethewey, the former poet laureate. Trethewey tends to blur the line between the nineteenth century and the twenty-first. As she attests in the prelude to *Native Guard* (2006), "You can get from there to here, though / there is no going home" because the "tome of memory" always retains "its random blank pages." Trethewey's suggestion—that memory is continuously remade, a tome that is incessantly written upon—is borne out in the ensuing poems, which migrate from the death of Trethewey's mother to the tangled web of Civil War history. When she travels to Vicksburg, Mississippi, the site of General Grant's famous siege, the "ghost of history," instead of fading away, "lies down beside me, / rolls over, [and] pins me beneath a heavy arm."[53]

That embrace, at once intimate and stifling, gives way to a series of poetic meditations on the Abolition War. "Native Guard," the poem that lends the book its title, conveys the lyric reflections of Francis E. Dumas, the son of "a white Creole father and a mulatto mother" who, after his father's death, inherits his slaves. Dumas discovers that he is legally prohibited from freeing them, so he joins the Union Army, manumits the slaves, and encourages them to volunteer in his unit. Eschewing the "flawed" vehicle of memory, Dumas uses "ink / to keep record," writing down his thoughts and experiences in a journal (presumably a Confederate's) that he stumbles across. Everything that he writes is therefore "crosshatched" with the journal's old words, "On every page, / his story intersecting with my own." Crosshatching, which involves marking with two separate but intersecting lines, is for Trethewey not simply Dumas's compositional method but the structure of history writ large: events do not merely succeed each other; they are continually restaged in parallel forms. That historical vision is fleshed out later in the poem. After the Pascagoula raid (1863), which ended in Confederate defeat, the slaves and the masters suddenly switch places, only to realize that their roles cannot be so easily reversed:

> We know it is our duty now to keep
> white men as prisoners—rebel soldiers,
> would-be masters. We're all bondsmen here, each
> to the other. Freedom has gotten them
> captivity. For us, a conscription
> we have chosen—jailors to those who still
> would have us slaves.

Emancipation brought about a momentous release, embodied by these black soldiers who fought against their former masters. Nonetheless, conditions such as captivity and freedom tend to be far more contiguous than we presume. As Trethewey puts it (in Dumas's voice), "we're all bondsmen here, each / to the other," ensnared in a vast web of mutual obligation and charged history.

The poem's final section, "1865," concludes by naming the "things which must be accounted for":

> slaughter under the white flag of surrender—
> black massacre at Fort Pillow; our new name,
> the Corps d'Afrique—words that take the *native*
> from our claim; mossbacks and freedmen—exiles
> in their own homeland; the diseased, the maimed,
> every lost limb, and what remains: phantom
> ache, memory haunting an empty sleeve;
> the hog-eaten at Gettysburg, unmarked
> in their graves; all the dead letters, unanswered;
> untold stories of those that time will render
> mute. Beneath battlefields, green again,
> the dead molder—a scaffolding of bone
> we tread upon, forgetting. Truth be told.

That bold injunction, "Truth be told," calls upon us, the Civil War's latter-day heirs, to remember the dark side of emancipation—the bloody executions at Fort Pillow, the inexorable sense of exile, the "phantom ache" of removal. Those untold truths, however, are buried forever "beneath battlefields," available only in fragments or haunted markers: empty sleeves, scaffoldings of bone, unmarked graves. That troubling erasure of emancipationist memory is revisited in "Elegy for the Native Guards." Trethewey begins by quoting Allen Tate's Lost Cause poem, "Ode for the Confederate Dead" ("Now that the salt of their blood / Stiffens the saltier oblivion of the sea"), and then wonders whether the war's black soldiers might be forgotten altogether. Unlike the Confederate soldiers, whose names are "raised hard / in bronze" across the South, there are no memorials for the Native Guards, that veritable "black phalanx." "What," Trethewey asks, "is monument to their legacy?"[54]

In a way, her book is that monument. But it is a monument full of faded images, crosshatches, and erasures, all of which suggest that, whether in the nineteenth century or the twenty-first, we have never been, and probably never will be, post-racial—or, for that matter, post-war. Literary history shows us that emancipation is neither a moment of accomplished liberation nor a point fixed in time to which we can return at will. Instead, it is a still unaccomplished, and perhaps unaccomplishable, project—an ideal as grand, and elusive, and irrepressible as the American dream itself.

Recent films about emancipation tend to veer in a different direction, figuring liberation as a form of violent entertainment. In Quentin Tarantino's *Django Unchained* (2012), a former slave (played by Jamie Foxx) gains his freedom, becomes a bounty hunter in West Texas, and then returns home to rescue his wife and kill her master. That revenge story brings together a wide variety of genres, from the Spaghetti Western bounty hunting sequences (in which Django becomes a black version of the "Man with No Name") to the Blaxploitation wrestling episode (in which two slaves are forced to fight to the death). Although it is not set during the Civil War, it is undeniably a film of and about emancipation, and it revolves around the very issues—regarding bondage and the relation between violence and freedom—that coalesced in the war.

Even more bodies pile up, creating a gory altar for emancipation, in Timur Bekmambetov's *Abraham Lincoln: Vampire Hunter* (2012). Bekmambetov's film reimagines the Civil War as a supernatural battle between Southern vampires (who created slavery to have a permanent food supply) and Northern vampire hunters, with Lincoln as the nation's zealous and athletic hunter in chief. The oft-repeated narrative of Lincoln's enlightenment, wherein he acquires a hatred of slavery through some witnessed trauma, is repeated here too, but with a twist: Lincoln awakens to the world's horrors when he discovers the terrible reality of Southern vampirism, and his subsequent political career—as well as the war itself—is launched by that awakening.[55]

Despite their patent differences, both *Django Unchained* and *Abraham Lincoln: Vampire Hunter* find joy and elation in subverting the standard stories about the Civil War. In that respect, they have a great deal in common with Terry Bisson's *Fire on the Mountain* (1988), which is one of the most inventive and inspiring works about the Great Emancipation. Bisson's novel asks, what if John Brown—who famously tried, and failed, to spark a war against the slaveholders in 1859—had actually *succeeded*? The grand antislavery revolution that John Brown attempted to bring about finally comes to fruition here. In Bisson's retelling, Harriet Tubman (who was supposed to join Brown but got sick, thus postponing the raid) never falls ill. "Moses," armed with her superior strategic mind, accompanies Brown, and this changes everything. She orders the bridge to be destroyed and the railroad to be spiked, cutting off Robert E. Lee and his militia and enabling Brown's men to flee into the mountains (as they had originally planned). They set up a base of operations in Roanoke and then carry out a guerilla war against the entire slaveholding class. To signal their strike against slavery, the abolitionists light fires on top of several mountains. Those fires, reaching from the mountain peaks up into the heavens, represent a sign of deliverance to the slaves, who flock to their aid.

That revolutionary blaze inspires people from every corner of the globe. Giuseppe Garibaldi and his fighters, fresh off their victories in the Second Italian War of Independence, push up from the South (and, in the process, return Texas and California to Mexico), while German Socialists (along with Walt Whitman) come down from New York. The Cherokee and Creek join the fight, allying with Brown and Tubman, as do the Molly Maguires in Pennsylvania (who later liberate Ireland) and the Charterists from England.[56] Even Marx himself musters a brigade that eventually finds its way to emancipated Appalachia. In Bisson's novel, the Civil War becomes an Abolition War that spans the earth, enveloping the whole world in a collective fight against exploitation.

After winning that fight, the abolitionists create a new country founded on radical social and economic equality, Nova Africa, which joins with Mexico, Haiti, Zimbabwe, Italy, and other countries to form a vast, multinational workers' government. That turn of events makes innumerable advances possible. There are flying cars; soaring, hypermodern cities; and plasma-powered airships. Nova Africa—or, more accurately, their space program, P.A.S.A. (the Pan African Space Administration)—is even preparing to colonize Mars. The novel's main storyline follows two descendants of John Brown's black doctor—Yasmin Abraham Martin Odinga, a Nova African anthropologist, and her daughter, Harriet—as they retrace the treacherous route of their revolutionary forbear one hundred years later, in 1959, and come to terms with the death of Leon, Yasmin's husband and Harriet's father. A cosmonaut for P.A.S.A., Leon died tragically in the failed Mars flyby of 1954. But in the novel's climactic scene, he symbolically returns: the new spacecraft, which successfully lands on Mars, is named after him, and the cosmonauts place an electronic plaque for him on the red planet whose digital letters will glow for a million years.

That refusal of loss, that transformation of disappointment into triumph, is redoubled in Bisson's treatment of the Civil War. The conflict occurs here but in inverted form. To suppress the rebellion, the slaveholders dispatch a squadron of young cadets, not one of whom survives: the abolitionists slit their throats and then lay their bodies out on a bridge as a warning. In the wake of that massacre, Lincoln, hoping to preserve the Union and destroy Nova Africa, sends in a battalion of white troops. "If the whites couldn't keep the slaves," Bisson explains, "they at least wanted the land back." Lincoln's plan fails, and he is executed for treason, but he becomes a "legend among the border whites in Kentucky, Virginia, and parts of Missouri"—the iconic leader of a new Lost Cause.

The Civil War as we know it also makes it appearance. At one point, while visiting the United States, which is now an underdeveloped country lagging far behind the socialist vanguard, Yasmin stumbles on a book that is popular there. Titled *John Brown's Body*, the book is an alternative history (like *Fire on the Mountain*), but the story it tells is the *actual* course of events during and after the Civil War. From Yasmin's perspective, the novel is nothing less than a "white nationalist fantasy." The plot of *John Brown's Body*, she discovers, turns on a "trick": "The idea is that instead

of going on the Fourth as planned, Tubman gets sick. The raid is de-
layed until fall . . . [and] Brown goes without her. . . . Without Tubman
he hesitates, takes hostages, lets the Washington train go through. You
know, in real life it was Tubman who insisted on blowing the Maryland
bridge and cutting off the train. Anyway, in the book they don't blow
the bridge; they get trapped in the town, captured, and hung as trai-
tors." There is still a war, but it is the opposite of a war for freedom and
equality: "it's fought to keep the old U.S. together rather than to free
Nova Africa." Once the Union is preserved, the violence does not even
end; it just pushes out west. The Americans "wipe out the buffalo, string
the country together with railroads and barbwire; annihilate, not just
defeat, the Sioux, the Crow, the Cheyenne, the Apache, one after the
other. Genocide is celebrated by adding stars to the flags. . . . Settlers run
the Mexicans out of California and Texas, or turn them into serfs, and
·move north to Alaska and south into the Caribbean, eventually seizing
the entire continent."[57]

Fire on the Mountain is a stunning reversal of that turn of events, a
dreamlike subversion of history that reimagines and celebrates emancipation's global march forward. In that regard, it is of a piece with recent
efforts by artists and activists to remake the public spaces claimed by the
Confederacy. In the past few years, people have tarred and feathered
some of the most prominent Lost Cause memorials. Others they have
pulled to the ground, or sprayed with graffiti to make them reflect their
true nature—emblazoning "RACIST" underneath a statue of Jefferson
Davis, or "Black Lives Matter" over the name of Robert E. Lee. In Florida, someone ingeniously splashed a Confederate memorial with red
paint, making it resemble the scene of a murder. These are not acts of
vandalism; they are acts of storytelling, attempts to reframe the war, in
highly visual ways, from the vantage point of black freedom. Fire on the
Mountain shares this same subversive energy and provides a complemen-
tary story about the war. It accomplishes in the realm of fiction what
these acts accomplish in the realm of public spectacle, reclaiming and
reviving the Great Emancipation.

In Bisson's retelling of the Civil War, John Brown still dies, but rather

Confederate Memorial Park in Tampa, Florida (2017). Courtesy of ABC News.

than asphyxiating under a Southern rope, he suffers a headshot four years later, and by then the revolution is nearly complete. When he dies, freedom has spread faster than the mountain's fires, and he is surrounded by his comrades, black and white, foreign and American. As Yasmin's great-grandfather (who tended to Brown in his final moments) recalls, he did not weep then,

> But I weep now, unashamed, an old man, almost fifty years later, not for Brown—God knows the Captain lived to see more of his dreams come true than most of us—I weep with some kind of joy remembering the square silently filling up with soldiers as twilight fell, mostly n'African but some foreign, some [American], even the silk-bloused Mexican Garibaldini (many of them black recruits by now) speaking that wild lingo I thought was Italian until I went to Italy. Nobody had to tell the men that Shenandoah Brown was dead. There was a drum roll, the longest I have ever heard. Tubman gave a nod, and . . . [one] thousand rifles fired into the air in a great rippling wave of sound. . . . And on the mountains that surrounded Roanoke

on every side, a fire sprang to life—two, four, six of them, lighted on the top of each of the brooding peaks that had nurtured our rebellion and birthed our independence.[58]

This is the funeral that Brown deserved but never received. The collective grief, the rippling of those waves, and the burning of those mountaintop fires all gesture toward freedom's continued expansion. And it is in literature that those fires remain lit, providing the imagination with "brooding peaks" that nurture emancipation and carry the past into the future.

Afterword
Recent and Future Civil Wars

WHETHER THEY FILL US WITH ELATION OR TERROR, whether they side with the North or the South, whether they come from the 1860s, the 1960s, or today, these stories all make one thing vividly clear: the Civil War is an ongoing struggle. Any doubt that the war continues was dispelled in June of 2015, when Dylann Roof, a young neo-Confederate, walked into a black church in Charleston—the former capital of the Confederacy—and murdered nine people. The parishioners had gathered there for an evening prayer service, a midweek respite and release from the pressures of the world. Although they had never seen Roof before, they greeted him with open arms and invited him to sit down and pray with them. As they lifted their hearts and voices to God, Roof rose from his pew, withdrew a gun, and shot Susie Jackson, an 87-year-old grandmother and the resident church "matriarch." Jackson's nephew, Tywanza Sanders, despite the shock and rage that flowed through him, tried to talk Roof down. "You don't have to do this," he pleaded. But by that moment Roof had been so thoroughly radicalized, and so committed to reviving the Confederacy, that Sanders's plea fell on deaf ears. Roof shot Sanders at point-blank range and then turned his gun on the other parishioners, murdering seven more people: Cynthia Hurd, Ethel Lee Lance, Depayne Middleton-Doctor, Clementa Pinckney, Daniel Simmons, Sharonda Coleman-Singleton, and Myra Thompson.[1]

What was this massacre but a scene from America's ongoing Civil War? To prepare for the battle, Roof went on Lost Cause pilgrimages, visiting the Museum and Library of Confederate History (a notorious neo-Confederate gallery in Greenville, South Carolina) and former plantations, where he took selfies in front of slave quarters.[2] After the shooting, multiple photographs surfaced in which Roof waves the Confederate battle flag and poses with the joyless, puckered look of a nineteenth-century soldier. In the malignant, half-articulate manifesto he left behind, he declared that the South was not yet "beyond saving."[3] The Confederacy, he dreamed, would rise again.

The events in Charleston revealed with brutal clarity just how toxic and dangerous the Lost Cause continues to be. It is not merely a story; it is a myth with lethal consequences, an ideology imbued with violent power. To challenge that myth, people immediately began to take action against the symbols that so inspired Roof by removing, dismantling, and destroying Confederate memorials. Lost Cause obelisks, plaques, and statues that had been standing for generations suddenly came crashing down. Bree Newsome, an artist and activist, courageously scaled the flagpole in front of the South Carolina statehouse and took down the Confederate flag that had been arrogantly waving over the city of Columbia since the 1960s, in symbolic defiance of the civil rights movement.[4]

In Tennessee, people splashed a statue of Nathan Bedford Forrest—a Confederate general and founder of the Ku Klux Klan who ruthlessly murdered black prisoners of war—with pink paint. In Durham, activists placed a rope around a Confederate memorial, pulled it to the ground, and spit on its shattered pieces. And in Charlotte, someone recorded the names of the Charleston 9, in heavy black paint, on a Confederate monument dedicated to "the Anglo-Saxon civilization of the South."[5] The reclaimed monument is an impromptu poem, a recitation in bold letters of names that must not be forgotten, superimposed on Confederate rock.

These efforts to reappropriate the Civil War's symbols are forms of what Martin Luther King Jr. called "direct action." As King explained in his "Letter from Birmingham Jail," "direct action seeks to create such a crisis and foster such a tension that a community which has constantly refused to negotiate is forced to confront the issue. It seeks to so dramatize

Todd Zimmer, *Bree Newsome removing the Confederate battle flag* (2015).

Confederate Monument in Charlotte, North Carolina (2015). Courtesy of WBTV.

the issue that it can no longer be ignored."[6] These direct actions against the Lost Cause have indeed "dramatized the issue," and they have been met with massive resistance. State legislators have passed laws barring the removal of Confederate memorials, activists have been arrested, and white supremacist groups are now recruiting and organizing with renewed fervor.

This tension came to a head in Charlottesville, Virginia, in the fall of 2017. Earlier that year, the city council voted to remove two prominent Confederate monuments—statues of Robert E. Lee and Stonewall Jackson, poised as valiant white heroes atop their docile horses—and rechristen the park, changing it from "Lee Park" to "Emancipation Park." White supremacists, incensed and itching for a fight, descended on Charlottesville. With torches in hand they sang "Dixie," chanted racist slogans ("Blood and soil!" and "One people, one nation, end immigration!"), and pummeled anyone who stood in their way. One black man, DeAndre Harris, was beaten to a pulp in a parking lot. Another anti-racist protester, Heather Heyer, was mowed down by a white supremacist who used his car as a weapon.[7] In perhaps the most iconic photograph taken of the riot, one of the neo-Confederates, a pasty racist wearing camo shorts and holding a furled Confederate battle flag, faces off against a masked black man (later identified as Corey Long), shirtless and wielding fire. Right before this moment, one of the fascists fired a gun near Long and then pointed the pistol at his head.[8] Long defended himself by converting his aerosol can into a makeshift flamethrower, while the fascist wielded the Confederate flag as if it were a religious icon, capable of otherworldly protection. The photograph seems to capture the long Civil War in a single image. Doreen St. Felix, writing in the *New Yorker*, noted the figures' symmetry, as though "a Dutch master has placed them just so": "The white supremacist, a little stout, is dressed in a sloppy kind of uniform; his mouth is puckered as he strains to threaten his adversary. He waves his flag strenuously, an incoherent blur. . . . Corey Long, is, by contrast, a figure of elegance. . . . Compared to his foe, Long handles his instrument easily, and wittily—when that flag catches on fire, the supremacist will be carrying the sacrilege that he fears."[9]

All of this recent turmoil could be seen as a contest over Civil War memory. But that's not quite right. The violence in Charleston and Charlottesville was not about the Civil War's "legacies," or how the past should be remembered. Rather, these events illustrate a lived relation between the past and the present, a state of lasting struggle born out by the Civil War's lack of an ending. The parameters of that struggle may

Steve Helber, *Charlottesville* (2017). Courtesy of Associated Press.

have changed, but in the ways that matter the war continues to rage on, making black life fragile and precarious.

As the Civil War endures, so do the stories we tell about it. In the wake of Charleston and Charlottesville, people shared poems—some old, some new—to process the violence and comprehend what had occurred. Friends posted poems that suddenly acquired new meaning, like Emily Dickinson's "After great pain, a formal feeling comes" and Dylan Thomas's "Do not go gently into that good night."[10] On Facebook, Sherman Alexie posted a newly written "Hymn" that called for love and empathy ("Will you be / Eyes for the blind? Will you become the feet / For the wounded? . . . Will you welcome the lost to your shore?"), while A. J. Haynes, the singer for the Seratones, struck an angrier tone in an elegy for Heather Heyer:

> Daughters of the Confederacy,
> My memory is as hot and sharp
> As the lingering scent of rust and steel
> That slices through Heather's torso
> Like a scythe to cane fields.[11]

Is it any wonder that poems followed pain? Storytelling is all the more important—indeed, existentially necessary—when the story has not ended.

One of the artists who went viral was the African American poet Lucille Clifton. Although Clifton died five years before Dylann Roof ever stepped foot in Charleston's Emanuel African Methodist Episcopal Church, her poems suddenly acquired a sense of fiery urgency. For some observers, Clifton's 1970 description of the narrow-minded guardsmen who massacred students at Kent State was an equally apt description of twenty-first-century neo-Confederates:

> only to keep
> his little fear
> he kills his cities
> and his trees
> even his children[12]

Clifton's "a visit to gettysburg" seemed even more prescient. "i will / touch stone," the poem begins, "yes i will / teach white rock to answer," referring to the giant white monument dedicated, in 1913, to the soldiers who fought in that fateful battle.[13] Measuring one hundred feet high and topped by a triumphal arch, the Gettysburg Memorial honors the soldiers who, as Lincoln said, "hallowed" the ground through their sacrifice. Yet the memorial bestows that honor very narrowly. It does not give any indication of why the soldiers died, or what they fought for. Nor does it say anything about slavery or emancipation—an erasure that, for Clifton, is symbolized by the blinding whiteness of the memorial itself. In the poem, Clifton imagines placing her black body against the pale granite, turning herself—rather than Gettysburg—into the war's touchstone:

> yes I will
> walk in the wake
> of the battle sir
> . . . . . .
> a touchstone
> and I will rub
> "where is my black blood

Doug Kerr, *Pennsylvania State Memorial, Gettysburg* (2009). Creative Commons
Attribution-Share Alike 2.0 Generic.

and black bone?"
and the grounds
and the graves
will throw off they clothes
and touch stone
for this touchstone.[14]

Of course, as W. H. Auden remarked, "poetry makes nothing happen."[15] It cannot resurrect the dead or change the world of the living.
But literature *can* help us understand where we come from and who
we wish to be. It aids us in creating stories for the world to come and
figuring out how to live within it. Many of the poems that made the
rounds after Charleston and Charlottesville fit this mold, tilting their
vision toward the future. In his "Hymn," Alexie says, "Alone we are
defenseless" but "Collective, we are sacred." In the coming days, "We
will be courageous with our love. We will risk danger / As we sing and
sing and sing to welcome strangers." Clifton's "the last day" dreams of

a future in which we find ourselves surrounded by friends, "all of them now / wearing the eyes they had / only imagined possible."[16]

Charleston's inaugural poet laureate, Marcus Amaker, similarly pivots from pain to liberation. Amaker's 2017 poem "Stagnation (a letter 2 America)" begins with a challenge and a critique. The United States, he declares, "has built / too many monuments to war," too many "man-made maladies / mounted on Mother Earth":

> I've seen scars on the skin
> of our country's landscape—
> blood-stained band aids
> covering exposed bones;
> a pain that has not healed.

However that does not mean we are doomed to simply live out the Civil War, again and again:

> No statue's spirit
> will wake up to apologize,
> but you can.
> No system rooted
> in racism
> will ever empathize,
> but you can.
> History can not
> re-write itself,
> but you can.
> . . . . . .
>
> Carve out stones
> for freedom fighters,
> do more to preserve and promote
> the feminine.
>
> Rip off the bandages
> without ignoring your bondage.
>
> It's going to hurt.[17]

These poems afford one final look at the Civil War, a glance at what might come to pass. They sketch out a future *after* the Civil War, a world in which the Great Emancipation has become a lived reality. Though literature cannot reveal what, exactly, such a future entails, it can convey what it feels like: the thrill of release, warmth of recognition, and sense of boundless community that comes when fascisms old and new are destroyed and the "radical revolution in all the modes of thought," which Frederick Douglass declared to be the war's true purpose, has been achieved. W. E. B. Du Bois made a similar point a century later, in his updated biography of John Brown. The war's grandest ideal—the task we must continue to carry out, Du Bois said—is nothing less than universal liberation, abolishing "barriers between classes" and "hard and fast lines between races": "Only in this way can the best in humanity be discovered and conserved, and only thus can mankind live in peace and progress."[18] Such hopeful visions may strike some people as overly romantic. But literature is a record of hope as well as despair, and the literature of emancipation, for more than 150 years, has anticipated a moment in which the Civil War is finally resolved and equality is as solid as the stone out of which the war's memorials are carved.

To get from here to there—from today's Civil War to tomorrow's emancipation—"is going to hurt," as Amaker writes. It will require massive changes to the government, to the economy, and to the most intimate, hard-to-reach parts of society: people's values, identities, and feelings of belonging. When it comes to those more personal changes, storytelling is vitally important. If Civil War literature demonstrates anything, it is that we use stories not merely to reckon with the past but to see ourselves, and others, in a different light. It is through stories that we apprehend who we are and what we value. So to discover and preserve "the best in humanity," as Du Bois words it, we need new films, new poems, and new histories. We need new communities, and novels, and art. We need new laws, and myths, and direct actions. Perhaps then, or at some further remove, the Civil War will finally come to a close and another story will emerge: a story of real equality, a story whose beginning is only now coming into view.

Acknowledgments

I wish to thank the many people who shaped this book in one way or another. *Not Even Past* would not exist without the guidance and encouragement of my editor, Matt McAdam. Matt is an editor's editor, and this book has benefited immensely from his advice and acumen. I am also grateful for the superb work done by my copy editor, Jeremy Horsefield, and by the people at Johns Hopkins University Press who put such thought and care into creating this book: Catherine Goldstead, William Krause, Hilary Jacqmin, and Juliana McCarthy. To the anonymous readers who responded to the manuscript with such wisdom and generosity: thank you so much.

At the University of Georgia I have been fortunate to work in a department that provides me with the freedom to pursue my ever-evolving interests. I am grateful to Jed Rasula and Michelle Balliff, who served as departmental chairs during this book's composition, for their support, and to my colleagues throughout Park Hall for their commitment to literary studies and the value of writing. I especially wish to thank Casie LeGette, Tricia Lootens, John W. Lowe, Barbara McCaskill, Eric Morales-Franceschini, Jason Payton, Nancee Reeves, Susan Rosenbaum, Esra Santesso, and Aidan Wasley. My view of the Civil War's narratives has also been influenced by my students at the University of Georgia, whose insightfulness and curiosity remind me almost daily just how lucky I am. Two of those students, Sidonia Serafini and Zachary Anderson, were particularly instrumental, since they tracked down sources and helped me proofread the manuscript.

As the "Suggested Further Reading" section suggests, my understanding of the Civil War's stories is also indebted to friends a bit farther away. I shared some of this work in its early stages at several venues—Trinity College, the University of Texas, the University of Paris, Amherst College, the Midwest MLA, and

C19—where colleagues pointed me toward different sources, helped me clarify ideas, and provided a fresh perspective on old materials. I wish to thank, in particular, John Levi Barnard, Faith Barrett, Jill Spivey Caddell, Kathleen Diffley, Elizabeth Duquette, Benjamin Fagan, Ian Finseth, Randall Fuller, Eric Gardner, Nathan Grant, Christopher Hager, Christopher Hanlon, Paul Hurh, Coleman Hutchison, Jeffrey Insko, Michelle Kohler, Andrew Kopec, Gregory Laski, Robert S. Levine, Dominic Mastroianni, Justine Murison, Samuel Otter, Matthew Rebhorn, Elizabeth Renker, Eliza Richards, Kelly Ross, Cécile Roudeau, Jane Schultz, Julia Stern, Edward Sugden, Timothy Sweet, and Kristen Treen.

This book wouldn't be possible without my family. My parents, Monte and Betty Marrs, have been unflagging in their love and support. My wife, Kristin Lenore Marrs, who read and responded to a terrible early version of this book, is the best partner any man could hope for. My children, Harper and Caleb, light up my world in ways I cannot even begin to enumerate. Thank you, all of you, from the bottom of my heart.

Notes

Introduction

1. Stephen J. Ochs, *A Black Patriot and a White Priest: André Cailloux and Claude Paschal* (Baton Rouge: LSU Press, 2000), 40–94.

2. William Wells Brown, *The Negro in the American Rebellion: His Heroism and His Fidelity* (Boston: Lee & Shepard, 1867), 169.

3. *New York Times*, August 8 and 9, 1863.

4. Rodolphe Desdunes, *Our People and Our History: Fifty Creole Portraits*, ed. and trans. Sister Dorothea Olga McCants, Daughter of the Cross (Baton Rouge: LSU Press, 1973), 124; George Washington Williams, *A History of the Negro Troops in the War of the Rebellion, 1861–1865* (New York: Harper & Brothers, 1888), 218–19.

5. Paul Laurence Dunbar, "The Unsung Heroes," in *The Collected Poetry of Paul Laurence Dunbar*, ed. Joanne M. Braxton (Charlottesville: Univ. of Virginia Press, 1993), 197; Joseph T. Wilson, *The Black Phalanx: A History of the Negro Soldiers of the United States in the Wars of 1775–1812, 1861–'65* (Hartford: American, 1890), 217; Natasha Trethewey, *Native Guard* (Boston: Mariner Books, 2007), 44. The poem Wilson quotes is an anonymous elegy that had a long afterlife.

6. Trethewey, *Native Guard*, 40.

7. Walter Mitchell, "Harvard's Heroes," *Atlantic Monthly*, September 1863, 385–87.

8. John William de Forest, *Miss Ravenel's Conversion from Secession to Loyalty* (New York: Harper & Brothers, 1867), 279.

9. Lawrence Lee Hewitt, *Port Hudson, Confederate Bastion on the Mississippi* (Baton Rouge: LSU Press, 1987).

10. Herman Melville, *Battle-Pieces* (1866), in *Published Poems*, vol. 11 of *The Writings of Herman Melville*, ed. Robert C. Ryan and Hershel Parker (Evanston, IL: Newberry Library; Chicago: Northwestern Univ. Press, 2009), 44.

11. Paul Francis de Gournay, "Defending Port Hudson," in *Battles and Leaders of the Civil War*, ed. Peter Cozzens (Urbana: Univ. of Illinois Press, 2002), 5:392–410.

12. This statistic resulted from a 2019 Boolean search on WorldCat (https://www.worldcat.org/).

13. Robert Penn Warren, *The Legacy of the Civil War* (Lincoln: Univ. of Nebraska Press, 1998), 1.

14. Matt Pearce, "Chanting 'Blood and Soil!' White Nationalists with Torches March on University of Virginia," *Los Angeles Times*, August 11, 2017; A. C. Thompson, Ali Winston, and Jake Hanrahan, "U.S. Marine to Be Imprisoned over Involvement with Hate Groups," *ProPublica*, June 20, 2018.

15. David W. Blight, *American Oracle: The Civil War in the Civil Rights Era* (Cambridge, MA: Harvard Univ. Press, 2011), 6 (my emphasis).

16. *Gone with the Wind*, dir. Victor Fleming (MGM, 1939); W. E. B. Du Bois, *John Brown* (New York: International Editions, 1962); Trethewey, *Native Guard*, 31.

Chapter 1. A Family Squabble

1. Johnny Cash, *Johnny 99* (Columbia Records, 1983).

2. For a closer look at some of these actual cases, see Amy Murrell Taylor, *The Divided Family in Civil War America* (Chapel Hill: Univ. of North Carolina Press, 2005).

3. On mid-nineteenth-century political identities, see Anne Norton, *Alternative Americas* (Chicago: Univ. of Chicago Press, 1986); on the era's family-based politics, see Michael Paul Rogin, *Subversive Genealogy: The Politics and Art of Herman Melville* (Berkeley: Univ. of California Press, 1979).

4. See Ruth L. Bohan, *Looking into Walt Whitman: American Art, 1850–1920* (University Park: Pennsylvania State Univ. Press, 2006).

5. Mark Twain, "Letter to Walt Whitman" (May 24, 1889), Walt Whitman Collection in the Beinecke Library, Yale University.

6. Walt Whitman, "Preface, 1855, to first issue of 'Leaves of Grass,'" in *Prose Works 1892*, ed. Floyd Stovall, vol. 2, *Collect and Other Prose* (New York: New York Univ. Press, 2007), 434–35.

7. Walt Whitman, *Leaves of Grass: A Textual Variorum of the Printed Poems*, ed. Sculley Bradley et al., 3 vols. (New York: New York Univ. Press, 1980), 1:83, 2:400–401.

8. Whitman, *Leaves of Grass*, 2:505.

9. Roy Morris Jr., *The Better Angel: Walt Whitman in the Civil War* (New York:

Oxford Univ. Press, 2000); Drew Gilpin Faust, *This Republic of Suffering* (New York: Random House, 2008), 5.

10. Morris, *Better Angel*, 175.

11. Walt Whitman, "Our Sick and Wounded Soldiers," *New York Times*, December 11, 1864, repr. in *Prose Works 1892*, ed. Floyd Stovall, vol. 1, *Specimen Days* (New York: New York Univ. Press, 2007), 302.

12. For an illuminating account of this, see Peter Coviello, "Whitman's Children," *PMLA* 128, no. 1 (January 2013): 73–86.

13. Walt Whitman, "To James Redpath (?)" (August 6, 1863) in *The Correspondence, 1842–1867*, ed. Edwin Haviland Miller (New York: New York Univ. Press, 1961), 121–23; "To Mr. and Mrs. S. B. Haskell" (August 10, 1863), in *The Correspondence, 1842–1867*, 127–29.

14. Walt Whitman, 1891 version of "Vigil Strange I Kept on the Field One Night," from the Walt Whitman Archive, https://whitmanarchive.org/.

15. Abraham Lincoln, "House Divided" speech (1858), in *Speeches and Writings, 1832–1858* (New York: Library of America, 1989), 426; "First Inaugural Address" (1861), in *Speeches and Writings, 1859–1865* (New York: Library of America, 1989), 224; "Second Inaugural Address" (1865), in *Speeches and Writings, 1859–1865*, 686.

16. "Incidents in the Battle of Belmont," in *The Rebellion Record: A Diary of American Events*, ed. Frank Moore (New York: G. P. Putnam, 1862), 3:70.

17. Richard Devins, *The Pictorial Book of Anecdotes and Incidents of the War of the Rebellion* (Hartford: Hartford, 1866), 241.

18. *New York Express*, April 15, 1861, as quoted by Horace Greeley in *The American Conflict: A History of the Great Rebellion in the United States, 1860–1864* (Hartford: O. D. Case, 1865), 455.

19. For a fuller account of the Civil War's visual cultures, see Shirley Samuels, *Facing America: Iconography and the Civil War* (New York: Oxford Univ. Press, 2004); and Kathleen Diffley and Benjamin Fagan, eds., *Visions of Glory: The Civil War in Word and Image* (Athens: Univ. of Georgia Press, 2019).

20. "At South Mountain," *Harper's Weekly*, October 25, 1862, 674.

21. Frederick W. Seward, *Seward at Washington, as Senator and Secretary of State* (New York: Derby & Miller, 1891), 200–201.

22. John Brown Gordon, *Reminiscences of the Civil War* (New York: Scribner's, 1903), 464.

23. Herman Melville, *Published Poems*, vol. 11 of *The Writings of Herman Melville*, ed. Robert C. Ryan and Hershel Parker (Evanston, IL: Newberry Library; Chicago: Northwestern Univ. Press, 2009), 19.

24. Katherine Bjork, *Prairie Imperialists: The Indian Country Origins of American Empire* (Philadelphia: Univ. of Pennsylvania Press, 2018); Paul Giles, *The Global Remapping of American Literature* (Princeton, NJ: Princeton Univ. Press, 2011), 9.

25. Oliver Optic, *A Lieutenant at Eighteen* (Boston: Lee & Shepard, 1896), 7; *At the Front* (Boston: Lee & Shepard, 1897), 487.

26. John Musick, *Brother against Brother; or, The Tompkins Mystery: A Story of the Great American Rebellion* (Chicago: J. S. Ogilvie, 1897), 12, 19, 252–53.

27. Koritha Mitchell, *Living with Lynching: African American Lynching Plays, Performance, and Citizenship, 1890–1930* (Urbana: Univ. of Illinois Press, 2011), 1, 30.

28. Walt Whitman, "Ethiopia Saluting the Colors" (1871), in *Leaves of Grass,* 1:631–32.

29. Ulysses S. Grant III, "Here Comes the Greatest Centennial in U.S. History!," *This Week Magazine,* October 16, 1960, 8; Library of Congress, *The American Civil War: A Centennial Exhibition* (Washington, DC: Library of Congress, 1961), 1.

30. William H. Price, *The Civil War Centennial Handbook* (Arlington, VA: Prince Lithograph, 1961), 2, 6–7.

31. Martin Luther King Jr., "Address to the New York State Civil War Centennial Commission" (September 12, 1962), ser. 3, box 3, Martin Luther King Jr. Papers, Martin Luther King Jr. Center for Nonviolent Change, Atlanta, GA.

32. Robert Penn Warren, *The Legacy of the Civil War* (Lincoln: Univ. of Nebraska Press, 1998), 1, 3–4, 6.

33. Aaron Copland, *Lincoln Portrait* (New York: Boosey & Hawkes, 1951).

34. On the Lincolns' own wartime struggles, see Michael Burlingame, *Abraham Lincoln: A Life,* vol. 2 (Baltimore: Johns Hopkins Univ. Press, 2008); and Stephen Berry, *The House of Abraham: Lincoln and the Todds, a Family Divided by War* (Boston: Houghton Mifflin, 2007).

35. "Editor's Easy Chair," *Harper's Monthly* 31 (June–November, 1865): 126; Henry Howard Brownell, "Abraham Lincoln (Summer, 1865)," in *War-Lyrics, and Other Poems* (Boston: Ticknor & Fields, 1865), 117; Walt Whitman, "O Captain! My Captain!," *New-York Saturday Press,* November 4, 1865, 218; Anonymous, "America, Mourn!," in *Poetical Tributes to the Memory of Abraham Lincoln* (Philadelphia: J. B. Lippincott, 1865), 165.

36. Whitman, *Prose Works 1892,* 2:60.

37. Walt Whitman, "When Lilacs Last in Dooryard Bloom'd" (1865), in *Leaves of Grass,* 2:531.

38. Whitman, *Prose Works 1892*, 2:114–15.

39. Whitman, "Lilacs," 535.

40. *Of Human Hearts*, dir. Clarence Brown (Metro-Goldwyn-Mayer, 1938); *The Reprieve: An Episode in the Life of Abraham Lincoln*, dir. Van Dyke Brooke (Vitagraph, 1908); *Abraham Lincoln's Clemency*, dir. Theodore Wharton (Pathé Films, 1910); and *The Sleeping Sentinel* (Lubin, 1914).

41. Irving Bacheller, *Father Abraham* (Indianapolis: Bobbs Merrill, 1925), 150–51.

42. Henry Jarvis Raymond, *History of the Administration of President Lincoln* (New York: J. C. Derby & N. C. Miller, 1864), 469; Frederick Douglass, "Oration in Memory of Abraham Lincoln" (1876), in *Frederick Douglass: Selected Speeches and Writings*, ed. Philip S. Foner and Yuval Taylor (Chicago: Lawrence Hill Books, 1999), 618. On Lincoln's expansion of presidential power, see Mark E. Neely's *The Fate of Liberty: Abraham Lincoln and Civil Liberties* (New York: Oxford Univ. Press, 1991); on the evolution of Lincoln's racial views, see Eric Foner, *The Fiery Trial: Abraham Lincoln and American Slavery* (New York: Norton, 2011).

43. Irving Stone, *Love Is Eternal: A Novel about Mary Todd and Abraham Lincoln* (New York: Bantam Doubleday Dell, 1954), 57.

44. Gore Vidal, *Lincoln: A Novel* (New York: Vintage, 2000), 313.

45. Adam Braver, *Mr. Lincoln's Wars: A Novel in Thirteen Stories* (New York: HarperCollins, 2003), 4, 8–9.

46. Braver, *Mr. Lincoln's Wars*, 13, 15, 16–18, 20.

47. *Lincoln*, dir. Steven Spielberg (Walt Disney Studios, 2012). On the importance of compromise to Spielberg's film, see also Aaron Bady, "*Lincoln* against the Radicals," *Jacobin*, November 26, 2012, https://www.jacobinmag.com/2012/11/lincoln-against-the-radicals-2/.

Chapter 2. A Dark and Cruel War

1. Mark Twain, "The Private History of a Campaign That Failed," in *Collected Tales, Sketches, Speeches, and Essays*, vol. 1, *1852–1890*, ed. Louis J. Budd (New York: Library of America, 1992), 863, 866.

2. Twain, "Private History," 1:870–72, 874.

3. Mark Twain, "Man's Place in the Animal World" (1896), in *Collected Tales, Sketches, Speeches, and Essays*, vol. 2, *1891–1910*, ed. Louis J. Budd (New York: Library of America, 1992), 210; "Private History," 1:879.

4. William T. Sherman, *Memoirs of General William T. Sherman* (New York: Library of America, 1990), 601.

5. Ken Burns, *The Civil War* (PBS, 1990).

6. Oliver Wendell Holmes, "The Soldier's Faith" (1895) and "In Our Youth Our Hearts Were Touched by Fire" (1884), in *The Essential Holmes: Selections from the Letters, Speeches, Judicial Opinions, and Other Writings*, ed. Richard Posner (Chicago: Univ. of Chicago Press, 1992).

7. J. D. Hacker, "A Census-Based Count of the Civil War Dead," *Civil War History* 57, no. 4 (December 2011): 307–48.

8. Drew Gilpin Faust, *This Republic of Suffering* (New York: Random House, 2008), 92–96.

9. Abraham Lincoln, "Second Inaugural Address," in *Speeches and Writings, 1859–1865* (New York: Library of America, 1989), 687.

10. Walt Whitman, *Prose Works 1892*, ed. Floyd Stovall, vol. 1, *Specimen Days* (New York: New York Univ. Press, 2007), 114–15.

11. Whitman, *Prose Works 1892*, 1:80–81.

12. The story behind these photographs is a bit more complicated than the images indicate. Many of the shots, such as Gardner's photograph of the sharp-shooter in Devil's Den at Gettysburg, were posed: he moved the body to make the shot more effective. See William Frassanito, *Gettysburg: A Journey in Time* (New York: Scribner's, 1975), 186–92.

13. James M. McPherson, *Hallowed Ground: A Walk at Gettysburg* (New York: Random House, 2009).

14. Abraham Lincoln, "Gettysburg Address" (1863), in *Speeches and Writings, 1859–1865*, 536.

15. Henry Timrod, "Ethnogenesis," and Julia Ward Howe, "Battle Hymn of the Republic," in *"Words for the Hour": A New Anthology of American Civil War Poetry*, ed. Faith Barrett and Cristanne Miller (Amherst: Univ. of Massachusetts Press, 2005), 313, 75.

16. Abraham Lincoln, "Second Inaugural Address" and "Meditation on the Divine Will," in *Speeches and Writings, 1859–1865*, 687, 359.

17. Emily Dickinson, *The Poems of Emily Dickinson: Reading Edition*, ed. R. W. Franklin (Cambridge, MA: Harvard Univ. Press, 1999), 238, 214, 246.

18. John Milton, *Paradise Lost*, ed. Gordon Teskey (New York: Norton, 2005), bk. 1, line 345.

19. Emily Dickinson, letter no. 280 to T. W. Higginson (February 1863), in *The Letters of Emily Dickinson*, ed. Thomas Johnson (Cambridge, MA: Belknap

Press of Harvard Univ. Press, 1958), 423; Dickinson, *Poems*, 276; *Oxford English Dictionary* (online).

20. Joseph Lawson, in *The Civil War: The Second Year Told by Those Who Lived It*, ed. Stephen W. Sears (New York: Library of America, 2014), 665–66, 667.

21. Mary Boykin Miller Chestnut, *Mary Chesnut's Civil War*, ed. C. Vann Woodward (New Haven, CT: Yale Univ. Press, 1981), 814.

22. Chestnut, *Mary Chesnut's Civil War*, 370, 768, 356, 29–31, 181.

23. Nathaniel Hawthorne, "Chiefly about War Matters, by a Peaceable Man," *Atlantic Monthly*, July 1862.

24. Hawthorne, "Chiefly about War Matters."

25. Stephen Crane, *The Red Badge of Courage: An Episode of the American Civil War*, ed. James Nagel (New York: Broadview, 2014), 39, 46, 48.

26. Crane, *Red Badge of Courage*, 48, 65.

27. See Wilfred Owen, *Poems* (New York: Viking, 1921); and Paul Fussell, *The Great War and Modern Memory* (New York: Oxford Univ. Press, 1975).

28. Stephen Crane, *Black Riders and Other Lines* (Boston: Copeland, 1896), 15.

29. Crane, *Red Badge of Courage*, 65, 120.

30. Frederick Jackson Turner, "The Significance of the Frontier in American History" (1893), in *The Frontier in American History* (New York: Henry Holt, 1921); Centre for Research on Globalization, "The U.S. Has Only Been at Peace for 21 Years Total since Its Birth" (2015), https://www.globalresearch.ca/amer ica-has-been-at-war-93-of-the-time-222-out-of-239-years-since-1776/5565946. The phrase "regeneration through violence" comes from Richard Slotkin, *Regeneration through Violence: The Mythology of the American Frontier, 1600–1860* (Norman: Univ. of Oklahoma Press, 1973).

31. Mark Twain, "The War Prayer" (1905), in *Collected Tales*, 2:652, 655.

32. Mark Twain, *A Connecticut Yankee in King Arthur's Court* (Berkeley: Univ. of California Press, 1983), 4, 65, 423.

33. Twain, *Connecticut Yankee*, 430, 432.

34. Ambrose Bierce, "What I Saw of Shiloh" (1874), in *The Devil's Dictionary, Tales, and Memoirs* (New York: Library of America, 2011).

35. Ambrose Bierce, *Tales of Soldiers and Civilians* (New York: Lovell, Coryell, 1891), 45, 47–48.

36. Bierce, *Tales of Soldiers and Civilians*, 95, 98.

37. Robert Underwood Johnson, preface to *The Story of a Great Conflict: A*

History of the War of Secession, 1861–1865, by Rossiter Johnson (New York: Bryan, Taylor, 1894), iii; David Thompson, "With Burnside at Antietam," in *Battles and Leaders of the Civil War* (New York: Century, 1887), 2:661.

38. Ulysses S. Grant, *Memoirs and Selected Letters*, ed. William McFeely (New York: Library of America, 1990), 147, 227, 232.

39. Edward Porter Alexander, *Fighting for the Confederacy: The Personal Recollections of Edward Porter Alexander*, ed. Gary W. Gallagher (Chapel Hill: Univ. of North Carolina Press, 1989), 95–96.

40. Sherman, *Memoirs*, 877, 3, 466.

41. Sherman, *Memoirs*, 885, 76.

42. Sherman, *Memoirs*, 601. Sherman's commentary comes from two letters, one addressed to Hood and another (beginning with "You cannot qualify . . .") addressed to officials in Atlanta who had informed him of the "appalling and heart-rending" consequences of his army's actions, stating that "the woe, the horrors, and the suffering, cannot be described by words; imagination can only conceive of it" (599).

43. James Longstreet, *From Manassas to Appomattox: Memoirs of the Civil War in America* (Philadelphia: J. B. Lippincott, 1896), 328–30.

44. Longstreet, *From Manassas to Appomattox*, 32–33.

45. Michael Shaara, *The Killer Angels* (New York: Ballantine, 2002), i, 106.

46. Shaara, *Killer Angels*, xx, 364–65.

47. *Gettysburg*, dir. Ronald F. Maxwell (New Line Cinema, 1993).

48. Jeffrey Shaara, *The Last Full Measure: A Novel* (New York: Ballantine Books, 1998), 3 (my emphasis).

49. Jeffrey Shaara, *Gods and Generals: A Novel of the Civil War* (New York: Ballantine Books, 2011), x, 3–4.

50. Edmund Wilson, *Patriotic Gore: Studies in the Literature of the American Civil War* (New York: Norton, 1994), 479, 99, xi–xiii.

51. Wilson, *Patriotic Gore*, xv, xvi.

52. Wilson, *Patriotic Gore*, xi–xii.

53. Shelby Foote, *Jordan County: A Landscape in Narrative* (New York: Vintage Books, 1992), 234, 236, 238.

54. Foote, *Jordan County*, 239, 248–49, 261, 269, 271, 277, 234.

55. MacKinlay Kantor, *Andersonville* (New York: Penguin, 1993), 104, 183, 220.

56. Kantor, *Andersonville*, 184, 395.

57. Richard Cheney, "Vice President's Remarks at 30th Political Action Confer-

ence" (January 30, 2003), https://georgewbush-whitehouse.archives.gov/news/releases/2003/01/20030130-16.html; Donald Trump, "Inaugural Address" (January 20, 2017), from *The American Presidency Project*, http://www.presidency.ucsb.edu/index.php.

58. Taylor Brown, *Fallen Land: A Novel* (New York: St. Martin's, 2015), 9.

59. Stephen Wright, *The Amalgamation Polka* (New York: Knopf, 2007), 167, 240, 177, 180.

60. Stephen Wright, *Meditations in Green* (New York: Scribner's, 1983); *Amalgamation Polka*, 167.

61. William Faulkner, *Requiem for a Nun* (New York: Vintage, 1994), 73.

62. Christopher Hager, "The Arc of the Moral Universe, and Other Long Things," *Common-place.org* 17, no. 1 (Fall 2016), http://common-place.org/book/the-arc-of-the-moral-universe-and-other-long-things/.

Chapter 3. The Lost Cause

1. Winston Churchill, "If Lee Had Not Won the Battle of Gettysburg," *Scribner's*, December 1930, 587–97.

2. Churchill, "If Lee Had Not Won," 588.

3. Drew Gilpin Faust, *This Republic of Suffering* (New York: Random House, 2008), xi; and *Mothers of Invention: Women of the Slaveholding South in the American Civil War* (Chapel Hill: Univ. of North Carolina Press, 2004).

4. Donald Trump, as quoted in Harriet Alexander, "'Our Great Country Being Ripped Apart': Donald Trump Criticizes 'Foolish' Removal of Confederate Monuments in New Tweets," *Telegraph*, August 17, 2017.

5. Jefferson Davis, *The Rise and Fall of the Confederate Government* (New York: D. Appleton, 1881), 1:1, vi, 518; Edward Pollard, *The Lost Cause: A New Southern History of the War of the Confederates* (New York: E. B. Treat, 1866), 47.

6. Pollard, *Lost Cause*, 711, 743, 750–52.

7. "The Constitution of the Confederate States of America" and Alexander Stephens's "Corner-Stone Speech," in *The Confederate and Neo-Confederate Reader: The "Great Truth" about the "Lost Cause,"* ed. James W. Loewen and Edward H. Sebesta (Jackson: Univ. Press of Mississippi, 2010).

8. William Gilmore Simms, *War Poetry of the South* (New York: Richardson, 1866), v.

9. Henry Timrod, "A Call to Arms" (1862) and "Ethnogenesis" (1861), in *"Words for the Hour": A New Anthology of American Civil War Poetry*, ed. Faith

Barrett and Cristanne Miller (Amherst: Univ. of Massachusetts Press, 2005), 321, 313, 315.

10. Walter Brian Cisco, *Henry Timrod: A Biography* (Cranbury, NJ: Associated Univ. Presses, 2010).

11. Henry Timrod, "Ode" (1866), in *The Collected Poems of Henry Timrod: A Variorum Edition*, ed. Edd Winfield Parks and Aileen Wells Parks (Athens: Univ. of Georgia Press, 2007), 129–30.

12. David O'Connell, *Furl That Banner: The Life of Abram J. Ryan, Poet-Priest of the South* (Macon, GA: Mercer Univ. Press, 2006), 57.

13. Abram Ryan, "C.S.A.," in *Father Ryan's Poems* (Mobile, AL: Jno. L. Rapier, 1879), 215.

14. Charles Reagan Wilson, *Baptized in Blood: The Religion of the Lost Cause, 1865–1920* (Athens: Univ. of Georgia Press, 1980).

15. Abram Ryan, *Poems: Patriotic, Religious, Miscellaneous* (New York: P. J. Kennedy & Sons, 1880), vii, 24, 51, 37, 240.

16. Joel Chandler Harris, *The Life and Letters of Joel Chandler Harris*, ed. Julia Collier Harris and Katherine H. Wootten (Boston: Houghton Mifflin, 1918), 159.

17. Southern Poverty Law Center, *Whose Heritage? Public Symbols of the Confederacy* (April 21, 2016), https://www.splcenter.org/20160421/whose-heritage-public-symbols-confederacy.

18. B. A. C. Emerson, *Historic Southern Monuments: Representative Memorials of the Heroic Dead of the Southern Confederacy* (New York: Neale, 1911), 21, 55.

19. Tyler Estep, "Big Boi Endorses Petition for Outkast Carving on Stone Mountain," *Atlanta Journal-Constitution*, July 15, 2015.

20. Mildred Rutherford, *The History of Stone Mountain* (Georgia Division of the United Daughters of the Confederacy, 1923).

21. Wilson, *Baptized in Blood*, 115–16.

22. "Recumbent Figure of Robert E. Lee," *Confederate Veteran* 7 (1899): 513.

23. Thomas Dixon Jr., *The Victim: A Romance of the Real Jefferson Davis* (Toronto: Copp Clark, 1914), 84–85.

24. Dixon, *Victim*, 75.

25. Dixon, *The Clansman: An Historical Romance of the Ku Klux Klan* (New York: A. Wessels, 1907), 329, 42, 46, 47.

26. Dixon, *Clansman*, 315–16, 46.

27. *The Birth of a Nation*, dir. D. W. Griffith (1915).

28. Wilson, *Baptized in Blood*, 115–16.

29. Katharine Du Pre Lumpkin, *The Making of a Southerner* (1946; repr., Athens: Univ. of Georgia Press, 1991), 200.

30. John Crowe Ransom, "Introduction: A Statement of Principles," in *I'll Take My Stand: The South and the Agrarian Tradition* (Baton Rouge: LSU Press, 1977), xxxviii; George Wallace, "Inaugural Speech" (January 14, 1963). The Agrarians' fiction tended to be less programmatic than their histories. Robert Penn Warren's *Wilderness* (1960) and Caroline Gordon's *None Shall Look Back* (1937), in particular, present the Civil War in ways that move beyond the neo-Confederate politics laid out in *I'll Take My Stand.*

31. Margaret Mitchell, *Gone with the Wind* (New York: Scribner, 2011), 109, 137, 440.

32. Mitchell, *Gone with the Wind,* 492, 641, 642–43.

33. Mitchell, *Gone with the Wind,* 206.

34. John Coski, *The Confederate Battle Flag: America's Most Embattled Emblem* (Cambridge, MA: Harvard Univ. Press, 2009), 109.

35. Malcolm X, *The Autobiography of Malcolm X: As Told to Alex Haley* (New York: Random House, 1964), 38.

36. Robert W. Hamblin, *Myself and the World: A Biography of William Faulkner* (Jackson: Univ. of Mississippi Press, 2016), 1.

37. Federal Writers' Project of the WPA, *Mississippi: A Guide to the Magnolia State* (New York: Hastings House, 1949), 256; William Faulkner, *Requiem for a Nun* (New York: Random House, 1951).

38. William Faulkner, *Intruder in the Dust* (1948; repr., New York: Vintage House, 1972), 194–95.

39. William Faulkner, *Sartoris* (1929), republished in its original form as *Flags in the Dust* (New York: Random House, 1973), 1–3, 45.

40. Faulkner, *Sartoris,* 156.

41. William Faulkner, *The Unvanquished,* in *Novels, 1936–1940,* ed. Joseph Blotner and Noel Polk (New York: Library of America, 1990) 321, 373–74.

42. Faulkner, *Unvanquished,* 489, 491.

43. Southern Poverty Law Center, "Neo-Confederate," https://www.splcenter.org/fighting-hate/extremist-files/ideology/neo-confederate.

44. Harry Turtledove, *The Guns of the South: A Novel of the Civil War* (New York: Del Rey, 1992), 5, 259.

45. MacKinlay Kantor, *If The South Had Won the Civil War* (New York: Bantam Books, 1961), 2, 16, 19, 24, 112.

46. Ron Paul, interview by Tim Russert, *Meet the Press*, NBC, December 23, 2007.

47. Constance Sublette and Ned Sublette, *The American Slave Coast: A History of the Slave-Breeding Industry* (Chicago: Chicago Review Press, 2015).

Chapter 4. The Great Emancipation

1. Andrew Billingsley, *Robert Smalls of South Carolina and His Families* (Columbia: Univ. of South Carolina Press, 2007), 59; Stephen G. N. Tuck, *We Ain't What We Ought to Be: The Black Freedom Struggle from Emancipation to Obama* (Cambridge, MA: Harvard Univ. Press, 2010), 11.

2. William Wells Brown, *The Negro in the American Rebellion: His Heroism and His Fidelity* (Boston: Lee & Shepard, 1867), 79, 77.

3. Frederick Douglass, "The Mission of the War" (1864), in *Selected Speeches and Writings*, ed. Philip S. Foner and Yuval Taylor (Chicago: Lawrence Hill Books, 1999), 558, 562.

4. Abraham Lincoln to Horace Greeley, August 22, 1862, in *Speeches and Writings, 1859–1865* (New York: Library of America, 1989), 358; W. E. B. Du Bois, *Black Reconstruction in America, 1860–1880* (New York: Free Press, 1992), 55.

5. James Madison Bell, "The Day and the War" (1863), in *"Words for the Hour": A New Anthology of American Civil War Poetry*, ed. Faith Barrett and Cristanne Miller (Amherst: Univ. of Massachusetts Press, 2005), 135–37.

6. Sarah Shuften, "Ethiopia's Dead" (1865), in *"Words for the Hour,"* 177–78.

7. John Cimprich, *Fort Pillow: A Civil War Massacre, and Public Memory* (Baton Rouge: LSU Press, 2005).

8. Paul Laurence Dunbar, "Robert Gould Shaw" (1900), in *The Collected Poetry of Paul Laurence Dunbar*, ed. Joanne M. Braxton (Charlottesville: Univ. of Virginia Press, 1993), 221; William James, "Robert Gould Shaw" (1897), in *Memories and Studies* (New York: Longmans, Green, 1912), 39; Harriet Jacobs to Lydia Marie Child, March 26, 1864, in *Freedom's Journey: African American Voices of the Civil War*, ed. Donald Yacovone (Chicago: Lawrence Hill Books, 2004), 201.

9. "The Escaped Slave," *Harper's Weekly*, July 2, 1864.

10. William Wells Brown, *Clotel; or, The President's Daughter*, ed. Robert S. Levine (Boston: Bedford / St. Martin's, 2000), 207.

11. Brown, *Negro in the American Rebellion*, 46, 169, 212, 74–75.

12. Brown, *Negro in the American Rebellion*, 111, 118–19.

13. Dan Emmett, "I Wish I Was in Dixie's Land" (1859/1860), in *The Civil*

War Songbook, ed. Richard Crawford (Mineola: Dover, 1977); Brown, *Negro in the American Rebellion*, 119.

14. W. E. B. Du Bois, *The Souls of Black Folk: Essays and Sketches*, 3rd ed. (Chicago: A. C. McClurg, 1909), 261.

15. *Slave Songs of the United States*, ed. William Francis Allen, Charles Ware, and Lucy McKim Garrison (New York: A. Simpson, 1867), 48.

16. Douglas Blackmon, *Slavery by Another Name: The Re-enslavement of African Americans from the Civil War to World War II* (New York: Doubleday, 2008).

17. Frederick Douglass, *My Bondage and My Freedom* (1855), ed. John David Smith (New York: Penguin, 2003), 161.

18. Douglass, *My Bondage*, 249–50.

19. See Isaiah Berlin, *Liberty* (New York: Oxford Univ. Press, 2004).

20. Frederick Douglass, "The Revolution of 1848," in *Selected Speeches and Writings*.

21. Frederick Douglass, "The Mission of the War" (1864), in *Selected Speeches and Writings*, 557.

22. Frederick Douglass, "Why Should a Colored Man Enlist?" (1862), in *Selected Speeches and Writings*, 530.

23. Frederick Douglass, "The Unknown Loyal Dead" (1871), in *Selected Speeches and Writings*, 609–10; "There Was a Right Side in the Late War" (1878), in *Selected Speeches and Writings*, 629, 631.

24. Douglass, "There Was a Right Side," 628; Frederick Douglass, *Life and Times of Frederick Douglass* (1881/1892), in *Autobiographies*, ed. Henry Louis Gates Jr. (New York: Library of America, 1994), 811, 966.

25. F. E. W. Harper, "Words for the Hour" (1871), in *Complete Poems*, ed. Maryemma Graham (New York: Oxford Univ. Press, 1988), 102–3.

26. Renée Ater, *Remaking Race and History: The Sculpture of Meta Warrick Fuller* (Berkeley: Univ. of California Press, 2011), 77.

27. Ater, *Remaking Race and History*, 73.

28. John Quincy Adams, *Narrative of the Life of John Quincy Adams, When in Slavery, and Now as a Freeman* (Harrisburg, PA: Sieg, 1872), 35–36.

29. Elizabeth Keckley, *Behind the Scenes; or, Thirty Years a Slave, and Four Years in the White House* (New York: G. W. Carleton, 1868), 111, 112, 117.

30. Harriet Tubman and Sarah Bradford, *Scenes in the Life of Harriet Tubman* (Auburn: W. J. Moses, 1869), 40–42.

31. Edward J. Blum, *W. E. B. Du Bois, American Prophet* (Philadelphia: Univ. of Pennsylvania Press, 2007), 189–90.

32. W. E. B. Du Bois, *Dusk to Dawn: An Essay toward an Autobiography of a Race Concept* (1940; repr., New York: Transaction, 2011), 3.

33. W. E. B. Du Bois, *The Star of Ethiopia* (1913), in *The Oxford W. E. B. Du Bois Reader*, ed. Eric Sundquist (New York: Oxford Univ. Press, 1996), 309–10.

34. W. E. B. Du Bois, "Robert E. Lee" (1928), in *Oxford W. E. B. Du Bois Reader*.

35. C. Vann Woodward, *The Strange Career of Jim Crow: A Commemorative Edition* (New York: Oxford Univ. Press, 2001).

36. James Q. Whitman, *Hitler's American Model: The United States and the Making of Nazi Race Law* (Princeton, NJ: Princeton Univ. Press, 2017), 1.

37. Whitman, *Hitler's American Model*, 5, 17.

38. W. E. B. Du Bois, *The Souls of Black Folk* (1903), vol. 3 of *The Oxford W. E. B. Du Bois*, ed. Henry Louis Gates Jr. (New York: Oxford Univ. Press, 2007), 8; *Black Reconstruction*, 727, 67, 126.

39. Mary L. Dudziak, *Cold War Civil Rights: Race and the Image of American Democracy* (Princeton, NJ: Princeton Univ. Press, 2011).

40. Civil Rights Congress, *We Charge Genocide: The Historic Petition to the United Nations for Relief from a Crime of the United States Government against the Negro People* (New York: CRC, 1951), 23–24.

41. W. E. B. Du Bois, *John Brown* (New York: Oxford Univ. Press, 2007), 147, 166, 171–72.

42. Gerald Sorin, *Howard Fast: Life and Literature in the Left Lane* (Bloomington: Indiana Univ. Press, 2012).

43. Howard Fast, *Freedom Road* (1944), ed. Eric Foner (London: Routledge, 2015), 72, 69, 201; W. E. B. Du Bois, foreword to *Freedom Road*, xviii.

44. Martin Luther King Jr., "I Have a Dream" (1963), in *The Norton Anthology of African American Literature*, vol. 2, 3rd ed., ed. Henry Louis Gates Jr. et al. (New York: Norton, 2014).

45. Martin Luther King Jr., "Letter from Birmingham Jail" (1963), in *Norton Anthology of African American Literature*.

46. Martin Luther King Jr., "Address to the New York State Civil War Centennial Commission" (1962), transcribed by the New York State Museum, http://exhibitions.nysm.nysed.gov/mlk/images/MLK-Transcription.pdf.

47. James Baldwin, "The White Man's Guilt," *Ebony* 20, no. 10 (August 1865): 47.

48. Ishmael Reed, *Flight to Canada: A Novel* (New York: Scribner, 1998); *Roots: The Next Generations* (ABC, 1979); and Robert Lowell, *Life Studies and For the Union Dead* (New York: Farrar, Straus & Giroux, 2007), 63–64.

49. Margaret Walker, *Jubilee* (Boston: Mariner Books, 1999), 198, 242–43, 302, 234.

50. King, "Address to the New York State Civil War Centennial Commission," 4.

51. Walker, *Jubilee*, 206, 174, 485.

52. Ta-Nehisi Coates, "The Case for Reparations," *Atlantic*, May 2014, http:// www.theatlantic.com/magazine/archive/2014/06/the-case-for-reparations /361631/.

53. Natasha Trethewey, *Native Guard* (Boston: Mariner Books, 2007), 1, 20.

54. Trethewey, *Native Guard*, 25–27, 44.

55. *Django Unchained*, dir. Quentin Tarantino (Columbia Pictures and The Weinstein Company, 2012); *Abraham Lincoln: Vampire Hunter*, dir. Timur Bekmambetov (20th Century Fox, 2012).

56. Terry Bisson, *Fire on the Mountain* (Oakland, CA: PM Press, 1988), 28.

57. Bisson, *Fire on the Mountain*, 66–67, 143, 75.

58. Bisson, *Fire on the Mountain*, 153.

Afterword

1. Adam Parker, "Susie Jackson," *Post and Courier*, June 17, 2015; Ed Pilkington, "'He Was My Hero': Charleston Mother Hails 26-Year-Old Killed Shielding Victims," *Guardian*, June 19, 2015; BBC News, "Charleston Church Shooting— As It Happened," https://www.bbc.com/news/live/world-us-canada-33181651.

2. Rachel Kaadzi Ghansah, "A Most American Terrorist: The Making of Dylann Roof," *GQ*, August 21, 2017.

3. Dylann Roof, "The Last Rhodesian" (2015), https://www.documentcloud .org/documents/2108059-lastrhodesian-manifesto.html.

4. David S. Reynolds, "Hauling Down the Confederate Flag," *New Yorker*, July 3, 2015.

5. WBTV, "Confederate Monument Vandalized with Names of Charleston Church Shooting Victims," August 4, 2015, http://www.wbtv.com/story/2970 5145/confederate-monument-vandalized-with-names-of-charleston-church -shooting-victims.

6. Martin Luther King Jr., "Letter from Birmingham Jail" (1963), in *The Norton Anthology of African American Literature*, vol. 2, 3rd ed., ed. Henry Louis Gates Jr. et al. (New York: Norton, 2014).

7. Joel Gunter, "A Reckoning in Charlottesville," BBC News, August 13, 2017.

8. Yesha Callahan, "Interview: How Corey Long Fought White Supremacy

with Fire," *Root*, August 14, 2017, https://www.theroot.com/interview-how
-corey-long-fought-white-supremacy-with-f-1797831277.

9. Doreen St. Felix, "An Image of Revolutionary Fire at Charlottesville," *New Yorker*, August 14, 2017.

10. "Poems for Charlottesville" (2017), episode 19 of *On Poetry* (podcast), https://www.on-poetry.com/episode-19-poems-for-charlottesville/.

11. Sherman Alexie, "Hymn," https://earlybirdbooks.com/hymn-a-new-poem -by-sherman-alexie; A. J. Haynes, "A Poem for Heather Heyer, from Shreveport," *Shreveport Times*, August 14, 2017.

12. Lucille Clifton, "after kent state," in *The Collected Poems of Lucille Clifton, 1965–2010* (Rochester, NY: BOA Editions, 2015).

13. Lucille Clifton, "a visit to gettysburg," in *Collected Poems*.

14. Clifton, "visit to gettysburg."

15. W. H. Auden, "In Memory of W. B. Yeats," in *Collected Poems* (New York: Random House, 1976), 248.

16. Alexie, "Hymn"; Lucille Clifton, "the last day," in *Collected Poems*.

17. Marcus Amaker, "Stagnation (a letter 2 America)" (2017), http://marcusa maker.com/stagnation/.

18. Frederick Douglass, "The Mission of the War" (1864), in *Selected Speeches and Writings*, ed. Philip S. Foner and Yuval Taylor (Chicago: Lawrence Hill Books, 1999); W. E. B. Du Bois, *John Brown* (New York: International Editions, 1962).

Suggested Further Reading

Intellectual inquiry is a curious thing. In *Moby-Dick*, Ishmael knows all too well that it is impossible to pin down the cosmic meaning of the whale, the great leviathan, in human culture, yet he does his damnedest to try. The novel begins not with his famous invitation, "Call me Ishmael," but with an etymology that attempts—and fails—to extract the whale's secret from its name. One of the strangest chapters is simply called "Cetology," in which Ishmael endeavors— and again, fails—to categorize whale species according to their size and shape. At one point, Ishmael thinks he's finally landed on the secret: the whale's tail. *This is it*, he imagines, *the key to it all!* "Five great motions," he says excitedly, "are peculiar to it": swimming, battling, sweeping, lobbing, and fluking. But as soon as he finishes analyzing those movements, Ishmael discovers he is still wandering through the dark. "The more I consider this mighty tail," he con- cludes, not with disappointment but with a sense of sharpened awe, "the more do I deplore my inability to express it. At times there are gestures in it, which, though they would well grace the hand of man, remain wholly inexplicable. . . . Dissect him how I may . . . I but go skin deep; I know him not, and never will."

I sympathize with Ishmael. When viewed through literature, the Civil War is disturbingly whale-like in its elusiveness. Few events in human history have been revisited so prolifically, or with such astounding passion. Over the past century and a half, the war has spawned about 10,000 memoirs, 6,000 novels, and 2,000 books of poetry, as well as countless songs, statues, speeches, essays, films, paintings, plays, fables, and films. My aim throughout has not been to offer a final word on these copious materials but to better understand the pri- mal stories they impart and the influence those stories have had on American culture. In that same spirit, I would like to offer a brief guide for further reading.

This, too, will inevitably go but skin deep. Nonetheless, that seems to be entirely in keeping with the nature of the war's lack of an ending. What is the Civil War but an unfinished revolution with which we still reckon—a revolution that can still be won or lost? Since the war has not yet concluded, it is impossible to reach a point of full understanding, but we owe it to ourselves—and to those who come before and after us—to try.

On the Civil War as a War

To assess the Civil War in a single book is a gargantuan task. For that reason presses tend to publish books on the topic as part of a longer series. Two particularly strong series are Civil War America, published by the University of North Carolina Press, and UnCivil Wars, published by the University of Georgia Press. The Library of America has also reprinted many of the war's major primary documents as part of a four-volume set, *The Civil War: Told by Those Who Lived It*. (The Library of America's series is solid; it is also *very* tilted toward firsthand accounts.) Nevertheless, some stand-alone books do capture the spirit of the event almost in its entirety. James McPherson's *Battle Cry of Freedom* (1988) approaches the Civil War as a single, cohesive era that begins with the political furor over slavery's westward expansion and ends with dissolution of the Confederacy in 1865. *Battle Cry of Freedom* continues to be a necessary chronicle and intellectual resource. Louis Masur's *The Civil War: A Concise History* (2011) elegantly accomplishes what its subtitle suggests by surveying the war's origins, consequences, and turning points, devoting one chapter to each year of the struggle. Williamson Murray and Wayne Wei-Siang Hsieh offer a more military-focused account in *A Savage War* (2016), which recounts the battles, strategies, and technologies that made the Civil War the first example of modern, industrialized warfare.

On Civil War Memory

The best overall guide to the Civil War memory, which everyone should read at least once, is David W. Blight's *Race and Reunion: The Civil War in American Memory* (2001). It chronicles how the dominant forms of Civil War remembrance —reconciliationist, emancipationist, and white supremacist—developed and spread from the end of the war through the early twentieth century. It is interdisciplinary (in the best sense of that fraught word), lucidly written, and bracing in its historical insights.

David S. Reynolds's cultural histories of the Civil War era are also indispensable. *John Brown, Abolitionist* (2006) recasts Brown as a founding figure of modern America. According to Reynolds, Brown did not merely anticipate the Civil War; he sparked a revolution against slavery and set off an enduring debate about the relation between violence and justice. The book tracks the growth of Brown's legend, from the antebellum era to the civil rights era and beyond. In *Mightier than the Sword* (2011), Reynolds charts the astounding impact of Harriet Beecher Stowe's *Uncle Tom's Cabin*—the most influential novel of the nineteenth century—as it was read, used, and interpreted by people far and wide, from Confederate soldiers to Union leaders and Russian oligarchs.

Other books focus on how the Civil War has been remixed and repackaged over time. Gary Gallagher's *Causes Won, Lost, and Forgotten* (2008) is an insightful, wide-ranging meditation on the influence of popular art and culture on Civil War memory. Gallagher looks at an array of works of art and Hollywood films, from *Gone with the Wind* to *Gettysburg*, but the most fascinating chapter, to my mind, is the one about Confederate themes in recent Civil War paintings. Further inquiries into the weird twists and turns of Civil War remembrance can be found in essay collections. Alice Fahs and Joan Waugh's *The Memory of the Civil War in American Culture* (2004) examines the eclectic ways in which the war has taken shape in American society, from the advent of Memorial Day as a holiday to the resurrection of the Lost Cause in Southern textbooks. Kirk Savage's *The Civil War in Art and Memory* (2016) focuses on artistic and commemorative reconsiderations of the war, with essays organized around memory's defining locations: "Home," "Battlefield," "Public Space," and "Heroism." The essays in Thomas J. Brown's *Remixing the Civil War* (2013) similarly assess the war's cultural impact, but with a different emphasis. *Remixing the Civil War* approaches the conflict as an "undead" event, the enduring life of which is evident in everything from Juneteenth festivals to the abiding use of the Confederate battle flag as a Southern emblem. Speaking of the Confederate flag, the requisite history of that symbol's use and appropriation is John Coski's *The Confederate Battle Flag* (2005).

On Civil War Literature in General

Unlike historians, who started to obsess over the Civil War's meaning as soon as it began, literary critics have tended to be more interested in what came before and after the conflict. Edmund Wilson and Daniel Aaron, who wrote the first in-depth studies of Civil War literature, changed that. Wilson's *Patriotic Gore* (1962) is a searching inquiry into the war's writings. Those writings, he argues, don't amount to much in terms of aesthetic value, but they are of paramount importance for understanding American civilization. Though Wilson tends to dismiss the aesthetic qualities of Civil War literature too hastily, he provides rich and provocative accounts of the era's writers. Daniel Aaron is more attuned to matters of race. In *The Unwritten War* (1973), he contends that this is why there is no Civil War epic or masterpiece: racism "blurred literary insight," and white writers' "self-appointed roles as bards and prophets removed them too effectually from the theatres of conflict." *The Unwritten War* also provides a helpful schematic, grouping writers according to their relation to the conflict, from "Drawing-Room Warriors" like Ambrose Bierce to "Malingerers" like Mark Twain.

Recent years have witnessed a renaissance in Civil War literary studies. Scholars have found connections across wartime media, recovered lost archives, elevated neglected writers, and used fresh approaches to reassess the war's literature and culture. Coleman Hutchison's edited volume, *A History of American Civil War Literature* (2015), samples and summarizes many of these contributions. The essays range from considerations of the Civil War's international dimensions to brief histories of the Civil War book industry and overviews on writers such as Natasha Trethewey and Mary Chesnut. I also recommend Timothy Sweet's collection, *Literary Cultures of the Civil War* (2016), which features several essays about relatively unknown Civil War writers, genres, and works, such as African American wartime letters and the poems of George Moses Horton (an enslaved poet from North Carolina).

One of the major shifts in thinking has to do with what counts as Civil War literature and where it comes from. For a long time Northern authors were viewed as the Civil War's representative voices. That disregard was partly a response to the ideological taint of Confederate and neo-Confederate writing: few literatures, if any, are so conspicuously tied to an odious politics of white supremacy. Yet overlooking Confederate literature not only yields a blinkered view of the conflict and the literary works it has produced but also reinforces the nationalist triumphalism that has long reigned in American cultural memory.

Several important books have challenged this tendency. Sarah Gardner's *Blood and Irony* (2004) looks at the narratives written by Southern white women during and after the conflict. Throughout the South there are still countless unpublished manuscripts "with titles such as 'My Recollections of the War' and 'A Confederate Girlhood'" (3). Those manuscripts, Gardner demonstrates, preserved Southern memory up through the twentieth century; indeed, many white Southern women approached writing as a means not only for finding their voice but also for helping the South reckon with defeat. A different but no less significant recovery takes place in Coleman Hutchison's *Apples and Ashes* (2013). Hutchison's book is the first full-scale literary history of the wartime South. It moves insightfully across Confederate culture, analyzing the multitude of songs, poems, and novels that tried to imagine the Confederate nation into being.

This does not mean that Northern literature has been neglected of late. On the contrary, there is a veritable cornucopia of studies of the North's literary and cultural history. In addition to classic books such as George Frederickson's *The Inner Civil War* (1965), which explores the intellectual upheavals of the wartime North, there are excellent recent studies such as Randall Fuller's *From Battlefields Rising* (2011), which considers the responses of Northern writers such as Ralph Waldo Emerson, Louisa May Alcott, and Nathaniel Hawthorne to the war. Fuller provides a sharp, engrossing account of these writers' lives, perspectives, and milieux, capturing how and why they "helped to create a literary culture that ... play[ed] a significant role in the escalation of hostilities" (9). Alice Fahs's *The Imagined Civil War* (2004) focuses on popular Northern books, disclosing how the war was depicted in various best sellers, while Elizabeth Young's *Disarming the Nation* (1999) analyzes writings by women and the ways in which they dealt with the intersections of race, gender, and class. (*Disarming the Nation* also has a very good chapter on Confederate cross-dressers.)

For an insightful study of Northern writers and their uses of memory, one should read Stephen Cushman's *Belligerent Muse* (2014). Cushman does a deep dive into five authors who participated in the war and significantly shaped how it was to be remembered: Abraham Lincoln, Walt Whitman, William T. Sherman, Ambrose Bierce, and Joshua Lawrence Chamberlain. As Cushman reveals, these writers must be read through a dual lens, since they sought to simultaneously chronicle the war and frame its public memory. Cushman's book also makes a very strong case for Chamberlain as a writer who has been woefully overlooked.

Philip Gura's *Man's Better Angels: Romantic Reformers and the Coming of the Civil War* (2017) starts further back in time, retracing the major influences on Northern reformers, such as John Brown and Horace Greeley, who went on to play a defining role in the war and its aftermath. Gura shows how antebellum events affected these reformers and anchored their subsequent understanding of justice, moral suasion, and the nature of institutions. Ian Finseth's *The Civil War Dead and American Modernity* (2018) is another perspicacious study of the North's contributions to Civil War literature, arguing that Northern writing often revolves around an attempt to do the impossible: faithfully represent the dead.

These books have taught us a great deal about the genres of wartime expression. When Edmund Wilson lamented, back in the 1960s, that the "period of the American Civil War was not one in which *belles lettres* flourished,"* he was mostly thinking about novels. But the most public and prolific literary forms during the Civil War era were songs, poems, and short stories, many of which were published in popular magazines. In *My Heart Is Turning Ever* (1992), Kathleen Diffley reveals that for many Americans during and after the Civil War literature was inseparable from those magazines: across the disunited states, people turned to *Harper's Weekly*, *Southern Magazine*, and other, similar periodicals to comprehend the crisis and assign it with a sense of order and meaning.

The Civil War's songs and poems have also been thoughtfully examined. In *To Flight Aloud Is Very Brave* (2012), Faith Barrett looks at the full and astounding range of poetic responses to the struggle, from the lyrics of Emily Dickinson to popular songs and other, more obscure poems written by Union and Confederate soldiers. These poems, Barrett shows, share an investment in perspective: political ideals were bound up with acts of rhetorical positioning, and vice versa. Eliza Richards, in *Battle Lines* (2018), reframes Civil War poetry as an integral part of the broader system of Civil War media: nearly every poem was immersed in a vast media ecology, which Richards deftly reconstructs. Timothy Sweet's *Traces of War* (1990) casts the war's poetry in a different light, examining its formal and philosophical ties to wartime photography. Sweet recaptures how Walt Whitman, Herman Melville, and other wartime poets engaged with photographic attempts to record the conflict.

Other genres and archives still need to be examined in greater depth, particularly Civil War letters. One book that paves a path in that regard is Christopher Hager's *I Remain Yours: Common Lives in Civil War Letters* (2017). *I Remain Yours*

---

*Edmund Wilson, *Patriotic Gore: Studies in the Literature of the American Civil War* (New York: Norton, 1994), ix.

documents a remarkable range of letters and epistolary practices: the silhou-
ette of a child's hand, traced on correspondence paper and ferried to a soldier
far away on the front; letters crosshatched in black and red ink, as a wife and a
husband respond to one another and maintain their relationship on the space
of the page, in spite of the distance and the violence that separates them. These
letters—which Hager says number in the range of about half a billion—are vital
to understanding the war and its meaning, not only for the people who lived
through it but also for us who live in its wake.

On the Family Squabble

The Family Squabble is Unionism's narrative form. So studies of Unionism
are crucial for understanding the story's ethos and appeal. Gary Gallagher's
The Union War (2011) is an excellent resource in that regard. Gallagher untan-
gles the development of Unionist thought and feeling, showing how and why
many soldiers, officers, writers, and politicians considered the war's rationale
to consist in preserving the nation. David Blight's *Race and Reunion* (2001) shows
how Unionist and emancipationist views of the war differed—sometimes quite
radically—from one another, and how those differences molded American memory. Some of the most intriguing recent books in this vein focus on Southern
Unionists. John Inscoe and Robert Kenzer's *Enemies of the Country* (2004) surveys
Unionist resistance throughout the wartime South, while Victoria Bynum's *The
Free State of Jones* (2001) and Sally Jenkins and John Stauffer's *The State of Jones*
(2010) chronicle a Unionist counterrevolution in southeast Mississippi, famously
led by Newton Knight.

There are also fine books about the history and meanings of interfamilial
struggle. The most thorough guide to the war's domestic divisions is Amy
Murrell Taylor's *The Divided Family in Civil War America* (2005). Taylor chronicles fractured families in Missouri, Kentucky, Tennessee, and other slaveholding states in the Upper South. Each of the chapters looks at real examples of
much-mythologized divisions, from "Union Father, Rebel Son" to "Brothers
and Sisters." *The Divided Family in Civil War America* overlooks crucial differences
between literary history and history as such, approaching mythmaking as if
it simply reflects the prevalence and importance of these individual cases, but
it does provide a searching account of the domestic relations that were frayed
by the war.

Walt Whitman, who helped invent and popularize the Family Squabble, has become a cynosure for scholars and students alike. In *The Better Angel* (2000), Roy Morris Jr. contends that "the Civil War saved Walt Whitman" (3): it renewed his faith in the nation and revived his poetic career. Morris recounts Whitman's wartime experiences, discussing his work as a nurse, his friendships with the soldiers, and his responses to the era's events. The friendships that Whitman developed might have been much more than friendships, though. The nature of Whitman's relations with the wounded soldiers is further explored by Robert Leigh Davis in *Whitman and the Romance of Medicine* (1997) and by Peter Coviello in *All Tomorrow's Parties* (2011). Davis and Coviello reveal that some of these relationships were actually erotic, and that Whitman's view of the Civil War is bound up with his feelings about same-sex love.

Whitman's connections to Melville are thoughtfully explored in Christopher Sten and Tyler Hoffman's edited collection, *This Mighty Convulsion* (2019). The essays in *This Mighty Convulsion* reconsider Whitman vis-à-vis Melville, assessing the similarities and differences in their poetry, philosophy, and worldviews. Other books focus primarily on Whitman's racial politics. Betsy Erkkila's *Whitman the Political Poet* (1996), David S. Reynolds's *Walt Whitman's America* (1995), and Martin Buinicki's *Walt Whitman's Reconstruction* (2011) chronicle how, throughout his life, Whitman was never able to reconcile his democratic politics with his views on race. Before the war Whitman came down, quite clearly, on the side of the abolitionists, but he was decidedly more ambivalent about black citizenship and multicultural democracy. Whitman's treatment of race is also the subject of Ivy Wilson's volume *Whitman Noir* (2014). The essays in *Whitman Noir* address the matter from a range of perspectives, exploring the gradual whitening of *Leaves of Grass*, Whitman's time in New Orleans, and Whitman's legacies for contemporary writers of color.

Abraham Lincoln, the man whom Whitman said was the living embodiment of "UNIONISM, in its truest and amplest sense," has been endlessly analyzed. I have been especially influenced by books about Lincoln's afterlife in American memory. Martha Hodes's *Mourning Lincoln* (2015) is a paragon in that respect. Hodes chronicles the variety of American responses to Lincoln's death—feelings of shock, tinges of glee, flashes of anger—and the ways they merged into broader reflections on death, justice, and nationality. Whereas *Mourning Lincoln* stays within the cultural milieu of 1865, Merrill D. Peterson's *Lincoln in American Memory* (1994) radiates outward to consider how Lincoln has been remembered long after the war's conclusion. Peterson documents Lincoln's apotheosis as a political icon, as well as the major themes and variations in cultural memory.

If one wants to know more about Lincoln's relation to American literature, one should read the essays in Shirley Samuels's *The Cambridge Companion to Abraham Lincoln* (2012). The volume discusses Lincoln's view of the Constitution, Lincoln's use of poetry and poets' use of Lincoln, and his afterlife in art and images. If one desires a more biographical approach, there is an embarrassment of riches. Stephen B. Oates's *With Malice toward None: A Life of Abraham Lincoln* (1977) is a classic biography that moves from Lincoln's childhood to his career as a lawyer to his experiences as a wartime president. In my opinion, the most incisive book about Lincoln as a writer and orator is John Burt's *Lincoln's Tragic Pragmatism* (2013). Burt approaches the Lincoln-Douglas debates as a launching point for understanding Lincoln's mind, and more specifically his evolving thoughts about moral conflict. It is more of a cultural biography than Oates's, but it is revelatory, and the final chapter includes splendid readings of Lincoln's wartime speeches.

On the Dark and Cruel War

The Civil War writings of Mark Twain, whose strange and short career as a Confederate officer begins chapter 2, are collected in David Rachel's *Mark Twain's Civil War*. Rachel's edition includes selections from everything Twain wrote about the conflict, from "The Private History of a Campaign That Failed" (1885) to *A Connecticut Yankee in King Arthur's Court* (1889) and beyond. Ron Powers's biography *Mark Twain: A Life* (2005) disentangles how Samuel Clemens became Mark Twain, and the chapters on Twain's wartime experiences are illuminating, tying Twain's wartime desertion to his decision to light out for the West. Twain's Civil War experiences also frame Jerome Loving's *Confederate Bushwhacker* (2013). Loving answers a lingering question: why did Twain wait until the 1880s to talk about his brief stint as a Confederate soldier? *Confederate Bushwhacker* suggests that it had a lot to do with what was happening culturally and politically in the post-Reconstruction years, and with whom Twain was talking: Ulysses S. Grant (whose *Memoirs* Twain published) and George Washington Cable (who went on a lecture tour with Twain).

Twain's fellow philosophers, Ambrose Bierce and Stephen Crane, are some of the writers Cynthia Wachtell examines in her book about antiwar protest in American literature, *War No More* (2010). Wachtell focuses on the difference between popular treatments of the Civil War and Bierce's, arguing that Bierce not only documents the most brutal parts of battle but also "invents new outrages" (21). Crane's *The Red Badge of Courage*, according to Wachtell, is a depiction of warfare's industrialization, a vision of battle's cruel transformation into mechanistic slaughter. Ian Finseth's chapter on realist fiction in *A History of Civil War Literature* provides another astute interpretation of these writers, showing how they tried, both individually and collectively, to deromanticize the Civil War. The ethical and philosophical dimensions of these writings are probed in Lawrence Berkove's *The Moral Art of Ambrose Bierce* (2002). Berkove uses Bierce's service as a topographical engineer as an interpretive model for understanding the surfaces and depths of Bierce's writing. Of particular interest are the chapters about Bierce and war, which stress that Bierce tended to see the Civil War not as a singular event but as an example of warfare more generally and the moral dilemmas it provoked.

One of the more perceptive readings of officers' memoirs can be found in Edmund Wilson's *Patriotic Gore*. Wilson views Grant and Sherman as stylists whose clear, straightforward approach to language is a "unique expression of the national character." Wilson tends to overhype how personal and revealing the memoirs are ("[Grant] is all there in his book; the book is the man speaking"), but *Patriotic Gore* provides a trenchant account of their lives and worldviews. For another take on Grant, one should read Joan Waugh's essay in her coedited volume *The Civil War in American Memory*. Waugh reframes Grant as a historian—someone who tries to discern the logic of history from the course of events—and situates his *Personal Memoirs* in relation to other, post-Reconstruction reflections on the Civil War. John A. Casey views these officers as far more traumatized by their war experiences than they let on. In *New Men: Reconstructing the Image of the Veteran in Late-Nineteenth-Century American Literature and Culture* (2015), Casey reads these memoirs as trauma narratives, making a case that Sherman's dispassionate viewpoint covers up a psychic wound, an altered sense of himself and the world that cannot be otherwise expressed.

Anyone who reads *The Killer Angels* should also read Michael Kreyling's *The South That Wasn't There* (2010). Kreyling presents the novel as a story about the shock of the Vietnam War. That is part of the reason why Shaara approaches the Civil War in the way that he does: it seems to offer an antidote to contemporary, guerrilla-style warfare. As Kreyling puts it, "Shaara implicitly puts Civil War memory up against contemporary, Vietnam-era military shock: as brutal as Civil War battles surely were, our warriors fought them with honor and valor" (85). In advancing that vision of the past, Shaara conjures up the fiction of an honor-bound Old South, ostensibly embodied by Robert E. Lee and his Army of Northern Virginia. Throughout chapter 2, I was influenced by Kreyling's reading of *The Killer Angels* as a "memory text" that bears as much on the present as it does on the past. I also learned a great deal from books about post-9/11 fiction, such as Susana Araújo's *Transatlantic Fictions of 9/11 and the War on Terror* (2015) and Richard Gray's *After the Fall* (2011).

Several of the other writers mentioned in this chapter, such as Mary Chesnut, have been studied in depth. The only version of Chesnut's diary that should be read is C. Vann Woodward's Yale edition (1981), which documents the changes that Chesnut made to the manuscript at different points in her life. Chesnut's decades-long labor of writing and rewriting is the starting point for Julia Stern's splendid study *Mary Chesnut's Civil War Epic* (2010). Stern reveals how Chesnut's copious edits in the 1880s transformed the manuscript by filling out the narrative, adding layers of historical reflection, and clarifying its genre—in short, by making it into a single, vast, American epic. Stern also provides a lucid account of Chesnut's life and context, as well as Chesnut's ideas about race, gender, and power.

On the Lost Cause

The primary sources for the Lost Cause can be found in several books. Besides Edward Pollard's *The Lost Cause* (1867) and Jefferson Davis's *The Rise and Fall of Confederate Government* (1881), which I discuss in chapter 3, there is James W. Loewen and Edward H. Sebesta's *The Confederate and Neo-Confederate Reader* (2010). Loewen and Sebesta's volume contains a generous sampling of Lost Cause documents: convention proceedings, government reports, and military orders, along with proclamations, letters, and speeches by Robert E. Lee, Howell Cobb, and others. The last chapter covers the Lost Cause's revival during the civil rights era, reprinting statements from Strom Thurmond, Sonny Perdue, and white supremacist newspapers such as the *Citizens' Council*.

These primary documents should be read in conjunction with historical studies. Charles Reagan Wilson's *Baptized in Blood* (1980) and Gaines M. Foster's *Ghosts of the Confederacy* (1987) are first-rate histories of the Lost Cause and its transformation into a cultural mythology after the Civil War. Anne Sarah Rubin's *Shattered Nation* (2008) and Kevin M. Levin's *Searching for Black Confederates* (2019) are essential reading too. Rubin shows how the cultural symbols of the Confederacy developed within the C.S.A. but expanded far beyond it, while Levin dismantles the pervasive mythology of black Confederate soldiers, a mythology that primarily developed in the 1970s as a response to the civil rights movement. In *Confederate Visions* (2013), Ian Binnington documents the ways in which Confederate nationalism took hold by inventing fictions of white individuality and Southern autonomy. Secessionists imagined the Confederacy into being, Binnington demonstrates, by telling a new story about the South and inventing a series of symbolic characters: the Demonic Yankee, the Silent Slave, and the Noble Southerner.

The two major poets of the Lost Cause, Abram Ryan and Henry Timrod, have garnered less attention than one would assume. There are two solid biographies of Ryan: David O'Connell's *Furl That Banner* (2006) and Donald Robert Beagle and Bryan Albin Giemza's *A Life of Father Ryan* (2008). Both biographies migrate from Ryan's early years to his maturation, taking of rites, Confederate service, and ensuing travels. *Furl That Banner* situates Ryan within Irish Catholic communities of the antebellum South and establishes connections between his religion and politics. An incisive study of Timrod still needs to be written. Walter Cisco's *Henry Timrod: A Biography* (2004) is serviceable, but it doesn't explain the poems particularly well. For a shorter but more insightful account of Timrod's writings, one should read the last chapter in Christopher Hanlon's *America's England: Antebellum Literature and Atlantic Sectionalism* (2013).

Thomas Dixon's and D. W. Griffith's contributions to the Lost Cause are the subject of Anthony Slide's *American Racist: The Life and Films of Thomas Dixon* (2004). Slide is sometimes too much of an apologist—he tries to defend the imaginative vitality if not the social vision of *The Birth of a Nation*—but he does offer a succinct history of Dixon's mind and work. Tom Rice's *White Robes, Silver Screens* (2015) does not traffic in apologetics. Rice records and describes the influence exerted by *The Birth of a Nation* on the modern Ku Klux Klan. Melvyn Stokes's *D. W. Griffith's "The Birth of a Nation": A History of "The Most Controversial Film of All-Time"* (2007) also features a trenchant chapter on Griffith's view of the Civil War era. For a nuanced reading of Dixon's novels, one should turn to Brook Thomas's *The Literature of Reconstruction* (2017). Thomas connects Dixon to the broader arc of Reconstruction culture and argues that, for Dixon, the Civil War was ultimately necessary since it launched "America's imperial mission for the white race" (78).

The Southern Agrarian movement has long had admirers, and many peo-
ple continue to view it as a kind of wellspring for modern conservativism.
Nonetheless, as Robert Brinkmeyer shows in *The Fourth Ghost* (2009), Southern
Agrarianism had a great deal in common with European Fascism. Both were
white supremacist movements that presented themselves as something more
intellectually heady and socially salutary. Brinkmeyer's book explains why the
Agrarians repeatedly emphasize the South's European heritage throughout *I'll
Take My Stand*, and it reveals how this political entanglement ended up dooming
Agrarianism later on.

The Agrarian (or Agrarian-lite) writer who has received the most attention,
of course, is Margaret Mitchell. Tara McPherson's *Reconstructing Dixie* (2003)
is an important and well-researched study of Mitchell's story and its influence.
McPherson demonstrates how *Gone with the Wind* impacted America's racial
imaginary in both material and immaterial ways, grounding people's understanding of the South and solidifying certain stereotypes, in particular those of
"the lady, the mammy, and the plantation."

Other books interpret *Gone with the Wind* along different lines. In *Scarlett's
Women* (1989), Helen Taylor focuses on the film's female fans and the myriad
ways in which they have responded to Mitchell's story. In *Frankly, My Dear: "Gone
with the Wind" Revisited* (2009), Molly Haskell argues that we should look at the
story in two ways. On the one hand, it retells the myth of the Lost Cause and its
"portrait of a noble South," which "gave the region a kind of moral ascendancy
that allowed it to hold the rest of the country hostage as the 'Dixification' virus
spread . . . north of the Mason-Dixon Line." On the other hand, Scarlett is one
of the most indelible characters ever created, a heroine with a fierce independent
streak and an instinct for survival. A variety of smart perspectives on the film
can also be found in James Crank's *New Approaches to "Gone with the Wind"*
(2015), which considers *Gone with the Wind*'s racial philosophy, its transatlantic
reception, and its similarity to Frank Yerby's plantation romances.

Of all the writers discussed in chapter 3, William Faulkner has been written
about the most. John T. Matthews offers one of the most insightful readings of
Faulkner's depiction of the Civil War in his essay in *A History of American Civil
War Literature*. According to Matthews, Faulkner tends to view the Civil War not
as a single event situated in the past but as a catalyst for modernity. Matthews
also captures Faulkner's complicated treatment of the Civil War, which tends to

appear "in Faulkner's fiction as a node for simultaneously acknowledging and disavowing the full import of the South's history."* Joel Williamson provides another helpful framework in *William Faulkner and Southern History* (1993). Williamson considers the full scope of Faulkner's influences—his time, place, family, and culture—and devotes an entire chapter to Faulkner's Civil War predecessor, the Old Colonel. Finally, John T. Matthews's edited collection *William Faulkner in Context* (2015) is an excellent resource, containing essays on Faulkner's racial views, his uses of genre, and his ties to the American South.

On the Great Emancipation

Emancipation is as vast a subject as there can possibly be. Most histories of emancipation therefore focus on particular people, movements, and events. In *I Freed Myself* (2014), David Miller examines acts of self-emancipation. Though emancipation is often remembered as something handed down from above, it also rose up from below when enslaved people escaped, revolted, and fought back against the slave system. Miller's book recounts some of these acts of self-liberation, which led nearly 200,000 African Americans to join the Union's military. Ira Berlin's *The Long Emancipation* (2015) moves in a different direction, tracking the growth of abolitionism from the eighteenth century onward. The dismantling of chattel slavery in the 1860s, he shows, was not a spontaneous upheaval but the endpoint of an almost century-long process. Documentary books also complement such histories. Ira Berlin and Barbara J. Fields's *Free at Last* (1993) contains hundreds of letters, field orders, and other primary materials, while Deborah Willis and Barbara Krauthamer's *Envisioning Emancipation* (2017) reproduces numerous photographs of freedpeople.

As emancipation took shape in African American memory, it yielded new celebrations and traditions. Mitch Kachun offers a thorough chronicle of those celebrations in *Festivals of Freedom* (2006). Kachun's book reveals how emancipation was experienced as newly freed people incorporated older holidays, like Freedom Day, into the world remade by the war. Kachun's descriptions of the "watch nights" on December 31, 1862, are especially compelling. Emancipation was remembered and recorded by many former slaves, some of whom composed narratives about their lives. The University of North Carolina's North

---

* John T. Matthews, "Replay: William Faulkner and the Civil War," in *A History of American Civil War Literature*, ed. Coleman Hutchison (New York: Cambridge Univ. Press, 2015), 289.

American Slave Narratives website (https://docsouth.unc.edu/neh/) has pre-served many of those narratives, though a few—by Elizabeth Keckley, John Quincy Adams, and William Wells Brown, among others—are also available in William L. Andrews's edited volume *Slave Narratives after Slavery* (2011). Un-published narratives and diaries are the subject of Christopher Hager's *Word by Word: Emancipation and the Act of Writing* (2013). Hager artfully reconstructs the lives of several people—including Maria Perkins, John M. Washington, and a man who went by the nom de plume "A Coloured Man"—who did not play a central role in the Civil War and Reconstruction but whose lives and writings tell us a great deal about literacy, freedom, and the relation between them.

Books on black soldiers and black regiments began to be written as soon as the war came to a close. There is a distinguished African American tradition in this vein. William Wells Brown's *The Negro in the American Rebellion* (1867), which I discuss in chapter 4, covers the actions and legacies of these regiments, as do George Washington Williams's *A History of the Negro Troops in the War of the Rebellion* (1887) and Joseph T. Wilson's *The Black Phalanx* (1890). More recent historical studies tend to focus on the details of the men's wartime service. Keith Wilson's *Campfires of Freedom* (2002), for example, looks at the lived rhythms of camp life: the men's efforts to acquire literacy, as well as their music, religion, and politics. Joseph Glatthaar's *Forged in Battle* (1990) describes the sometimes-tense relationships between black soldiers and white officers, and John David Smith's edited volume *Black Soldiers in Blue* (2005) contains essays on particular battles, sieges, and engagements.

Some of the best books about the era convey the dual nature of liberation—the incredible promise of freedom on the one hand, and the failure to truly carry it out on the other. Reconstruction was nothing less than a radical exper-iment in democracy, and that is a running theme from W. E. B. Du Bois's *Black Reconstruction* (1935) to Eric Foner's *Reconstruction: America's Unfinished Revolution* (1988). Twenty-first-century histories of Reconstruction have expanded on this view of the period. In *Slavery by Another Name* (2009), David Blackmon explores how white supremacy secured its postwar future by effectively re-enslaving freedpeople by other means. The prison system, debt enforcement, and em-ployment contracts forged after the war all ensured that the racial hierarchy and living conditions that marked slavery continued even if the institution itself was outlawed. The tenuous and oftentimes quite unfree lives of freedpeople are also the topic of Jim Downs's *Sick from Freedom* (2012), which shows that for many ex-slaves emancipation precipitated a health crisis, as numerous freedpeople fell ill from the pathogens they encountered as they migrated northward.

There are superb books about many of the writers, artists, and activists featured in chapter 4. Renée Ater's *Remaking Race and History* (2011) is a luminous study of Meta Vaux Warrick Fuller that tracks the evolution of Fuller's art, as well as her views on race, aesthetics, and history. Maryemma Graham's edited collection, *Fields Watered with Blood* (2014), contains nine essays about Margaret Walker's *Jubilee*, addressing everything from the novel's relation to the blues to its uses of space. The first book-length treatment of Frances E. W. Harper, which initiated renewed attention to Harper's life and writings, was Melba Joyce Boyd's *Discarded Legacy* (1994). Michael Stancliff finely extends that recovery in *Frances Ellen Watkins Harper: African American Reform Rhetoric and the Rise of a Modern Nation State* (2011). For discerning accounts of Harper's poetry, one should read Faith Barrett's aforementioned *To Fight Aloud Is Very Brave* (2013), as well as Tricia Lootens's *The Political Poetess* (2016).

William Wells Brown is the subject of Geoffrey Sanborn's *Plagiarama!* (2016). Sanborn is chiefly interested in Brown's strange, theatric style—his penchant for drawing a whirlwind of texts together in a vast mélange, and making a show of it. Brown's literary and extraliterary performances, Sanborn argues, resemble nineteenth-century variety shows. Brown's life and times are also chronicled in two trenchant introductions: Robert S. Levine's 2010 edition of *Clotel*, and John Ernest's 2011 edition of *My Southern Home*. In *Race, Transnationalism, and Nineteenth-Century American Literary Studies* (2017), Levine also explores the relationship between Brown's antislavery and anti-alcohol views and shows how these reform movements were, for Brown, utterly contiguous.

Harriet Tubman first told her story to Sarah Bradford, who initially published it in a haphazardly edited book, *Scenes from the Life of Harriet Tubman* (1869). Years later Bradford expanded and refined that account, issuing *Harriet, the Moses of Her People* (1884). There are benefits to hindsight, though, and the best books about Tubman are the more recent ones. Catherine Clinton's *Harriet Tubman: The Road to Freedom* (2004) meticulously chronicles Tubman's life. The early chapters focus on Tubman's family and her early experiences as a slave on Maryland's eastern seaboard, while later chapters detail her antislavery work, first with the Underground Railroad and then with the Union Army. Kate Clifford Larson's *Bound for the Promised Land* (2004) similarly recovers Tubman's wartime actions and makes a convincing case for viewing Tubman's politics through her spirituality, and vice versa.

The most complete single-volume edition of Frederick Douglass's works is Philip S. Foner and Yuval Taylor's *Frederick Douglass: Selected Speeches and Writings* (2000). The fullest treatment of Douglass's response to the Civil War is David Blight's *Frederick Douglass' Civil War: Keeping Faith in Jubilee* (1991), which elucidates Douglass's political, theological, and commemorative views of the struggle. Though less concerned with the Civil War, Nicholas Buccola's *The Political Thought of Frederick Douglass* (2013) offers a trenchant reading of Douglass's views on morality, liberalism, and democracy. The most complete biographies, in my view, are Robert S. Levine's *The Lives of Frederick Douglass* (2016) and David Blight's *Frederick Douglass: Prophet of Freedom* (2018). Levine uses the defining feature of Douglass's writings—their investment in constant change—as a paradigm for understanding Douglass's life, while Blight constructs a nuanced psychological portrait out of historical events and biographical materials. These Douglass-centered books have been complemented by studies that pair Douglass and Lincoln together. The most successful of those paired studies are John Stauffer's *Giants: The Parallel Lives of Frederick Douglass and Abraham Lincoln* (2008) and James Oakes's *The Radical and the Republican* (2011).

On Recent and Future Civil Wars

The events in Charleston and Charlottesville prompted a range of spirited, insightful writing. Jamelle Bouie's essays in *Slate* are essential reading as far as I'm concerned. Bouie shows how and why the Charleston massacre and the "Unite the Right" rally, far from being aberrations, grew out of the long history of racial terror in the United States. Among the country's cornerstones, few have been as persistent or as consequential as—in Bouie's words—"notions of white hegemony," which consist in "the idea that white Americans have a stronger claim on national resources, that they are somehow more legitimate citizens."*

Of related interest are Eric Foner's "Confederate Statues and 'Our' History" (2017) and Sophie Abramowitz, Eva Latterner, and Gillet Rosenblith's "Tools of Displacement" (2017). Foner chronicles the relationship between race and citizenship in the United States and reflects on the political meaning conveyed by

---

*Jamelle Bouie, "Why Richard Spencer Matters," *Slate*, May 22, 2017.

Confederate statues, flags, and other symbols. These Lost Cause objects, Foner points out, are not impartial lessons in history but "expression[s] of power," indications "of who has the power to choose how history is remembered in public places." Abramowitz, Latterner, and Rosenblith offer a more situated, local account of Charlottesville, tracing the violence in 2017 to earlier (and ongoing) racial divides in the city, which has maintained connections to white supremacists for a very long time.*

One of the best resources is *Charleston Syllabus* (2016), edited by Chad Williams, Kidada Williams, and Keisha Blain. The volume contains short, relevant documents that span nearly all of African American history, moving from the era of enslavement to the twenty-first century. It reprints Barack Obama's eulogy for Clementa Pinckney and the lyrics to Kendrick Lamar's "The Blacker the Berry," as well as documents about the Civil War, Jim Crow, mass incarceration, and racial segregation in housing. The Civil War selections highlight emancipation and clarify just how pivotal slavery, as both an ideology and an institution, was to the Confederacy.

The essays in *Charlottesville 2017: The Legacy of Race and Inequity* (2018) are also perceptive. Edited by Louis P. Nelson and Claudrena N. Harold, the volume contextualizes the violence that erupted in July of 2017 by looking at the founding and development of the University of Virginia, as well as the broader history of racial violence and inequality in the United States. Organized around four different types of responses—Remembering, Speaking, Listening, and Responding—the essays range across a variety of topics, touching on everything from the role of eugenics at the University of Virginia to the history of desegregation in Charlottesville. I particularly recommend the introduction, which provides a detailed recap of the creation, dedication, and reception of the city's monuments. Nelson and Harold note that the Lee statue was partially funded by the KKK, and, shortly after its unveiling in 1924, the nearby theater rescreened *The Birth of a Nation* and hosted a traveling minstrel show.**

---

*Eric Foner, "Confederate Statues and 'Our' History," *New York Times*, August 20, 2017; Sophie Abramowitz, Eva Latterner, and Gillet Rosenblith, "Tools of Displacement," *Slate*, June 23, 2017.

**Louis P. Nelson and Claudrena N. Harold, introduction to *Charlottesville 2017: The Legacy of Race and Iniquity*, ed. Louis P. Nelson and Claudrena N. Harold (Charlottesville: Univ. of Virginia Press, 2018).

Index